# THEURGY

BY MOUNI SADHU

Concentration
The Tarot
Meditation
Samadhi

# THEURGY

## THE ART OF EFFECTIVE WORSHIP

BY

MOUNI SADHU

AEON

Originally published by George Allen and Unwin
under the title Theurgy by Mouni Sadhu


this edition published 2004
by Aeon Books
an imprint of Cortex Publishing
London W5
www.aeonbooks.co.uk



**British Library Cataloguing in Publication Data**
A C.I.P. is available for this book from the British Library

ISBN 1 904658 08 3

Printed and bound in Great Britain

*To Albert Schweitzer*
*dedicated with homage*

## ACKNOWLEDGEMENT

I wish to express my thanks to those mentioned below for the co-operation I received when preparing the Bibliography for this book:

Australian National Library
Chief Librarian
British Museum Reading Room
The Superintendent
Paul Derain Library, Lyons (France)
Miss Nona D. Lucas, Melbourne
Dr J. v. Moger, Melbourne
The Public Library of New South Wales

# CONTENTS

# FOREWORD

Since publication of my last book, *The Tarot: a Contemporary Course of the Quintessence of Hermetic Occultism,*[1] numerous inquiries have been directed to me by readers concerning theurgy, that important and very powerful occult way of contacting the Supreme to enable the student and seeker to act successfully in helping others and himself.

Therefore it was decided that this book should be written in order to answer these many inquiries.

The purely theoretical part of theurgy has been sufficiently expounded in *The Tarot* and it is its practical aspect which will be approached here. Moreover, this practical aspect is just the chief reason why some people decide to contact the Infinite Power, in the very moment when they realize that their own lives are only a spark of the Whole—God.

Here we should note, that the very meaning of the term 'theurgy' as used in the ancient Graeco-Roman world differs from that of the present day. Followers of Pythagoras and Iamblichus, as well as those of the Neoplatonist school (Plotinus) and the great magician called Apollonius of Tyana considered theurgy to be a means for entering into contact with their gods and nature spirits and to obtaining the desired result by ritual and worship, preceded by long and tedious training, both mental as well as physical.

But the theurgy of later times has had much loftier conceptions, aims and means of realization. Nowadays this pearl of spiritual attainment, which is parallel to the highest Eastern initiation intc Samadhi,[2] is based on Christian philosophy and initiation. However, it is not concerned much with the dogmatic side of Christianity.[3] Instead, full weight is placed on the individual preparation of the prospective theurgist and his moral and mental training, leading finally to the awakening of controlled intuition (the realm of the Fourth State

1 Published by George Allen & Unwin Ltd, London, 1962.

2 See my *Mystic Trilogy* (*In Days of Great Peace*, 1957, *Concentration*, 1959, *Samadhi*, 1962, all published by George Allen & Unwin Ltd, London) and also *Ways to Self-Realization: a Modern Evaluation of Occultism and Spiritual Paths* (published by The Julian Press, New York, 1962; George Allen & Unwin Ltd, London, 1964).

3 Here I am referring to the two traditional churches—Catholic and Orthodox.

in Hindu mysticism), resulting in the merging of the individual and mortal with the Infinite and Eternal, which we may call—God.

Instead of a multitude of factors and powers—such as gods, spirits and natural forces—acting upon man, as was the case with the ancient masters just mentioned, the great central concept of the 'One without a second' arises in the theurgy of our own day.

Man then strives directly towards the Highest forsaking the intermediate paths and passing over them in his supreme ecstasy, to the One Father as taught to us by Christ. The path of a theurgist is supremely simple, but by no means does this imply that it is the easiest.

The leading schools of French occultism at the end of the nineteenth and beginning of the twentieth centuries (Sédir and Master Philippe of Lyons), tell us, that since only the Almighty has the power to deal with every difficulty, problem and the destiny of man, the simplest and most effective attitude is to surrender everything to Him, Who will arrange all of our relations with the world and our worries once and for ever.

It would be interesting to note, that the great contemporary spiritual master, Ramana Maharshi (1879-1950), who was born in India and who basically taught the realization of the Self in man, knew all about the theurgic path, and advised it for those who were unable to storm the steep cliffs of Jnana, while underlining the equality of both ways to the final attainment (see all parts of the *Mystic Trilogy* and *Ways to Self-Realization*).

Everything depends upon ourselves: we have to find which path is most suited to us. This is not an easy search or decision, but no one other than a man himself can make this difficult choice. A right choice means success and attainment, but a wrong one only disappointment and frustration.

So, this work will speak to those who are intuitively attracted to the theurgic path. That is why I will not attempt to persuade or convince: the entering upon the spiritual path cannot come as a result of any discussion or logic. The position is quite simple: man has, or has not, a spiritual germ in him, and it cannot be created *ad hoc*. The supreme problem posed for us is—*Does God exist or not?* And it cannot be solved by any empiric philosophy or logic. It cannot be proved or disproved. Hence theurgy requires *spiritual certainty*, which is sometimes called *faith*. I do not wish to say that everyone is born with such a mystical power evident from his earliest years. Even the great teachers of humanity started to act only when their early youth was over.

But I know of many examples of the gradual development of spirituality in men and women in the course of the passing years, and spontaneously only in very exceptional cases.

Therefore I will not try to prove what cannot be proved, to convince where there cannot be any conviction for the outer mind. I will only explain, in current terminology, the path of theurgy as it is accessible to men of the twentieth century.

Finally, if you have an intuitional desire to adore and to be united with the Supreme, to obtain Its help in worthy aims, to worship It with your head bowed to the dust before the majesty of the Infinite and Perfect Being, which, in the ultimate depths of your heart, you feel to be the only Lord, then start this book. If things are otherwise, do not lose time: without faith no theurgist has yet been made.

The contents of this work include material chosen from the latest experiences of theurgic groups throughout the world with which the Melbourne groups are in steady contact, as well as the traditional teachings most appropriate for this period, some of which reach as far back as the first centuries after Christ. Great care had to be taken with the theurgic literature of the nineteenth and early twentieth centuries, in order to separate the wheat from the chaff. This was necessary because some authors were not able to discriminate sufficiently between ordinary magic practices and pure theurgy, while others seemed to include their sectarian and religious beliefs in their books. This is against the very idea of true theurgy, which basically makes no distinction between faiths if they permit spiritual practices.

For my own part, I tried to use only carefully selected material not tarnished by any prejudice or superstition.

I preferred to limit the number of operations and their rituals giving only proven methods and eliminating cumbersome and uncertain texts which are used for conjurations and prayers. It would be of little use to put a lot of ballast into a work, intended to present the reader with the clear-cut and usable practices of true theurgy.

It is not the number of words pronounced in prayers and meditations which is the deciding factor in theurgic operations and which really matter, but the *quality* of the performance by the aspirant, resulting from his *devotion, intelligence, power of concentration and endurance.* Those who are initiated know, that *a few well-performed inspiring sentences in prayers may perfectly well suffice for a lifetime's attainment.* The basic and irreplaceable formulas in mathematics, physics, chemistry, and so on, are mostly simple and rather short, although their derivatives may be expanded to a formidable size.

Nevertheless I have reserved a place at the end of this book, after the main body of the material has been expounded, for some important texts, which may interest those who might like to know how others have treated the same subject (see Chapter XXXV). Any comparison should be made by the reader himself.

I wish to point out that only material which has been proven through and through has been given in this manual. And therefore earnest aspirants can safely use the formulas for invocations and prayers, and the more assiduously all the chapters are studied, the more immediate and lasting will be the spiritual benefits gained.

To this end I would like to repeat the advice to all my readers, given in a footnote at the beginning of this Foreword: to study the second and third parts of my Mystic Trilogy and Ways to Self-Realization in parallel with this book. For those more advanced in occultism and symbolism there is also *The Tarot.* In it will be found several chapters dealing with the cabbalistic aspect of theurgy, together with a classical analysis of the Lord's Prayer and some Scriptures, through the system of the Sephiroth.

At this point it may be useful to give a final definition and explanation of theurgic methods, which—as you know—consist of invocations and prayers. What really are they? They are *channels* into which is directed the living force of the operator. When using them you will no longer be a plaything of your mind's moods, but will proceed directly to the goal you have set for yourself. They are also the *right means whereby to attract the attention of the Highest Power,* which can dispense the boons and assistance for which you pray. This is because, so far, that Power has directed your evolution until here and now, instead of a semi-conscious wandering through superstition and falsehood, you have started to turn to the *source.* The statement: *the right channel leads to right attainment* is important, for the Supreme *responds* when approached.

Rest assured that the best sons of humanity have accepted both of the following postulates:

1. The existence of the supreme central consciousness—Spirit, which possesses full power over Its manifestation in matter.
2. The possibility for us to approach this Power in the way shown by theurgy.

By meditation about (1) and (2) you will support your faith and so obtain peace of mind.

Among the known theurgists from ancient times to the present day it is worth mentioning only a few of the prominent ones. This is because, during their lifetimes, not all of these true theurgists left written works about their wisdom and activities, or cared whether or not the world recognized them. Many preferred to remain unknown in their service to humanity.

All the leading priests in ancient Egypt performed theurgic operations of many kinds, while in the Graeco-Roman tradition, Pythagoras, in his school, was the first to teach about theurgic methods of communication with the spiritual powers which he called 'gods'. Plotinus was well acquainted with this science, although, in the writings of his intellectual master—Plato, there was nothing divulged concerning the theurgic traditions the latter undoubtedly learned during his training in Egypt. The same applies to Socrates, who likewise must have known a good deal about the matter. Also the famous Apollonius of Tyana excelled in both high magic and theurgy. And when Christianity of the first centuries after Christ took over esotericism and mysticism from the pagan world, many of its saints followed the tradition of worship, fortified by devotion based on deep spiritual wisdom, which often manifested itself in miraculous cures, and so on.

Of course, the leading theurgist of the Old Testament was Moses, followed by some of the prophets. He took the tradition from his native land of Egypt and adapted it to suit his own great purpose of creating a framework for the idea of the One God and thereby preparing for the coming of the Messiah.

In medieval times Paracelsus possessed vast knowledge of theurgy and its theory, giving proof of this fact in his works. And before him, the elite of the Knights Templars' Order widely used theurgic methods, sometimes mixing them with magic. Their faith in the Supreme Being was so strong, that even in the time of the decline and ensuing destruction of their Order, the last Grand Master—*Jacobus Burgundus de Molay*—was able, by his powerful invocation when being burnt to death at the stake, to call both of the destroyers of his Order (the French King Philip IV and Pope Clement V) before God's tribunal, that is, to die shortly after himself, which events occurred even before the predicted time.

The French mystic and theurgist (*'Le Philosophe Inconnu'*) —Louis Claude de St Martin was prominent at the end of the eighteenth century. He was followed in the middle of the nineteenth century by the famous French occultist—Eliphas Lévi (Abbé Alphonse Constant), who greatly contributed to the renascence of theurgy—as well as of magic—in Europe. Then at the end of the nineteenth century his disciples—Papus (Dr Gérard Encausse) and the Marquis Stanislas de Guaita popularized theurgic ideas, although the latter was also occupied with the darker aspect of occultism. F. Barlet and P. Sédir were the spiritual children of the last known French theurgist of great calibre, the 'Maitre Philippe' of Lyons (1849-1905), otherwise—M. Philippe Nizier, whose astonishing and miraculous practices were known far beyond his native land.

Another important theurgist was Abbé Julio (M. Houssay), who performed a great service in the history of theurgy. He collected and edited a multitude of traditional Christian theurgic texts concerning invocations, prayers, exorcisms and rituals for different purposes and conditions, which before that time had been dispersed (often in a distorted form) throughout numerous old publications and manuscripts. It is to him that we are indebted for the great work of classifying everything into a clear, constructive and effective system.

Jean Sempé should also be mentioned, as it was he who inspired Abbé Julio by his saintly life, which was dedicated to theurgic cures and assistance. Abbé Schenebelin of France and the Russian priest John of Kronstadt (near St Petersburg, now Leningrad), who died shortly before the beginning of World War I also belong to the same category of theurgists as Abbé Julio.

Another prominent theurgist, who was also an occultist, was Prof. G. O. Mebes of the Imperial St Petersburg University, who died in 1918. He was the head of a group of Russian intellectuals and mystics in the period prior to the Russian Revolution of 1917. The well-known Russian novelist Kuprin dedicated one of his stories to his spiritual master, which is striking by its realistic narration and the strange facts given in it, which lift a small corner of the veil that hides the mystery of human death. Although the real name of the 'master' was not given by Kuprin, anyone acquainted with the occultism of the beginning of the twentieth century cannot fail to recognize Professor Mebes himself.

Among the German occultists connected with theurgy, mention can be made of the following: Gustav Meyrink, who died in 1935, wrote about the intellectual concepts of theurgy in the form of a novel, while Dr Alfred Strauss, G. W. Surya, H. Wilms, B. Ahhorn, J. Goerres, G. Heinzelmann and K. Reinhardt were also authors of works connected directly or indirectly with theurgic science.

In the English language theurgic writers of note include James Hastings, William Ralph Inge, Thomas Whittaker, Alexander Wilder (translator only).

Mouni Sadhu,
September, 1963,
Melbourne, Australia.

# PART I

# THE GENERAL TRADITION OF THEURGY

. . . For what doth it profit a man, if he gain the whole world, and suffer the loss of his own soul? Or what exchange shall a man give for his soul?

# CHAPTER I

# PRELIMINARIES

Among much of the nonsense spreading in certain circles interested in occultism, are such statements as: 'anyone can meditate'. But without a considerable degree of ability to direct one's mind according to one's will, no meditation is ever possible apart from a vague wandering of ideas or mental pictures and thoughts through the screen of awareness of the untrained beginner.

The ability to concentrate is an unavoidable precursor of meditation. In turn, this takes years of toil to develop, unless a man is one of those few geniuses known to human history, who are born with the uncommon power of domination of mind. All this refers equally well to the ability of true theurgic practice which is, as we already know, the deepest, mystical mute prayer.

Nevertheless, certain forms of this high art may sometimes be more accessible than concentration and meditation and there is a deep reason for this. When studying concentration, in order to approach the realm of meditation, man is primarily working for himself by trying to develop his own powers, which belong to the mental (that is, not yet spiritual) level of his consciousness. He may, or may not be helped by higher forces, which supervise our struggles on the long evolutionary path of successive incarnations. The reason for this is also, that everything belonging to the realm below that of pure *spirit* (that is, consciousness devoid of all egoism and personality) can still be used for both good (a progressive attitude) as well as evil, which is the retrograde path of merging into matter, sometimes called 'involution', based on egoism.

By means of specially well-directed efforts, evil and selfish human beings can possess and also obtain, mental abilities far beyond those of average men. In other words, they can gain considerable powers of concentration and thereby enlarge their forces, thus leading them to a certain degree of authority over weaker people and their environment. And there lies the actual danger.

There is no need to enlarge here upon the recent disastrous happenings in the world, when certain unscrupulous individuals have been able to exercize overwhelming influence on those around them and on nations, and the results which have arisen from this sad fact.

Most of us know of the rather pessimistic saying, which however is fundamentally true: 'Power (of course, only relative and materialistic) tends to corrupt and absolute power corrupts absolutely.' A powerful weapon in wrong hands will certainly bring destructive results.

That is why human striving to develop the most effective forces in man, that is, *concentration* and its twin— extraordinary will-power are not always supported by the higher Spiritual Authorities, who alone can help us to attain full achievement and success.

This explains why the vast majority of study done on concentration and its exercises seems to be 'boring', too difficult and finally not to turn out successfully.

In the second part of my trilogy (*Concentration*) I tried to elucidate all the necessary preliminaries, giving exercises in their most accessible and compact forms by limiting them to the bare minimum capable of giving practical results. And still I receive, among others, some letters complaining about difficulties and misunderstandings, which unripe, that is, not sufficiently able students have found in that book.

It is quite different with the practice of theurgy. This art belongs to the spiritual (absolutely selfless realm) and no harm can arise from it, just as we could not possibly expect a true saint to eventually turn out to be a rogue. The worst that can happen to an unsuccessful or unripe aspirant is simply a poor response, if any, from the powers he tried to conjure or implore.

Right from the very beginning a theurgist strives towards goodness, selflessness and the sublime, and to a certain extent usually practises the sacrificing of his time and efforts for the sake of his fellow-men. From the start he trains himself to forget his ego-personality when he is operating, and to act in tune with the great, all-pervading *Whole*. In other words, he seeks union with God. Sensible men, who are not even occultists or theurgists, know very well that there is *more satisfaction in giving than in receiving,* and that there is *more happiness in praying for others than for oneself.* It should be mentioned here, that it is a law, that prayers for others are much more effective and far more frequently fulfilled than those directed to our own purposes.

Techniques, which in other occult paths of development may be trying and complicated, are of little importance for a theurgist. He should certainly not be a completely ignorant person and, moreover, he should at least know what I have tried to explain in the first part of this book.

But there is little similarity to any dogma in the art of our relationship with the Whole (God), and the foremost factors are the presence of faith, good will and the spirit of sacrifice in the aspirant. The way in which these qualities express themselves is not essential: gold will always remain gold and of value even in the form of nuggets, and not just in the articles manufactured from it. This is one of the first things which we have to realize and practise in theurgy.

Finally, we have to answer the question, which concerns the title of this chapter: what sort of preliminary preparation is necessary for us on this path?

It differs from that of other occult ways. Just as *faith, hope* and *love* cannot be developed in a man *ad hoc,* from to-day to to-morrow, as and when he pleases, so an aspirant should first analyze for himself, whether or not the path attracts him, and whether or not he is prepared to act in accordance with it, without shunning the sacrifice expected of him, which he will almost certainly encounter as an introduction to the theurgic realm.

Briefly and bluntly, a man must take a short 'stock-taking' within himself, with full inner sincerity and zeal. If the result is positive he can continue with subsequent chapters, which have been written for him. If not, it would be better to employ his time otherwise.

Sometimes an example serves to illustrate a problem better than an explanation. I found an interesting and deeply mystical account of the true value of man's relation to the Supreme in the last work of Leo Tolstoy, which he compiled for his own use at the very end of his life. The book is called: *A Circle of Reading* and consists of selected proverbs and thoughts taken from many philosophers, writers and the author himself, arranged for every day of the week, and covering the period of a year. There is a longer item such as a legend or story added to each week-end, to serve as a kind of summary, or such was the intention of the famous writer.

The book itself is not at my disposal at the time of writing, but I will try to give a brief account of one of the legends in it.

In olden times in North Russia, on many of the numerous barren islands in the White Sea, beyond the ancient city of Archangel, there were lonely monasteries and solitary abodes of ascetics, who strove to save their souls by prayer, hard work and fasting. Only courageous fishermen passed through the stormy seas surrounding these islands, and the Bishops of Archangel, who held a nominal spiritual authority over the known monasteries, did not seem to bother much about them. In those days the solitary ascetics were left to themselves as this was considered the best service which the outer world could provide for saints, who shunned the worldly tumult.

However, the time came when a new bishop was ordained, who was evidently an energetic man, interested in the ascetics of his district. In particular there were legends in Archangel about three unnamed saints who lived on a desolate little island, without even a church on it. But fishermen insisted that the three men were miracle workers.

So, one day, when the weather was calm, the Bishop ordered a small oar-manned ship to take him to the mysterious island, with one or two fishermen to act as pilots.

After a few hours of rowing, the Bishop found himself on a deserted beach and then three tall, white-bearded figures respectfully approached him. They wore only the rudest possible clothes made of bark and hides and constantly held each other by the hand. After due prostration before the knight of the Church, they told him that they had lived on the island since their youth and had tried to save their souls by work, prayer and fasting. 'But we are illiterate and cannot even pray correctly,' said the eldest of the three. 'We know only one short prayer, as our memories are very weak.' 'What is your prayer?' asked the Bishop. It was very simple, merely: 'There are three of you and three of us: be gracious to us.' Evidently a rudimentary knowledge of the Holy Trinity was the basis of their prayer.

The Bishop considered this formula to be insufficient and said: 'The shortest way to address God is through the Lord's Prayer and you should learn it for your salvation.' 'Teach it to us! Teach it to us!' the old men begged him. And so he started the lesson, eager to enlighten the primitive ascetics.

Finally, after hours of hard work due to the weak memories of his pupils, they were able to repeat the Lord's Prayer faultlessly. Satisfied with his mission, the Bishop took leave and returned to his ship. After the vessel had been rowed for some miles he heard his oarsmen calling to him in fear: 'Your Eminence! Look back! See what is happening on the sea!' The Bishop, who was sitting facing the bow, turned his head and through the light mist of fading day, saw the three old men hastily walking over the waves towards him, giving signs to stop. When they came close, the eldest one bowed and said: 'Your Grace, in God's name forgive us for we are stupid old men: we were repeating the prayer you so graciously taught us when suddenly a word was missed and then the whole prayer fell to pieces. Let us hear it from you again!'

And then the Bishop fell on his knees before the Saints and said meekly: 'Your prayer will reach the Almighty as it is. It is I who have to ask for your grace and prayers.'

So runs the old legend. Apart from the naïve narrative, it shows us the very core of man's relation to the Supreme: faith and sincerity are the only values which count and not elaborate outer forms.

It remains to say but a few words concerning the physical side of preparation for theurgic action. There are no such complicated proceedings as in ritual magic, and so on, because, in theurgy, the operator is not dependent upon so many secondary factors as in occult operations. By turning directly to the Source, he can afford to omit worship of the entities from the higher planes, as well as astrological configurations.

Before the commencement of an operation, it is recommended that you change the clothes you wear every day during your worldly activities for some clean and rather soft attire, preferably made of cotton or silk, with avoidance of woollen materials. It is also desirable to bathe or shower before changing.

You should not be carrying any money on you at the time of worship, as it is too saturated with impure vibrations, which adhere to it from the many former owners, through whose hands it has passed.

All these conditions are to help facilitate your concentration and remove undesirable interference, which comes from physical objects. It cannot be said that a forgotten shilling in your pocket will annihilate all your efforts, in spite of your best will and inner tuning. But the fact remains, that distractions should be avoided, especially for beginners, who are still inexperienced and sensitive to all outer interference.

Finally, undesirable influences from the side of hostile powers, which come from the invisible parts of the universe, cannot be overlooked. Unfortunately they exist and they have more access to an operator when he is not in good order physically. All things in creation are related one to another. So, clothes which have been worn during trivial activities attract astro-mental currents of similar quality. Why unnecessarily add extra difficulties when unavoidable ones are already sufficiently irksome and depressing?

# CHAPTER II

# THE BASIC LAWS OF THEURGY

Three basic Laws rule all theurgic action and they provide justification and reason for it.

*First :*

Every incarnate being forges its own destiny by its deeds, feelings and thoughts. For an occultist there is nothing new in this conception. But let us look deeper.

Our behaviour prepares our reward, in accordance with another law, that of cause and effect. As a result we all have full 'stores' of events and conditions, in which we live, and through which we will have to live when the time is ripe. In brief, all this can be expressed by the well-known and generally accepted term of 'Karma', which comes from our Eastern brethren and their occult philosophy.

That particular part of the whole human karma of an individual, which has to be paid or rewarded in *this* incarnation is called 'Prarabdha Karma', in other words, our current destiny. It is the cup we have to drain in this life.

From this point of view it might appear, that everything is firmly predestined for us, and that nothing can change it, and therefore even theurgic influence would seem to be useless.

Fortunately it is not so. Some masters of theurgy, like the mysterious M. Andréas (as presented by Paul Sédir) and Mâitre Philippe of Lyons, tell us that human intervention, directed to the Supreme, may have response in the form of alleviation of suffering from which we pray for delivery. In his own words and style M. Andréas tells us: 'Heaven may alter the form of repayment.'

This is a very ponderous axiom and I would strongly recommend every earnest reader to think deeply about it, for on it is based every human hope for the best, amidst the troubles and sufferings of earthly life.

Creation, in which we play our modest rôles, is a *living*

organism, and not a dead, motionless and changeless casting. Everywhere forces are at work, every moment causes are born and followed by their results. By introducing immaterial, but most effective forces, like prayers, in a direct appeal to the highest we influence the macrocosm, the whole of creation, which is necessarily reflected on the microcosms, that is, the human beings like ourselves. This Law annihilates the untruth of the idea of the alleged unavoidable and inexorable destiny, promoted by some false prophets and misanthropes. Briefly, we can and we are entitled to act, since we are conscious actors and not merely dancing dolls.

*Second :*

This law teaches us that the most effective action is to turn for all our needs to the Supreme Ruler of creation—God, who knows what is best for everything and does not need our explanations. So Christ taught us, directing us to the One Father in His Lord's Prayer. A purely theurgic analysis and deciphering of this unique spiritual stream, which lifts us to Him to show how we should pray to the Supreme, has been given in Chapter X of *The Tarot.*

A striking example of the way in which truth manifests itself through very different channels (as the spiritual masters of humanity are often called) can be found in the teachings of the last great Rishi of India—Sri Ramana Maharshi (1879-1950). He says: 'Leave all your worries and burdens to God, and He will bear all of them. He created His Universe, and it is His duty to look after it, not yours!' And in yet another place the sage said: 'When taking your place in a train it would be unwise to continue holding your heavy luggage on your shoulders, believing that you are helping the motion of the train. Put it in the luggage-rack and do not burden yourselves unnecessarily.'

When Lafcadio Hearn asked a Buddhist priest to pray for him, the latter wanted to know what the request should be. 'Let the Lord grant me the best that may happen to a man' was the wise answer of the writer. He had a firm faith, and it enlightened his final years.

The keen student will note, that the delicate perfume of the cardinal virtue of theurgy, that of *faith,* penetrates all theurgic laws, attracting those, who are able to feel the extremely subtle vibrations of this spiritual Power.

The foregoing has been stated in order that the reader will have an adequate explanation of and justification for theurgic methods and activities, thereby discarding any doubt about the necessity and effectiveness of spiritual prayer when wisely directed to the Supreme Source of Life and Grace. The techniques and kind of ritual, which you will find in following chapters are only a further development of the central idea of theurgy. They may help you to take your first steps, and to follow the proven tradition of the great theurgists of the past, who succeeded in their immense tasks, and who left to us their spiritual inheritance as a sure guide and inspiration.

*Third :*

This law tells us about the reality of redemption. In the West this idea has been brought to its full power by Christ. Although almost two thousand years have passed since it was first proclaimed, it still remains like an unattainable peak, a lofty ideal, which has never been fully realized by the sons of man. The truth of redemption is, that a stronger being can take on his mighty shoulders the burdens of the weak and ailing, and so alleviate their suffering.

This is what we too have to do for 'others', to the measure of our own strength. It is a practical manifestation of the law of unity, justifying the assistance given by life enclosed in one form, to life hidden in another. In the whole multitude of separate cells in a beehive, it is the honey, filling all those cells, which matters. Everything else is of only secondary importance.

The law of redemption has always been known to the best representatives of the Eastern tradition. In Chapter VIII of *In Days of Great Peace* I quoted the words of a contemporary yogi, who referred to the Vedantic idea of the alleviation of human karmas by spiritual masters, in taking on all the sufferings of those around them as their own, despite the fact that they themselves long ago finished all karmic accounts.

Thus did Ramana Maharshi, the last great Indian Rishi, in this our epoch. May his life inspire you and give insight into this mystery.

# CHAPTER III

# GOD IN THEURGY

The whole construction of theurgic science is based on one cardinal concept: the idea of the Supreme Being we call God. This concept does not lend itself either to discussion or attempts to prove it, since both would merely lead to no conclusion. You have to accept (if you can do it sincerely in your heart) or reject God. In the latter case theurgy is not for you.

This decision is by no means just a mental process, simply because His existence or non-existence cannot be proved externally, that is, demonstrated by means of the mind and faced with all the limitations of human thought. No path leads through conviction, logic or other kind of mental activity to the true realization of God's existence, for numerous things are usually forgotten in deliberations about the supreme. Here I will mention only a few of the most essential ones:

a. *Limitations of the thinking process*

Complete sincerity within ourselves is a necessary condition if we really want to realize these, our limitations, which prevent any cognition of the supermental realm, extending far beyond the mortal mind (the so-called 'Fourth State' in Eastern Yogas). Within these limitations no successful search for the Absolute—God can be undertaken.

Our mind normally works only on the basis of its previous experiences: what we do not know remains a blank impenetrable wall of thought. In trying to learn the construction of the atom's nucleus, the physicist must first be well acquainted with all the latest discoveries about the structure of matter itself. In order to create a serum against a disease doctors must first find and isolate its cause, that is, the germs of that disease. If this cannot be done (as, for example, in the case of cancer) medical science must remain incapable of dealing the death blow to the sickness.

Examples can, of course, be extended *ad infinitum,* but it

is not necessary for the present investigation. All that I want to prove is that we cannot be experts in matters in which we normally have no previous experience and knowledge.

What experiences reaching beyond all mental activities are accessible to the human masses? Very few, and even these are highly problematical. Hence religions and some philosophies try to substitute this lack by superimposed beliefs and dogmas after having declared their 'source' to be divine inspiration. Millions accept all of this as a comfortable refuge from personal analytical research, thus absolving them from any toil and effort.

Actually, there is nothing wrong in the teachings of the great religions on this planet, which are derived from truly enlightened and spiritually experienced founders. At least all of them teach about the doing of good and avoidance of evil, which is only right, for it helps to improve the karmas of the believers and followers. And this means better conditions for the search.

But this does not necessarily give men the real experience of the *Supreme, which alone counts*. It is true that in some religions there have been, and are, incarnate, a few exceptional souls, whom we call saints, who really possessed some wisdom beyond the mind's limitations, and who did not care whether or not others would be convinced as they themselves were, of the actual and experimental existence of the Supreme Power —God, Who is beyond all words and thoughts.

b. There are things which are beyond everyone's experience, that is, things to which we cannot refer as being known to other men, and cannot be expressed in words, without which there is no link between the cognizing elements of separate human consciousness.

c. Those who actually have higher spiritual experiences are not too eager to throw their pearls around, for they are well aware of the results of such unwise behaviour: the cruel, egoistic world would only ridicule them. This is because our inner world cannot be demonstrated for average men, who are not engaged in any higher search. Even so, between men of inner enlightenment, which is sometimes not too exactly called knowledge of God, there exists a mysterious link, which allows them to recognize the germ of spirituality present in those around them.

It is in this way that masters call their disciples and the selection of the apostles is a striking example.

In our own time, cautiousness in partaking of spiritual experiences, which are supposed to lead one to the Supreme, is especially indicated, because of the innumerable fallacies and humbug spread everywhere by the Father of lies, in order to discredit and ridicule the innate human search for the true fatherland of final peace and achievement, and to substitute the counterfeit for the genuine jewel. That is why there are now so many different nonsensical sects backed by false teachers, leading aspirants to bitter disappointment and the denial of any true spirituality. They operate through the vice of curiosity and instead of the inner temple of the soul, create only a tomb for all hope.

d. The next limitation is rather a technical one and lies in our usual inability to concentrate our awareness firmly on the required goal. This is a prevalent malady of the day, which can be cured only by a well directed and persistent, individual effort, involving years of hard work (see the Mystic Trilogy, Part II—*Concentration*).

To resume, it can be stated in general that real experience of the central fulcrum of theurgy, which is God, cannot be available to all and sundry. And those who are already united with Him, as with the unique cause, source and aim, do not need any manuals of theurgy, just as a highly educated person does not need to look into the primers of his childhood.

Hence I will limit the present theme to an exposition of ideas, into which can be translated the personal experiences of God by our older brethren, who have by far surpassed the average level of human development in this period (see Part I of the *Trilogy: In Days of Great Peace:* the Highest Yoga as Lived).

You may accept the following concepts as channels into which you can direct your awareness, when you try to practise theurgy.

Although we often use roads built by others and not ourselves, we can still safely reach our destinations when using these highways, which were planned and constructed by engineers, who knew more about them than we did at the time.

It is necessary to create some workable ideas about the Supreme in ourselves, to which a prospective theurgist can direct all his best feelings, thoughts and intuitive powers, inspiring him to high flight.

The first one would be the building in us of realization of the greatness and incomparable power of the Almighty. This greatness is *absolute* and can be conceived only by adequate (that is, His own) intelligence, and the *Whole*. What then remains for us?

The way of comparison, which alone is accessible to our micro-intelligence, is merely an attempt to catch even a few rays of the majestic sun of Infinite Light. It must be done, and not just spoken about. But how can we convey anything without words? Such a way is open to the masters, it is true. One who sits at the feet of the perfect man, benefits from infinity made into a form accessible to his finite understanding. But this is a rare opportunity and happens to only a few. So the majority of prospective theurgists cannot count on it.

When I sat at the feet of the master Maharshi, everything came of itself without words being exchanged. This mute initiation is for ever, remaining as a source from which the mind can sometimes draw a trickle. Then a book is born.

But the past cannot be turned into the present for contemporary generations: they must also get some guidance, even if not in a direct way.

The following exercises might seem very elementary to you. But do not be deluded by their apparent simplicity: their performance, if it is to be done effectively as intended, needs an all-out effort on the part of the aspirant, and not everyone is able to achieve this aim.

a. Take an empty match-box and look attentively at both its outside and inside, in order to memorize well the form and details of the small article. Then close your eyes and try to build a mental picture of the box. Firstly its outer appearance, and at this moment pay not attention to its inside. The time necessary to perform this first part of the exercise depends upon your ability to concentrate. It may take hours, days or even months. This exercise, well known to occultists, comes from the Eastern Schools of Yoga. Forty years ago I had plenty of difficulty with it, and on occasions believed it to be impossible. Now it is looked back on as child's play. All depends on our steady and sincere effort and endurance. Without these qualities nothing can be achieved. But the task is by no means a superhuman one.

Finally, when the exercise is satisfactorily performed, that is, you can 'see' the outside of the little box clearly enough, turn your attention to its *inside*.

Study the inner surfaces and their general appearance just as you did for the outside. How can this be done? Some people have achieved good results by imagining that they were *inside* the box and observing it from the central point. It is quite an acceptable method, but if you find something better, go right ahead in your own way. The result is what we are seeking.

Now, with two separate mental pictures already formed, proceed further by imagining the box *simultaneously* from both inside and outside as a unit, which it actually is. On the face of it, this might seem to be a pretty hard task, but it is quite feasible.

In any case, a perfect image of the match-box is not what is required for our present purpose, but just the realization of the amount of effort and expansion of our mental pictures, necessary for a good performance, coupled with an understanding of the weakness of the mind, which finds it almost impossible to do such an easy exercise.

For the next stage, slip a few matches inside and then start the whole exercise again. Now it is the entire match-box, plus a dozen or so small wooden sticks all of which are apparently similar in size and shape. Difficulties are sure to arise, so think quietly about the fact.

A good engineer or motor mechanic has a fairly clear picture in his mind of the engine he services or repairs. Otherwise he would not be able to help you when your car is in trouble. And certainly he is not a superman, for there are millions of equally well, or even far better, trained minds.

Now we have reached the main point of this exercise, which is that your consciousness had difficulty in retaining in it an idea about an infinitesimal amount of matter. You know that all the matter of the universe is composed of atoms, and atoms in turn, of still smaller particles which are actually only points of energy. Now imagine the number of atoms in the whole of the visible universe, being as they are miniature solar systems. And try to visualize this conception.

Then turn your attention to the *immense consciousness,*

which retains, at all times, all the smallest particles of matter together with their combinations into elements, planets, solar systems and galaxies.

The human mind often becomes dizzy at such an effort of the imagination. But there is no need to be afraid of this. Meditate tenaciously with the maximum of endurance, at certain appropriate times, when you are not likely to be interrupted or otherwise distracted.

Learn by this meditation that this unimaginably vast consciousness is merely a fragment of His consciousness. This is one of the best conceptions of the Supreme accessible to us in an unbiased form.

From this attribute of immenseness about which you will meditate, it is easy to derive ALL the others which are usually ascribed to the divinity. The *greatness* of His all-penetrating consciousness MUST include all the virtues which men—in their imperfect language of the mind—try to attribute to God.

You will probably find, as others have done before you, that such a greatness must necessarily be *omniscient, omnipotent* (for It embraces everything), perfectly *just, good* and is—*love* (this being a form of the universal law of attraction). To such a being you can turn with the utmost *faith* and *hope.*

b. The next exercise will be a modification of the former one. Meditate about the idea of Him being all-penetrating. Also turn your attention to yourself, your mind, feelings and finally, your body. See that all of these are penetrated by the consciousness of the ONE. That is what great saints and occultists realized in their lives. From their experiences arose religious dogma, which, unfortunately—for the inexperienced masses—appear to be abstruse and devoid of life. Now you may see for yourself, that it is not so. The masses are wrong and the advanced units are right. Be one of them!

# CHAPTER IV

# FAITH IN THE SUPREME

All the operations of theurgy are directed to the *One Source*. It is the Supreme Being, the absolute ruling and creative power, which we call 'God'. There is no need for long deliberation about the fact, that without a living faith in this deciding factor, which alone can fulfil the entreaties of the theurgist, no action whatsoever is possible. The most punctiliously performed ritual and exact form of prayer will be useless and without any wings if the operator does not believe in the power which he tries to invoke.

This means that a *living faith* is a condition for any successful theurgic action. It seems that no other conception has been more misunderstood, confused and abused than that of *faith*. The aim of the present chapter will be to give a brief introduction to the realization of the true meaning of *faith*.

Firstly I will explain what faith *is not*, for this is much easier at the start of the study for beginners, than a direct assertion.

If we merely guess about the possibility of the existence of the Supreme (no matter in what religious or philosophical form), we have no *faith* and consequently, no power of realization. If we *try to convince* ourselves of the probability and the logical necessity and usefulness of the idea of God, we are perhaps starting a long journey in the direction of a true and realizable *faith*, but by no means do we possess It. Indeed, practical research shows, that there is very little chance of obtaining *faith* in such a way. Some eminent saints and theurgists bluntly deny the possibility of acquiring *faith* by mental efforts. We can conclude how right such an attitude is when we read certain parts of a book about religious conceptions, recently published in London, which is a striking example of the absurdity to which even a relatively developed outer mind can come, when it is far distant from the reality of *faith*.

As one of the conclusions in this book we find the idea of the probability of beings, which possess certain divine (in the author's conception) qualities, extending their realms to the different galaxies. In this way we are presented with quite a considerable number of deities, equal to that of the galaxies, if not the solar systems. This is only a minor example of where a questing into the superphysical and spiritual realms by the limited means of the mortal brain can lead.

No materialistic research can ever give us *faith,* if it has not already been germinating in us. If it has been then it will manifest itself in due time and in the proper circumstances. These are so numerous that it would be impossible to give any general rule, which, moreover, does not seem to exist, as we know by means of our thinking apparatus.

The only thing that matters is: do we have *faith* or not?

Real *faith* has nothing in common with such popular sayings as: 'Yes, I believe in God' which is usually only a verbalization of a well-known theme. There is no deeper sense in it, and therefore, no realizable power, as is always the case with any truism: for *faith* is one of the chief powers, as we will see further on in this chapter.

*Faith* is quite different from any blind belief or superstition. The saying 'he has a blind faith' is without any meaning for those who really know something about *faith.* Also, superstition is rather just the absence of *faith,* a worthless ersatz, a substitute of the lowest quality. It cannot be doubted that, in spite of all the materialism in our 'progressive' age as well as in the former, 'barbaric' periods of humanity's life, the mysterious inner feeling about 'something' beyond the visible and tangible objects of the world was and is invariably present in our species on this planet.

A cardinal point of discrimination here will be the difference between *faith* and *beliefs,* a difference which is too often disregarded, so that both of these incompatible concepts get confused with each other. Every belief is a product of one's emotional and mental life, and in every case, can be clearly traced to its origin. Even the official science of psychology knows a lot about this and uses the tracing of some wrong beliefs and mental attitudes to their origins, in order to find the cause and then try to remove it from the patient.

Finally, the difference between *faith* and *beliefs* can be shown in another way. Every belief must have an object as its basis, no matter in which realm it is found—physical, emotional or mental. It is not a power, but an attitude, usually connected with the play of imagination. All this is unnecessary and not desirable for theurgic action, which operates on a much higher level: true *faith* being one of the corner-stones of the art of effective prayer.

Having gradually finished with the explanations which show what *faith* IS NOT, we come to the most difficult problem—that of giving *positive* indications of what *faith* IS.

The reader will certainly agree, that if *faith* did belong to the realm of mind's consciousness, then it could be successfully translated into minds main sphere, that of human speech. But this is not so and there lies the whole difficulty. Whoever thinks otherwise simply does not understand the position.

So, in attempting to describe the indescribable, it will be necessary for us to make statements, which, while not departing from the truth about *faith,* are, because of what has just been said, a little incomplete. Still, we have to agree that even a 'little' is better than nothing.

*Faith* is a power, which possesses all the attributes we ascribe to that aspect of power and force which we know acts in this world, but which, at the same time, infinitely transcends both of them. Gravity, magnetic forces, inertia, the power in atoms, light, electric currents, and so on, are—to a certain limited degree—comparable with the power of *faith.* And it is through this comparison that I am trying to convey the idea of one of the dynamic manifestations of *faith.*

The most striking—at the same time—perhaps the most mysterious definition of *faith's* attributes was given to us by Christ: '. . . if you have faith as a grain of mustard-seed, you shall say to this mountain: Remove from hence hither, and it shall remove. . . .' Incidentally, a 'prophet' who, while trying to found a 'new religion', constantly plagiarized the Old and New Testaments and added some earlier primitive beliefs of his tribe, knew of this saying of the great master and tried to cover his own lack of *faith* (and therefore possession of any higher powers) with the following ambiguous little statement: 'If the mountain will not go to Mahomet, let Mahomet go to the mountain.' But theurgy, which aims at real results, does not indulge in such jokes.

From those few who have possessed *faith* and have been able to lift a small corner of this great mystery, we can see that rather it is a *state* than an experience. This is because true *faith* cannot be lost. It is a permanent state of an advanced human being and belongs to his innermost treasure.

If someone tells us that he 'had faith but later lost it' it simply means that he *never* possessed any *faith*.

Now we come to the most difficult problem, that of giving to the student of this book an approximate description of *faith*: not *faith* itself, which is beyond our possibilities, but what the fortunate person, who has found his final peace in *faith* thinks and feels. Firstly there is some affinity with the supermental, spiritual state of *Samadhi*, which is the chief aim of Eastern Yogis, and the privilege of their great sages, or rishis.

The common factor is the lack of any visions and other occult phenomena, which are only a certain form of satisfied curiosity, merely extended into worlds other than the physical. But no matter how different and at times apparently lofty these phenomena may be, they are as temporary (that is, mortal) as the person who experiences them.

From the foregoing we may see that *faith* is and can be only ONE! But apparently the problem is dual: *faith* has a universal character, it is a homogeneous, unique power, and we can either have It, or not have It. Then comes the 'second aspect of *faith*'. It can be directed only to the Supreme, no matter how we define IT. And here lies the difficulty: to express in human language what is beyond it. How is it possible to have pure, absolute *faith*, and at the same time to direct it only to God? All that can be said is, that only *faith* in the Supreme has power, while all other 'faiths' are illusions or superstitions and we have already dealt with the latter at the beginning of this chapter.

Briefly, if you wish to be a theurgist, you must first of all have *faith* in the omnipotent, supreme power, which alone can answer your prayers and strivings. It is a fact, just as that of being, say, a man and not otherwise, no matter how much we may like or dislike it. And it is just the same with *faith*.

*Faith* is a force far beyond all physical ones: we know that martyrs, animated by it, completely disregarded their bodies and all their physical relationships, fearlessly allowing themselves to be destroyed (often in a dreadful way while still living), in order not to betray by even the slightest word or movement, the Lord in whom they had their true *faith*. We know from history, that in most cases, where Christian proselytes were condemned to be thrown to wild animals or tortured to death, the only thing which was required of them in order to avoid such a fate was the burning of a little incense before the Emperor's statue. And yet they refused.

There is another mysterious power which can be equally likened to *faith*: it is, of course—*love*. And all that has been said about *faith*, can also be applied to *love*. This is because both of them are usually found together, and those who are fortunate enough to have faith in God, also necessarily have love for Him.

In the case of perfect theurgists, such as certain saints, both of these two facets of spiritual achievement seem to be united, as if melted into oneness.

As this does not yet apply to us, who are still seeking theurgy alone, we had best return to a further developing of the theme of this chapter.

When those who know what *faith* is speak about It, they state that there is a mysterious element of knowledge or, better, wisdom, which parallels *faith*. These men do not complain about any lack of knowledge or certainty, for they have full inner peace, derived from a lack of *curiosity* and the *expectancy* of 'something new which might happen to them'. This can be only because they already possess the deep-seated inner wisdom, which makes all other forms of cognition appear too trivial and childish to them.

It can be mentioned here, that curiosity and anxiety (or the mood of constant expectancy) are the chief obstacles to concentration, preventing domination of one's mind. More concerning this particular study will be found in *Concentration*.

*Faith* is neither identical nor necessarily concomitant with a special intellectual development. We would find it hard to believe that many of the saints or sages were, at the same time, eager students of worldly knowledge, or that they were keen speakers or philosophers (in our everyday meaning of these words).

One of these great men—whom I was privileged to see—the Indian Rishi Ramana, although in general a fairly well-educated man (he was trained in a Missionary High School) was not interested in any special problems of contemporary science or official philosophy, and would not discuss Einstein's famous equations, or any current theories on cosmogony, or existentionalism, and so on. This was because he knew that all of these things cannot give us the wisdom and high morality, so necessary for spiritual realization.

To conclude, I would like to mention a strange fact: two men in whom *faith* is developed, will always recognize one another, even without much talking. Sometimes just a few words will suffice for them to know.

The motto for this chapter will be: If you want to be a theurgist, you should have *faith* in the power you want to implore. This is only logical, but how many will forget this and try to perform the impossible feat of being successful in theurgy without *faith* in their hearts?

# CHAPTER V

# INSTRUCTION FOR ACTION

Theurgic actions are divided into different categories, the two main groups being:

1. Individual action
2. Collective action

In 1 we find further sub-divisions:

a. Action for the benefit of the operator himself
b. Action for the benefit of other persons
c. Action for the benefit of living persons
d. Action for the benefits of deceased persons

For 2, that is, collective action, the sub-divisions are identical, with the slight difference that 'a' action for the benefit of the operator is deleted. A group is NOT supposed to pray for itself, because it is an artificial unit composed of separate individuals, all of whom have their own karmas, and each member of a Group should be treated individually, if the need for assistance occurs.

Every operation *must start with a turning to the Supreme Lord,* followed by the basic request.

*Formula I*

BLESSED BE THOU, O LORD, ENLIGHTEN ME THROUGH THY INITIATION

This is an initial addressing, which must precede every theurgic operation, personal as well as collective. As can be seen, the first half is an expression of our reverence and love for the Almighty: for He is the *absolute good* for the theurgist, and He is the sole dispenser of every boon, the unique Source of all help, bliss and life for us. How otherwise would we turn to Him, if not with our humble blessing? In theurgy, as in other branches of true occultism, the instructions given are *firmly based on a positive knowledge of the human psyche and its attitudes.* Then, through the use of formulas, their explanation and operation, the path necessary in order to follow the great theurgists is shown, and also how to approach their achievements. Simply, those who give you these instructions know very well what will happen to you if you faithfully carry them out. Think deeply about this so that you may realize how you have to act in a certain way and not another. If your mind is still your overlord, and by its whims and doubts does not permit you to raise your consciousness beyond it (the mind is certainly not happy about such an alternative), then forsake any attempt to take advantage of theurgy. In such a case, your brain is still unable to reflect any glimpse of the imperishable, which lies hidden deep within you, as in every being.

It yet remains for me to make you aware of something, which even your mind cannot deny: that mind and brain are mortal twins. You cannot expect your brain's consciousness to act as your instrument after the destruction of your physical body, which cannot be avoided. You will not take the possessions of your brain—considered by so many to be the highest in man—in your further wandering through the forms of manifested life, to which you still belong. Is this not so?

To those ripe enough theurgy offers to set them free from the slavery of mortal factors: it is a way in which the non-perishable, eternal elements of man's consciousness may be opened to you. The choice is yours alone, as nobody else can live your life.

Be well aware of the significance of the foregoing. Theurgy is one of the paths, but, of course, not a unique one. There are also others about which I have spoken in my other books.

But the *deifying of the mortal elements* in man (an example of which has just been given) and the stressing and placing of one's whole hope in them, is *not a path at all,* but merely a tragic blundering, no matter how 'brilliant' the forms it may sometimes seem to take to undiscriminating people.

No reasonable man would put his life's savings into a bank, which he knows will inevitably become bankrupt. I hope you realize what I mean.

There is also an inner, mystical side to Formula I. It establishes the proper relation of the operator towards the source, from which he expects to obtain that for which he prays. Beginners, who, as yet, do not possess much practice and experience in invoking the Lord, should repeat it many times beforehand and learn to feel its meaning deeply in their hearts, so that, when the time for the action proper arrives, the pronouncing of this invocation *will immediately tune* the operator to the right mood and attitude. This means that he will then think only about what he intends to perform and, for the time being, merge into adoration of the Lord, forgetting his everyday interests.

I do not again need to underline the absolute necessity and decisive importance of the invocation for any further theurgic work. It is simply a condition for any possible success and you should never forget it.

The second half of Formula I is the request, and its mystical importance cannot be overestimated. We ask the omnipotent Giver for His enlightenment. What can be more reasonable and essential for the start of theurgic action? Enlightenment alone can preserve us from erring and inspire us to a right performance of our task.

All failures and wrongdoing come from the darkness in us. We need certainty and the light of wisdom. And where is the surest source from which we can obtain both of them, if not from Him?

Such is the simple but efficient philosophy for a true aspirant of theurgy. At the end of his life, St Augustine, himself an eminent philosopher and a wise man, expressed a final idea of achievement by saying that: 'The anxieties of human hearts can be stilled only when we find ultimate repose in the Lord.' And His enlightenment is, at the same time, the genuine and most efficient initiation. Theurgic tradition recommends a few technicalities which can be applied before and during an action and these are now presented for your consideration. They are not absolutely indispensable, especially for well-advanced people, but for beginners, they bring the desired results more easily.

If you intend to work alone, then no other person should be present in the chosen room except yourself. Naturally, the fully-trained operator can inwardly perform the whole of the necessary ritual, while being little affected by conditions around him, as his power of concentration permits him to exclude all outer impressions and disturbances from his field of awareness. But, so as to make a good start we should be careful and not risk any disappointment right from the very beginning, if we are still only aspirants and not masters, which latter is surely not the case. Do avoid any disorder in the room where you propose to operate, making sure that everything around you is tidy and clean. It is quite astonishing how improper surroundings, in the form of neglect of order around us, can prevent, or, at least, delay success.

Choose the right time, when there is a minimum of noise and the risk of being disturbed by calls and visits. Early morning and the quiet of evenings are usually recognized as the best times, but if you have to arrange otherwise, do not worry about it.

Never take meals, smoke or use alcohol just before starting your action. Allow at least two hours to elapse before you begin. A small amount of good incense burned in the room will purify the atmosphere and a not too bright light is recommended.

Theurgists operate in the worlds where there are no material veils, just as they do on the physical plane, on which the outer, fleshy shell may very well hide the astro-mental processes which find their place in man. I am referring to the currents of emotions and thoughts which pass through man's consciousness. Our eyes cannot always see human feelings and mental activities as they really are. Self-possessed individuals may be able to conceal their emotions under an outer mask of indifference or even just the opposite of what they really feel. But in the less material worlds where feelings (astral) and thoughts (mental) move and act, just as our physical bodies do here, neither of these two functions can be hidden. Even so, we sometimes hear of so-called 'thought-reading' by persons known as 'clairvoyants' or 'telepathists' and everyone knows from his or her own experience that, though invisible, feelings and thoughts are undoubtedly potent forces. Some people also know that these forces can be modified, directed and dominated (see my *Trilogy*, Part II—*Concentration*). Therefore our attitude, which is a complex of both astral and mental elements, is a deciding factor in every action in the invisible realms in which theurgists operate. In order to make this problem clearer still I will give only a simile in simple terms: our physical bodies, which belong to the material plane, perform on that plane according to their abilities, powers, state of health, and so on. Exactly the same happens when a man operates in the two subtle worlds—those of feelings and thoughts. The stronger a man is and the more able to concentrate his efforts in these two realms, the better and more enduring will be the results of the action.

The prayer of a trained theurgist is like the majestic flow of a large river; but an ignorant and weak person can produce only something similar to an irregular trickle from a half-clogged tap.

Different causes bring different results and it is a truth you have to fully realize, so as to avoid errors and disappointment.

Here may be mentioned two physical means, practice of which will greatly facilitate concentration during prayer and at the same time, lessen nervous tension and anxiety, which are such formidable obstacles to any spiritual work by beginners.

a. Breathing exercises, as given in Chapter XV of *Concentration*. There an aspirant will find a full description of pranayama, as these exercises have been called in Eastern Yoga.

b. When you meditate or pray and decide to do so with closed eyes, turn your eyeballs upwards as high as you can, and keep them in that position throughout the course of your action. The more you practise this simple rule, the more you will appreciate its effectiveness. Greater inspiration and less distracting earthly thoughts will result.

Some people practise turning up the eyeballs even with the eyes open (naturally when they are alone) and in certain theurgic groups members find both of the rules a and b indispensable for their work, personal as well as collective.

Now that we are acquainted with the correct way to start we can proceed to further steps in the next chapters.

# CHAPTER VI

## TECHNICALITIES OF THE RITUAL

In the preceding chapter (Instructions for Action) you found material and direction on how to use the basic Formula I, which is indispensable before every invocation. Now comes the time to use it practically and some indication must be given here of how to deal with outer activities (ritual) and techniques. At the end of Chapter V some special exercises were given, which contribute to the creation of the most favourable conditions for an action.

Now, if you feel due inspiration and a desire to turn to the Almighty with all your knowledge, in order to gain enlightenment and inner peace, choose a suitable time when no one can disturb you, and with full attention start to study the prayer of St Ephraem the Syrian (see Formula II in Chapter XV—Action for Liberation from Inner Troubles), so that when you will have occasion to use it, no uncertainty or forgetfulness will stand in your way. Items a. to m. in Chapter XV must be worked right through and the formula written down on a separate piece of paper if it is not convenient to use the book during an operation.

1. Sit as advised in Chapter V.
2. Perform pranayama if you feel it will be helpful (see Chapter XV of *Concentration*).
3. Commence with Formula 1, pronouncing every word slowly and with full understanding. In turning to the Almighty you must do so with the utmost reverence and humility, in the full realization of your mere nothingness in comparison with the Great Whole (God). In Chapter IX dealing with collective action you will find a special formula, which prevents an improper attitude and teaches the right way in which to act.
4. Now pronounce the first part of Formula II, that is, item a. the invocation, and since you are supposed to study the explanations concerning the items in Chapter XV beforehand, the idea contained in it should come readily to your mind. Slowly repeat the words aloud or mentally, at least three times

or more if you feel it will be more effective and capable of giving you greater concentration. Under the old tradition the operator sits or stands facing east, and bows each time he pronounces the prayer. Have full faith in it. In the same way pass to the next parts of Formula II until you reach the end. Close the operation with the final blessing (n).

The length of time you take depends entirely upon yourself and the degree of concentration attained, that is, freedom from intruding thoughts, which gives purity to an operation. In the beginning you will probably have to take longer because of the difficulty in avoiding thinking about things that have nothing in common with the operation. Remember, if you decide to use every part of the formula, say, three times, you must perform it, in spite of intruding thoughts.

When you have finished take rest, sitting quietly at peace with eyes closed and try not think about any trivial matter.

As a matter of interest, some theurgic groups in various parts of the world use a more complicated ritual and wear a special linen or silk garment, usually white, styled like a full-length, loose-fitting shirt with long, wide sleeves and a white cord worn round the waist to serve as a belt. Soft, white shoes without heels are also worn. Such groups usually accompany invocations and blessings by the sign of the cross; chant prayers instead of just saying them; choose hours and days according to the corresponding astrological times; fast from six to twenty-four hours before an operation, and some theurgists use a few drops of holy water taken from a church in a little sponge, to moisten their foreheads before an operation.

All these additional paraphernalia are NOT essential for the success of an operation, but rather they serve as a means of adding solemnity and concentration, which benefit an operator if he is in agreement with them. Hence their use is left to your own discretion. The *essential* factors are, as has already been mentioned, sincerity, *faith,* devotion of the operator, the solemnity of his intention to operate theurgically and concentration in order to give a clear and trouble-free performance. Everything else is of secondary importance. All of the aforesaid is equally valid for group operations. Sick persons cannot perform actions directed to the regaining of their health; but the task must be delegated to other theurgists, preferably a group.

# CHAPTER VII

# CONDUCT OF OPERATIONS

It seems to be appropriate to collect together in a separate chapter all the requisite conditions and rules, which are obligatory in theurgic activities, instead of spreading them over other chapters as additions to actual rituals and operations.

Read them before you study the chapters explaining the techniques and methods used in theurgy. This will facilitate understanding and prevent many mistakes, which otherwise could not be avoided. Every misunderstanding leads to errors, and errors mean lack of success by creating dangerous frustrations.

1. Never act immediately after meals. The best time would be after two hours have elapsed since food was last taken. The same refers to alcohol and tobacco, if you are unfortunate enough to still use them. Apart from the undermining of our physical strength, their greatest harm lies in their weakening of our will-power. When he is obedient to such physical habits a man allows himself to commit something which he knows (if he is intelligent enough) to be nonsense from the common sense point of view.

2. The standard rules of hygiene must be observed before every theurgic invocation or prayer. So far as you are still an incarnate being your body is somewhat a part of you, and its conditions do affect your consciousness. In wishing to obtain the best results, it is necessary to use the best means available, as they will greatly diminish the manifold obstacles which face every beginner.

3. Before every major operation, the leader, at least, should don fresh clothing and avoid wearing metal or money on himself.

4. If there is to be a major personal, or group invocation, tradition recommends at least six hours of absolute fasting beforehand. This rule refers equally well to the second part of this book, where traditional religious worship and formulas

are indicated. You simply cannot enter another person's home for worship and help concerning your vital problems, without strict observance of the rules given in this chapter. If not, who can be blamed for lack of success in your operation?

5. It is strongly recommended to perform at least a half-dozen pranayamas before every major theurgic action, whether alone or in a group. In most theurgic groups throughout the world, common exercises in pranayama are performed before worship with excellent results for the purpose of the action and for the operators themselves.

6. Sexual relations also have to be similarly arranged as in items 2. and 3. of this chapter.

7. Mentally and emotionally forgive all your 'real' and supposed enemies before you engage yourself in prayer for yourself or others. Worship performed, when at the bottom of your heart there remain hidden hatreds or fears, is useless, for then it does not have any ascending power and can even be dangerous, since it can attract forces which are quite different from the desired good ones.

8. If you are a member of a theurgic group, unswervingly follow the words of the leader when he is acting. Listen to his directives in whatever you have to do during every moment of the operation, whilst in the circle.

9. If you are performing healing work, remember that you may easily become involved in the same position as that of the 'patient' whom you are now trying to help. The *quality* of your effort is what counts. Some day you may urgently need the same help from the side of other operators. There is an occult law: *as you are for others, so they will be for you.*

10. If you happen to lack a solemn, dignified attitude towards the operation about to be performed, or if you have some mental doubts about it, *do not start at all.* Adjourn the meeting or personal session. Better to delay and wait until one is in a more desirable frame of mind than spoil the results, reap disappointment and so bear the responsibility for frustration of the effort of your brother theurgists.

11. When a group is assembled there should be no chatting among the members. A quiet attitude and silence are the best. Questions, if they arise, should be answered before the actual meeting.

12. It is inconceivable that you will accept even the most

insignificant material reward for your spiritual action in helping others. Even in a magic operation of a high degree, the acceptance of any money or other payment is strictly forbidden. In theurgy there is absolutely no exemption from this rule. No matter whether the help is of a minor or major character, everything must be unselfish and devoid of any thought of reward.

13. Intense and very ardent worship and operations can be accompanied by bowing and genuflections. In the Christian methods of ritual (Part II) both are essential from the traditional point of view and the sign of the Holy Cross should be used every time as indicated in the text, by following the example of the leader.

14. Similarly, if use of blessed water is prescribed, it can be obtained from a church, or blessing may be performed by the operator himself, according to the ritual as given in Part II.

15. Salt and incense should be blessed before use, as prescribed in Part II, Chapter XXII.

16. If special clothes are used, they should be treated as in items 14. and 15.

17. The texts for every operation and worship may be copied from the book in writing or typed on separate pieces of paper, so that they can be clipped together in the order of their use for the convenience of the operator. It may be impracticable to use the whole book for this purpose, as this will involve interruptions while seeking the appropriate texts and is undesirable for concentration and the general solemnity of the operation.

18. No sick person should take an active part in the circle of a group operation, even if it is performed for his or her benefit. Some theurgists allow the patient to be present in the room, but outside the circle. Generally speaking it is better when the patient is apart and praying in his own home, just at the time when he knows that the group is acting on his behalf.

19. In operations for the blessing of a home or expulsion of evil forces, the theurgists may go from one room to another, reciting the ritual and using blessed water and salt, as prescribed.

20. Worship for a dying person may be held in his room. It is not advisable to use the ritual for the dead when the corpse is still in the room. It should be removed as soon as possible

to the church or funeral chapel, and left there in peace for the rest of the time before burial. Do not try to mix theurgic rituals with those of the officiating priest or other minister; let them perform their own duties without any (even mental) interference. Churches have their own egregors and rights, which should be respected. Funeral masses are also theurgic operations of great efficiency, even if the minister is ignorant and not attentive from our point of view. This is because of the power of the egregor of the religion involved in the funeral rites, and the mass is one of the channels for that power, conducting it to earth.

21. The candles to be used should be made of wax, as prescribed for churches. For some especially urgent and important cases, such as a service for the dying, someone in extreme danger, or facing an important trial, tradition recommends candles which have been used during the Easter midnight service (Catholic and Orthodox Churches) and taken home, according to custom, after the Church celebration of the Resurrection.

22. The best type of incense is that in the form of sandalwood sticks, as used in India and other Eastern countries. These are now readily available in the West. Powder-like church incense is also excellent, but it requires more attention because of the need for charcoal.

In brief, any incense made from natural resins is acceptable, but not chemically perfumed materials, because they are of doubtful purity and efficiency.

Finally, I would again like to repeat a warning. Do not try to engage in any theurgic ritual merely to satisfy your curiosity, and without due respect to the powers involved, or for a so-called 'test'. In the best of cases under such circumstances the result will be nil. Otherwise, it can bring swift retribution from the offended forces, which are infinitely superior to all human resources (see Chapter XII, Invocation to the Holy Spirit).

## CHAPTER VIII

# PERSONAL ACTION

In this chapter we will consider the first category of theurgic action, the simplest and most frequently used. From their everyday practice many people know that by no means are all of their prayers fulfilled and the obtaining of desired results is rather rare indeed. There must be a definite reason for this. But we must realize that the sphere of theurgic science and action is unlike any other branch of human knowledge and activity.

Why is this so? Man-made science, its methods and further, all products of the human mind and hand—as, for example, apparatus and machinery—belong solely to the realm of man himself, his activities and possibilities. But even here we have good and not-so-good scientists and engineers and the outcome of their labours are according to the qualities of the men involved in the work. Even so, there are and always will be, men who are able to handle and direct man-made things to the full, and who will not complain that these things are beyond their control. This is clear, as, in this case, all the factors are within human reach.

Does the same apply to theurgic science? *Certainly not!* We have to realize that it is rather fragments of laws and principles belonging to theurgic actions which are known, and then, only to a limited number of men. Many influences, upon which depend certain fulfilment of a prayer are unknown and inaccessible to us. We know only the general outline and a few rules directing how we should act in order to ensure the greatest possible chance of success. But in this field our actions will never be equal to that of say, a scientist who knows exactly the potential of a current he has to apply so as to obtain a definite and wanted result in his experiments. You know that if you get thirty miles per gallon from your car, you cannot expect to travel a hundred miles in it with just a gallon of fuel in the tank. But you never will be able to say, that for a quarter of an hour of prayer you will get such and such a result. It seems to be so simple and perhaps even childish, but many people are not aware of this and still need to be told about it.

Finally, what are the known and unknown factors in the realm of theurgic action and how can we define them? The main weapon is an intelligent, sincere, selfless and well-directed prayer, but not a confused repetition of some pious texts from a prayer-book. This is the corner-stone of our present knowledge in the matter. As we will see later on in this book, in the course of further unfolding of our problems, there are still some other conditions, all of which are within the limits of human reach. Similarly, we will also speak about things beyond that reach: conditions unknown to us which may counterbalance our efforts and which simply leave our prayers unfulfilled.

Now, what is an intelligent prayer? Firstly, we should know where we are directing our action. Having already studied the chapter dealing with *faith* and *God*, there should not be any difficulty in realizing this. In theurgy, every prayer should be directed to the Central, absolute, creative power: that all-embracing Whole which we call 'God'.

Here you may notice a difference when compared with some religious creeds which advise their faithful to pray to the saints as being closer to us, ordinary human beings: the saints, who can also be the 'channels', directing, assisting and fortifying our weak efforts. While not denying the usefulness of this kind of worship, theurgy, which is an advanced spiritual science, deals, as has already been mentioned, with *tuning* the operator directly to the Source of all, because, in any case, even when going through intermediaries, prayer must rise to the Highest if it is to have any chance of success. And this knowledge we call *'intelligent action'*.

The necessity of absolute sincerity in prayer is so evident, that very little can be added by way of explanation. Perhaps a simple example will be more enlightening than a lengthy deliberation.

Imagine that you give information to a person, upon whom depends the fulfilment of a request you have made, while being aware that its falseness *is known* to that person. Could you, under such circumstances, expect a positive answer and agreement?

When praying you turn yourself to the Power which *knows* and penetrates everything and cannot be deceived in any way. Is there even the slightest chance of any successful cheating, which term also covers every insincere prayer? Judge for yourself!

Moreover, know that in such an event, the indignity of an insincere turning to the Highest Power will fall on your head as a disastrous damnation resulting from an unwise and impure action. If one cannot manage to remain open and unspoiled throughout the period of turning to the Almighty, it would be better not to engage oneself in such a way. That is until, at least during the time of worship, one's feelings and thoughts are sufficiently cleansed, so that in the very moment of turning to the Supreme, one's heart will not be like a cloak full of offensive impurities.

A *selfless* prayer means that one should not request anything which may be in conflict with the rightful interests of our fellow men. This means that *you dare not pray* for, say, a plague of pests, which is devastating your land, to be expelled and settle in your neighbour's fields.

This is only a simple example, but it is also one into which you may fit your own deeds. If there is a drought do not pray for rain just for your own garden. If you want someone to do something for you, make sure that it is not contrary to his legitimate interests, and that it does not limit or offend against his free-will.

You may tell me that there are occult means to obtain what is wanted without being bound by the moral obligations of an action. Of course this is so. Forced suggestions, hypnosis, magic compulsion and similar offenses can bring some short-lived and limited results; but always followed by the inevitable, bitter retribution consequent upon wrong deeds, just as your shadow follows your body. And this way is not a form of theurgy, but is an occult fraud (see Chapter XLIV of my *Ways to Self-Realization*).

So, when you want to pray for yourself do not be too exact in your requests. The best form, which will never take a dangerous, offensive or selfish shape, would be a *mute adoration* of the Supreme. If you cannot yet achieve this because of a lack of ability to concentrate passively and if you must still use thoughts (that is, verbalize your requests), then ask about light, grace, solace, and so on. Remember that HE KNOWS better what you really need, HE KNOWS far beyond all your conceptions and problems. Open your heart in silence and listen: let Him speak, not you. This is the way in which even 'miracles' are achieved, if you like to use this expression which is not very exact from a theurgic point of view.

Are we then allowed to pray for some definite purposes, such as deliverance from sickness, hardship, danger, fear, enemies, and so on? Yes! We can, but only under the foregoing conditions. The 'universal' way of prayer (mute, with an open heart) will serve best. However, some people still need to express themselves in speech. Then let them talk to Him, as to a great, all-understanding friend and protector of infinite power and wisdom, who sees into our hearts and minds. This effort, like every true prayer will not be wasted. But always be aware that not every request can be fulfilled, as we have a lot of 'debts' and our difficulties may be a payment for them, which has already commenced in the form of suffering. It cannot be stopped. As you already know from former chapters Easterners call this part of Karma—Prarabdha.

Sometimes the form of 'repayment' may be altered according to our prayers, but it is by no means certain, as we can see from the foregoing.

Here occur the 'unknown' and 'incalculable' factors which, as we said at the beginning of this chapter, may prevent the apparent success of any theurgic action, no matter whether the operator directs it for himself or others. Here perhaps we can realize the meaning of some of the 'evils' affecting us, which have little or no chance of being removed. A striking example is that of the so-called 'incurable diseases', although cases are known, where even these stubborn ailments have been subdued. If an incurable disease attacks a body, it may be a clear hint that Prarabdha Karma will not alter its designs, which will then mean death of the physical body.

That is why a theurgist in concluding his prayers and conjurations will always add the final words of the great teacher: '. . . But yet not my will, but thine be done.

In the theurgic tradition of the nineteenth century we find some powerful and inspired invocations, which are also suitable for our own day. A condensation of such formulas used for personal worship as well as for the benefit of other people will now be given and these intimate prayers can be successfully used not only in the day-time, but also at night, especially when we are sleepless and feel fear, loneliness or anxiety. At night-time a man is more vulnerable than by day as far as the psychical states which occur to us are concerned.

*O Eternal Absolute,* whose infinitesimal ray struggling through eons of incarnations am I, deign to direct my steps to Thee!

*O Light* in which there is no shadow, enlighten my path!

*O Goodness* without measure, ennoble my heart towards my fellow men!

*O Infinite,* all penetrating wisdom, make me understand even the smallest fraction of Thy designs!

*O Absolute, pure Love,* destroy every trace of the primordial sin in me, which is the feeling of separateness in existence!

*O Unique Truth,* beyond all images and thoughts, let Thy reflection dwell in me, blinded as I am by ignorance and tortured by doubts!

*O Thou the Only Aim,* guide my steps to union with Thee, thus letting me fulfil Thy will and attain peace!

In my struggles send me the power to endure, O Lord!
In my despair send me the angel of Thy hope!
In my sadness allow me to taste of Thy illimitable joy!
In my troubles let me feel Thy absolute harmony!
For see here comes the prodigal son to his Father's feet,
Taught his hard lessons by the eternal book of life.

This prayer can also be used for those whom we want to help simply by changing the 'me' in it to 'him' or 'her' and the 'my' to 'his' or 'her', and so on.

The following Mahayanistic Buddhist worship is held in high esteem by theurgists:

O Amitabha, illimitable light, penetrating the whole world,
O Lord of Compassion, following in the steps of Thy precursors,
O Master of Nirvana, who reigns in the full bliss of attainment,

Bless my path along the innumerable spokes of the wheel of life.
Teach me to recognize Maya in all its infinite forms,
Thereby destroying the roof of my prison's illusion!
Aum Mani Padme Hum! The attainment is sure!

*A Hindu Prayer*

We can find a splendid example of Vedantic theurgy in the ancient initiatory worship of the Gayatri, which I am including here:

Let us meditate upon the glory of the ONE who created this universe.
Let him illumine our minds!

In these few words we find an immense lake of peace and wisdom, when we practise this inspiring worship.

*A Shinto Prayer*

O Lord, deign to grant me (or him or her) the best that I (or he or she) can live through.

## CHAPTER IX

# RITUAL FOR COLLECTIVE OPERATIONS

For the purpose of collective action, theurgists should be chosen who, to a certain degree, are already experienced in individual operation (see Chapters V—'Instruction for Action' and VIII—'Personal Action'). This is necessary because harmonious co-operation is possible only under such conditions. It is impracticable to start instructing new members about elementary rules for spiritual work during an actual meeting, thereby wasting time and the attention of the remaining trained participants.

When all those who are supposed to take part in an operation are assembled in the chosen room, the leader invites them to form a circle and places a small table in the middle, on which he puts a list of names and photographs (if available) of those who are to be helped (in other words—patients).

The traditional 'Cord of Union' is then placed in the hands of those forming the circle and each member winds it once round his left thumb, leaving the right hand free. The cord should be soft and may be of silk or nylon, about 5/16ths of an inch thick and green, blue or dark red. It will most likely be readily obtainable from any good haberdashery. The length should be sufficient to go round the largest circle that can be made in the room (which will have several chairs and the table in it), plus two or three yards to surround the photographs.

The free ends of the cord remain in the hands of the leader, who takes his place close to the table, so that he can read the list of names and prayers relevant to the meeting. Two wax candles are usually lit on the table, and all other lights are extinguished during the time of the operation.

When lighting the candles and incense sticks, the leader *three times* softly pronounces: 'In the name of Almighty God, who created the universe and all of us who are in it!' The members respond with a whispered 'Amen'.

Everyone sits in a perfectly erect position on their chairs, knees together, hands resting palm downwards on them, according to the 'Westernized' asana taken from Chapter XV of *Concentration.*

The middle part of the cord is left on the table to form a circle round the photographs of the patients.

After lighting the candles and incense, the leader greets the members and says to them: 'This meeting is dedicated to the help of our suffering fellow men, who are in need of God's grace and pardon.' Then, very slowly, he reads or chants with the utmost concentration, the invocation to the Holy Spirit (see Chapter XII) and all members simultaneously repeat the words.

This being done, the action proper commences.

The leader begins the ritual for collective operation, by slowly reading the following verses *three times* each:

*Verse 1: I know that a sincere prayer is a blessing from the Almighty, but a negligent invocation of the Lord falls as a damnation on a foolish man.*

One minute of meditation follows during which members mentally repeat the verse.

*Verse 2: There is no man born who has not committed a sin: so, before I turn to Thee, O Lord with my prayer, I beseech Thee to be gracious to me, a sinner, who, with head humbled deep in the dust before Thee, is sorry for all his iniquities.*

At this point all bow their heads and then there is one minute of meditative prayer, with full concentration.

*Verse 3: I pray O Lord for my brother/sister (give full name* THREE TIMES*) who is in distress because of errors committed against Thy goodness and wisdom, but Thou who art the whole of grace and compassion, may lighten the burden of my brother/sister (again give the name three times) if Thou hearest my prayer for him/her.*

All join in intense, silent, prayer for one minute. Then the leader invites members to rise and stand around the table, each placing two fingers of their right hands on the edge of the photograph of the person for whom they now pray, while the cord still remains twined round each member's left thumb, and ready to repeat with him the conjuration for the imposition of hands:

*Verse 4:* *May help and solace be given to you, brother/sister* (slowly aloud and with intense concentration all repeat the name of the patient three times together with the leader) *and may Grace flow through my hands into you. Let the Lord's will be done!*

This formula is the culminating point of the whole operation and success depends upon it. Silent prayer follows for one minute.

*Verse 5:* *Blessed be Thou, O Lord, enlighten me through Thy initiation! Let my prayer join the unceasing current of worship of Thy saints, and rise to Thee as the smoke of incense.*

If there is more than one patient, verses 1, 2 and 5 are used in common for all of them, but *verses 3 and 4 must be repeated three times for each person.*

When standing in the circle with fingers placed on the patient's picture, members must memorize it and the mental image is then joined to the ritual of the imposition of hands, so that when pronouncing the name, you have the face of the person before you.

This finished, the leader invites members to resume their seats, thanks them for their co-operation, extinguishes the candles and switches on the normal lighting.

In theurgic groups all over the world, every meeting used for helping others is usually conducted by voluntary leaders, who must, of course, be fully conversant with their duties for the meetings, so that the ritual and action flow smoothly and without any undue delay. Normally, the leader is given a typed copy of his duties, taken from this chapter. Meetings intended to give assistance to others, like the one just described, are a very intimate activity, and no member should ever speak about them in public or boast of his participation, for this will rob everything of its effectiveness. That is why it is an accepted practice not to advertise a theurgic group in any way.

Leaders usually note the exact time when verses 3 and 4 are

read, as evidence for the absent patient. Physically sick persons, for whose benefit the operation is performed, should not be present at these meetings while the action is in progress. In certain theurgic groups no person who is to be helped is even admitted to that meeting.

This is done for a number of very good reasons:

a. It is very hard for the person mentioned in the operation to be in the circle and, at the same time, retain full emotional and mental composure. The egoistic, if even subconscious element is still too strong in average human beings and it may easily be excited by the ritual. On the other hand, the operating members themselves feel better and less restrained when they do not see the patients among them. If there is a physical illness to be alleviated, it is a definite rule *to exclude* such a patient from the meetings of healing theurgic groups, during the time of their action, and the reasons for this are simple.

b. The most effective operations can be best performed by physically healthy healers, that is, those whose physical and astral auras (radiations) are normal. Full harmony within the group is then preserved, and no transmission of the suffering of the patient(s) to the operators is possible, unless such an event has deliberately been sought.

c. There are cases where a selfless operator agrees to accept the suffering of his brother on his own shoulders, in order to alleviate the latter's Prarabdha Karma. This very seldom happens, for great spiritual power, courage and wisdom are needed for such a sacrifice. It is beyond the average level of development in the present epoch.

So we have to accept that, in general, no one within a healing group wants to be 'infected' by his brother's ailment, and therefore the precautions just mentioned must be fully enforced during every theurgic meeting.

Every prayer or invocation, as given in this book, can be included in the the programme for a meeting, according to the needs that arise and at the leader's discretion. In fact, theurgic groups throughout the world, as a matter of course, adjust their programmes to fit their needs as sometimes they may require healing power, spiritual support, help in material conditions, defence against evil influences, or simply an open-hearted worship of the Lord. And for all of these things they will find suitable material in the theurgic tradition. Some groups end their meetings with the following invocation, which the leader says as he stands and faces the gathering:

'May every day of your life take you closer to spiritual enlightenment, so that your present incarnation will not be a wasted, but an evolutionary one, in accordance with your own efforts to obtain the awareness of the Eternal Light, which lies hidden in every being. And when the hour of your departure comes, may you meet it, not with confusion and fear, but with joy, hope and certainty, invoking the holy presence of your spiritual master, who will then support and guide you to the light.'

The leader then announces the date and purpose of the next meeting, advising members to study certain prayers or invocations, as given in this book, which he intends to use next time.

This is an appropriate point at which to explain the theurgic conception of all diseases and suffering. Tradition recognizes that every manifestation has its 'soul', or better still, a 'spirit'. If Karma requires that an ailment should descend upon a man, the 'spirit' of the sickness (or the cliché of the accident, and so on) is sent towards the subtle bodies of the man (that is, astral and mental). From there the trouble is gradually transferred to the gross, physical matter, and then we have a disease, which develops in the affected body. From this we can see that, theoretically and logically, it would be possible to expel the 'spirit' of the sickness and a man could be cured, providing the operator is strong and knowledgeable enough, and knows how to deal with the invisible invaders (see *The Tarot,* Chapter III). Occultism, and especially its 'magic' branch uses this method of help.

The magician acts upon the astrosome, compelling the spirit of disease to quit the patient, and then we have a classical example of a 'magic cure'. In practice, magnetism, mesmerism and hypnotism, if successful, also do similar work: they try to *expel* the evil. But, say theurgists, the expelled disease (that is, its spirit) has to go somewhere. Whom will it then attack? The magician has his answer to this doubt. He tries to 'transplant' the disease to a lower organism, such as a plant or animal, which is unable to defend itself in any way. And that is the end of his ability to deal with the unwanted manifestations of life. But even this is strongly objected to by the great theurgists.

In remarking about the expulsion and transplanting of diseases, the mysterious Master Andréas, so often quoted by Paul Sédir, said: 'How would you feel if you had the disease of a giant transplanted into your body? For plants and animals suffer similarly when used as a cloak for magic operations.'

But the idea behind theurgy is different. It is to implore the Supreme, Who holds everything in His might, and who alone can arrange everything in the most just and best possible way. As we can see and as all true occultists recognize, the theurgic way is the purest and surest one, which does not involve the operator in any karmic complications, nor injustice towards weaker creatures, as is often the case with magic and other branches of not too clean occultism. Humanity is now living in the most critical epoch of its whole existence on this planet, being almost on the verge of catastrophic suicide on a global scale. For those who like to dabble in the old apocrypha and scriptural traditions, some facts which are evident today, may give a lot to think about. The establishment of the Jewish National State; the efforts at unification of all Christian faiths; the open persecution of religion among almost half of the world's population (Russia and China with their satellites); the obtaining by mankind of powers which can destroy all life on this planet; the prophecies (including the Revelation of St John) about annihiliation of the earth and all things on it by fire from the sky; the savage animosity of many races and nations among themselves, and the terrific spread of general suffering, especially in the forms of hunger and poverty: all these can perhaps be considered as 'signs' of the approaching end. For a faithful theurgist or a 'white' occultist there is nothing to fear or regret: they know that everything that happens is eventually for the best. Whatever had a beginning must also have an end and the human family on this earth cannot be any exception. If the evolutionary way of one kind of population on a planet becomes doubtful, then another will take its place.

And at the same time, the spiritual search (again according to the old prophecies) in man grows and is reaching a never before equalled intensity. Many people are thirsty for the higher spiritual, imperishable values in their lives. Often these strivings are wrongly directed or simply, intentionally misguided by the forces of darkness, which lead men on dangerous by-paths (this too has been predicted) instead of towards the light. But there is a ray of hope: in all the mess, man starts to turn towards spiritual ideas, often abandoning certain unsafe occult paths, which were so prevalent in Europe during the second half of the nineteenth and first quarter of the twentieth centuries.

Now men ask for something better and safer. And sometimes they return to the almost forgotten conceptions of God. Interest in theurgy may be one of the first steps in that direction after infatuation with things Eastern.

That is why I decided to remind those who need it about the old path in a form appropriate for the present day, and hence this book is the result of that effort.

It by no means annuls the other paths I have mentioned in my former works: quite the opposite and if anything it rather compliments them, showing one more doorway to the unique temple.

There is a means to assist and hasten the immediate result of an action being done on behalf of our suffering brethren, which can be used by those members of a circle, who feel themselves to be healthy and strong.

Just before the culminating point of an operation is reached, that is, Verse 4: 'May help and solace . . .', the operator *inhales deeply and produces tension in all the muscles of his body,* as if he is about to leap forward or dive deep into water. This should last for only a few seconds (not more than five) and when the actual pronouncing of Verse 4 begins, a slow exhale accompanied by a gradual release of the body's tension must follow. In this case there is no need to asssist the action by any effort of imagination, as is done in some occult practices, for here the created astral energy of itself goes in the right direction, providing the mind of the operator has been duly concentrated on the significance of Verse 4 and the release extended over the whole of the reading of it.

# CHAPTER X

# LOVE AND HOPE IN THEURGY

In theurgy there are manifold conceptions of the power, usually called 'love' depending upon the way in which it manifests itself. And all these conceptions by far transcend that which is called 'love' in the current language of everyday life. Therefore it is important to determine the general principles or laws concerning this power, which has two levels.

The first one acting in the living substance of physical, astral and mental worlds can be defined as a 'tendency towards unification', a striving from diversity to unity. We can see that, although manifesting itself in the three worlds, which are the different states of matter, it also has a very close relation to the realm of the final union, which is the core of the idea of spirit. Spirit is *one* and *universal*, having no limitations of time or space. That is why everything which unites and does not divide always has some spiritual aspect.

On the second level we can best realize love in the human world. Those who feel affection towards others want to be united with them and this, of course, occurs in many varied forms such as the union of lovers and married people; of friends, parents and children; men of similar ethical, scientific or political convictions, and so on. Families, tribes, nations and races are only a few further examples of unifying efforts, showing different aspects of the same basic power. In the purely physical world it is called the 'law of universal attraction' or simply, *gravity*. The construction of atoms, molecules, elements and the whole variety of combinations in matter, ending with planets, solar systems and galaxies, are ruled by the same basic forces of attraction.

Meditation about and realization of the conceptions on which I have touched only briefly here lead to an understanding of the idea of creation and manifestation of the universe which is inexpressible in words. It is amazing how some sages of the distant past, while not having any of our modern technical facilities or instruments, knew about the unity of the universe and expressed it in words very close to those we use at the present time. Some of the terms borrowed from them (atoms, ether, elements, and so on) are still essential for modern science.

In theurgy the right conception of love means nothing less than our innate right to be finally united with the Whole, which Christ called the 'Father in Heaven'. That is why prayers and theurgic operations in general have a good foundation and a reason for existence, because they are based on the essential truth of love.

Another motive power in theurgy is hope. Without it there would be no action at all, for who could undertake anything without having a hope (in some cases, even certainty) of achievement in his strivings? Hope is the inspiration present in the toil and hardship of work. Remove it and you will create a very painful punishment like that sometimes inflicted on unrepentant and stubbornly disobedient prisoners by the aimless moving or crushing of stones in prison courtyards and the bearing of triangles with heavy and unnecessary loads, and so on. Human nature itself is opposed to and rebellious against anything lacking an aim and its possible achievement. Analysing further we see that hope is, in its essence, *a glimpse into the future,* the anticipation of the results of our toil and desires.

For theurgists, hope shows them the more or less distant, but certain final achievement. We can now see that hope has been rightly put into its place beside two other virtues (love and faith). Of the third virtue—*faith* we have already spoken in Chapter IV of this book.

## CHAPTER XI

# A GREAT INVOCATION TO GOD

This is a theurgic version of the Lord's Prayer:

O Father Who art in Heaven, may the blessed time soon come when Thy Will, which is the wholeness of perfection, will be understood and accepted by human beings and will serve them as law. Purify and sanctify our souls which unite themselves in the ardent desire to hasten those happy days. Enlighten our understanding, absorb our wills, inspire with Thy Holy Spirit all our thoughts, actions and our sufferings, which we bind together to make a bouquet of thorny roses, in order to offer their perfume to Thee. Make us worthy to be admitted to the ranks of those, who, in both the visible and invisible worlds, sacrifice themselves to achieve realization of Thy will on this earthly plane.

O Omnipotent God, good God, Who fills and governs the immensity of worlds created by Thee, may Thy Holy Name be glorified and Thy will fulfilled, so that everything which has received Thy immortal breath of life, will respect and follow Thy Holy Law.

Preserve me in sanity of spirit, so that I will not cease to glorify Thee, and also in health of body to allow me to work to provide for my family, and to help my neighbour and serve my country.

For I am a man, and a feeble one, therefore give me the power to resist evil and even if I fail grant me repentance. May my enemies not be punished because of me, for I forgive them. And finally, when I will be deprived of this sheath of corruption (the body), bring me nearer to Thee, that I may know and love Thee even more.

O Thou, who hast made everything and who will transform everything so that it will return to the primary source, that principle emanated from the depths of the eternal, the soul of the universe, the divine light, I invoke Thy aid.

Yes! Come O creative fluid and penetrate my faulty senses!

And you, august messengers of the Highest, angels of light, heavenly spirits, you who are all ministers of the will of my God, come to me for I implore your assistance.

Hasten to come to enlighten and guide me, and carry my prayer to Almighty God, for He knows my desires. I want to help my brothers, to fortify them, to maintain them and make them just in His sight.

O Lord, grant me the power of resistance, patience in suffering, firmness in endurance, ardour for Thy spirit and love for Thy name. Remove from me all erroneous doctrines; guard me from the influence of the evil spells of degenerate priests; purify me from all idolatry, no matter how degenerated it may be; teach me to love Thee, as Thou wishest to be loved and penetrate my whole being so deeply, that when the hour of separation from my body comes, my last breath will be accompanied by this invocation:

I AM NOT AFRAID OF ANYTHING, FOR NOTHING CAN HARM ME SINCE GOD IS MY ONLY LOVE AND HIS WILL IS MY WHOLE LAW.

## PRAYER FOR USE BEFORE ANY ACTIVITY OR ENTERPISE

O God the omnipotent, God the powerful, God the sweet, God the highest and most glorious, O God, the just sovereign, God full of grace and clemency, I (name . . .), an unworthy sinner, full of iniquities throw myself at Thy feet; I present myself before Thy majesty; I implore Thy mercy and Thy goodness!

Do not look upon the multitude of my sins, because Thou always hast compassion for those who sincerely repent.

Deign to grant my prayer fulfilment. Bless, I beg Thee, this activity (or enterprise) through Thy goodness, through Thy mercy and through Thy omnipotent virtue.

I ask Thee for grace, in the name of Thy Son, who reigns together with Thee and in the name of the Holy Spirit.

So may it be!

## A MYSTIC PRAYER BY PHILEMON OF PHILADELPHIA

O Eternal, immovable and infinite God,
From whom everything truly arises, for nothing is apart from Thee,

Who art good without qualities, great without quantity, eternal without duration, omnipresent without place!
The unique perfection, which embraces all other perfection and all things in Its extent,
Possessing such a degree of perfection, that it is beyond anything we can realize.
In contemplation of which we merge for such a long time,
Until finally we come to understand, that we may not be ignorant of our own ignorance.
Do not abandon us O God, when we seek Thee in secluded places; do not let us go astray.
Help us through Thy paternal and infinite goodness and mercy, to love more the glory of Thy only Son, Our Lord Jesus Christ, Who came into this world because of us.
Let us admire and adore Him and through this discover and embrace Thee.
We implore Thee about this and pray for Thy generous love.
We pray to Thee with weeping and moaning, Thou who art truly the Supreme God, the sovereignly good.
To Thee, Who is One in Three, the living and true God, let there be given every praise and honour, through the whole of eternity and the ages of ages.

**Amen.**

This inspired and lofty prayer of a wise and saintly man does not need any explanation. In its supreme simplicity it is accessible to the most simple heart capable of feeling the fraternal elation of a great soul trying to express for us, its most intimate mystical experiences.

The mystery of the Unique Supreme Father, while still in Three manifestations attracts the ripe soul of Philemon. His devotion and ecstasy find expression in meek crying. We know that tears of joy and admiration often stream abundantly from pure hearts, when they are able to contemplate the perfection of the One without a second.

It is for you to initiate yourself into this mystery.

Most people know how to cater for those closest to them, that is, their family. But the nation in which we live in our physical incarnation is also a family, although in a much broader sense.

Theurgy also takes care of this condition, under which we all live. Of course, things are different for great souls, who are beyond all earthly limitations and are rather cosmopolitan in their enlightened views. But we have nothing to teach them, since it is they who reveal to us some aspects of the Unique Truth, according to our ability to understand them.

I will now give a prayer for one's country:

O Lord, Who in Thy infinite wisdom hast set me to live in this nation, using its accumulated means and knowledge,
Deign to grant Thy most effective blessing on my people,
Who will return to Thee one day, according to Thy right will.
Thou hast said that the *hearts of rulers are in Thy hand*:
Give our leaders the inestimable grace of Thy enlightenment.
For it is Thou who hast allowed them to rule us, executing Thy great plan, in humility and awareness of their duties.
Let them understand their responsibilities and duties leaving aside their ordinary human weaknesses, egoism, and anger.
Let their hearts be filled with Thy peace and wisdom.
Blessed be Thou, O Lord, grant us Thy initiation!

# CHAPTER XII

# INVOCATION TO THE HOLY SPIRIT

Apart from the 'Last Supper' worship (see Chapter XIII) the invocation to the Holy Spirit is one of the most mystical and powerful prayers in theurgy. This third manifestation of the absolute (the First and Second being the Father and Son) is supremely mysterious and the most misunderstood by men. There is little to wonder at, since Christ said that the world cannot yet accept the Holy Spirit, *because it does not know Him.*

Again, the idea of God the Father, the beginning of everything and of the Son, the creative emanation can be more easily realized, for they are still expressed in terms, which have some corresponding concepts in human life and language. Not so with Spirit, for how numerous and eloquent are those who have had real spiritual experiences? There lies the difficulty and the innumerable substitutes, wrong definitions and approaches can be seen as unqualified efforts to explain this mystery.

Theurgy gives us some positive definitions, in so far as the transcendental being can ever be defined, and so we will do our best when analyzing the ancient original text of the invocation to the Holy Spirit.

O Ruler of Heaven, (1)
O Consoler! (2)
Spirit of Truth, (3)
Omnipresent and filling everything (4)
Giver of Life! (5)
Come to dwell in us, (6)
Purify us of all iniquities (7)
And save our souls, (8)
O Merciful Lord! (9)

1. *O Ruler of Heaven*

We know that the traditional theurgic term 'heaven' means

the final, blissful state (consciousness) of those, who have finished their long wandering through the evolution of incarnations, (births, lives and deaths) and who have attained the ultimate peace in the Lord. In the invocation the Holy Spirit is called 'Ruler' or 'King' of Heaven. What does this mean? Only that the Attainment (in the sense just mentioned) is the realm of the Holy Spirit, Who rules over it and inspires us to seek it. Manifold and wonderful are His powers: He enlightens, purifies, bestows unusual abilities (remember the results of the descent of the Holy Ghost upon the apostles on the day of Pentecost?), and is the source of life as is emphasized in the fifth line of the invocation. Inspiration and intuition are the direct results of His reflection in man.

2. *O Consoler!*

This means that in our karmic tribulations, the Holy Spirit is the power which brings consolation and peace in the midst of painful experiences in our incarnations, turning our attention from the lower, earthly and mortal things, to the spiritual and imperishable, which are devoid of all suffering and grief.

3. *Spirit of Truth*

If we wish to be exact and logical we must recognize that there is no direct definition of Truth; but there can be many more or less purposeful attempts to approach this idea. However, the full meaning of truth is beyond the language of the mortal mind. But in spite of the impossibility of providing an adequate definition, truth can be perfectly *lived* and experienced by a man who has raised his consciousness beyond the realm of the ordinary thinking processes. Reflected in this realm, truth can be described as That, which really IS. Here existence does not mean any temporary, relative being, but the permanent, the immortal substance, beyond any change, growth or decay and unaffected by time and space.

Whether these descriptions remain only words for you, without any substratum of life in them, or whether they will find, HERE and NOW, a living response in you, will depend entirely upon the degree of your own spiritual enlightenment. The search for truth seems to have been innate in the depths of human nature from even the most ancient times. Remember the tragic question that Pilate put to the Great Teacher:

'What is truth?' In such a question man confesses his ignorance of the cardinal wisdom, which he so desperately needs and cannot find. Finally, in theurgy truth can never be found as something 'apart', or as something to be looked at: *Truth can only be realized* and lived, and bring to us the Light of its dispenser—the Holy Spirit. Now you know Whom a theurgist addresses when seeking truth.

4. *Omnipresent and filling everything*

One of the attributes belonging to our conception of spirit is its omnipresence. This does not need much explanation or proof, for the very idea of immateriality means superiority over the cardinal attributes connected with matter, that is, *space* and *time*. Neither can affect the illimitable and eternal. The realization of this is possible, but only in the supramental state of consciousness, when it has acquired the same attributes, not otherwise.

If you attain union with the Supreme (see Chapter XVI) then you will know the truth about the Holy Spirit. The same thing happens in the superconsciousness, attained by other means, that is, the Eastern Samadhi. Saints and great occultists realized the Holy Spirit by merging into the ultimate depths of their own consciousness, where He dwells, and abandoning all the mental scum below them. This way is open to anyone who knows about it, under the condition that he is able to establish the *silence* in himself (that is, in his mind).

Spirit then fills the prepared temple and dwells in it for as long as the purity (absence of mental rubbish) is maintained.

5. *Giver of Life!*

There is no life without spirit. And what concerns us as human beings is the life in us. It manifests itself through movements in our consciousness, which are like a burning flame, enlightening the surrounding picture of the universe. This flame can be increased or decreased, according to the qualities of the being in which it manifests itself. The often ignored and still more often misunderstood occult belief, that everything has some degree of consciousness, even things which we call 'dead', is corroborated by theurgy. In this fragment of the invocation, the Holy Spirit is called 'Giver of Life', because everything possessing consciousness derives it only from Him.

In imploring this Spirit, the unique central sun of consciousness-life, theurgists know what they are doing: they try to put themselves directly (which here means consciously) into contact with Him, which will then enhance their own light. Expansion of conscious-life, as we know it, in the 'union with the Father' and in true Samadhi, are the results of communion with the Holy Spirit.

6. *Come to dwell in us*

Now that 5 has been explained, the coming of the Holy Ghost is clear in its meaning. We pray for more light in our lives, but it is only the beginning. We know that in the beginning, the union (Samadhi in the East) manifests itself only sporadically and for short periods of time, because then our whole nature is not yet sufficiently pure and prepared. Here in the sixth line we pray that the Holy Spirit will dwell in us, that is, will remain in us permanently. And this happens to those human beings who reach the 'top of the ladder'.

The Great Teacher even told us that He would send the Holy Spirit to those who are worthy of accepting Him. Such are the splendid horizons opening before us.

7. *Purify us of all iniquities*

Where there is light there cannot be any darkness, for darkness is only the absence of light. When the Holy Spirit enlightens the mortal mind, purity of the consciousness will result. This also means purity of feelings, which are dependent upon thoughts. With both astral and mental purified, no evil can be committed in the flesh, which is only a gross reflection of these two principles. Theurgists call this process liberation from sin and pray for it in this part of the invocation. Let us join this very worthy request!

8. *And save our souls*

You may already recognize this as another expression of the requests which we encountered in 6 and 7. The term 'salvation' is common to many religions and, because of its simplicity, is also used in theurgy. It means the combination of the dwelling of the Holy Spirit in us, with the inherent purification and elevation of our whole being.

It is because of the overwhelming importance of such an

achievement in the life of an evolving being (here a human one is meant), that three separate forms of invocation have been used in this prayer.

9. *O Merciful Lord!*

This is the hopeful emphasizing of a great truth, that the Lord is infinitely compassionate towards our weaknesses and transgressions. The only condition is that *we turn to Him* for His mercy and grace. Whoever has practised this incomparable means of spiritual resurrection from the deadly sleep in matter knows, why and what happens to us. A human being turning sincerely to the Lord, the Father, is unable to commit the same crimes, for forgiveness of which the man prays. Is it not an enormous step ahead?

Look attentively into the the depths of your own conscience —which is but a dimmed reflection of God's law in us—and you will discover this truth for yourself. And this counts first and foremost, because it gives you the unbeatable factor of enlightenment—the right experience.

Under such conditions, could the Lord remain other than merciful? If you have a deeper insight you will see, at the same moment, that His mercy does not oppose justice. Then full peace will enter into you.

This invocation to the Holy Spirit is a very powerful force in theurgy, which is used in many operations and precedes them as you will find recommended in subsequent chapters.

It now remains to explain the profound words of the Teacher concerning offences against the Holy Spirit by foolish men, as we know from the gospels: 'And whosoever shall speak a word against the Son of man, it shall be forgiven him: but he that shall speak against the Holy Ghost, it shall not be forgiven him neither in this world nor in the world to come.' We dare not claim any full understanding of the deep mystery in this statement. Does it mean the final failure in the chain of human incarnations, beyond all reprieve and thus—a final damnation? We do not know. It is better to confess this rather than plunge into doubtful deliberations and guesswork.

The only sure lesson is, not to commit such a crime for any price. We can make some attempt to find motives: to offend the Holy Spirit may well mean to deny one's own true self, the spiritual spark in man, which gives him life. Would it not be a kind of 'spiritual suicide' to blaspheme against this reflection of the highest in you? But spirit cannot be killed as in essence. It is the eternal confirmation of life, and the antithesis of death.

In a certain occult tradition there is a teaching, which tries to explain the possibility of a final failure in evolution for some individual entities, such as man.

The involutionary tendencies, in such unfortunate cases, are so strong, that despite karmic retributions in every incarnation, the individual does not abandon his evil ways and limitless egoism, using every opportunity to sink further and further into matter and to suppress every upward movement in himself. The accumulated karma becomes so enormous and heavy, growing with each new physical life, that there is no more possibility of exhausting and repaying it in the present aeon of creation (sometimes called 'relative eternity'). Then the spiritual monad (the self) seeing that there is no more hope of any advancement throughout the incarnations in this cycle of life, abandons the remaining elements that form the individuality (physical, astral and mental) and returns to the point of departure. The individual can still live an apparently normal human life until his death. He does not know about the supreme tragedy that has touched his being. But then, his astro-mental double, now being only a conglomeration of the subtle astro-mental matter without a spark of true life, begins to decompose in a way similar to the putrefaction of the physical body, while not losing awareness of his dreadful condition. It is said that this abominable process of decomposition is much longer than any physical decay, and endures until every trace of consciousness and adherence of the particles of the astro-mental body disappears forever.

In the ancient Graeco-Roman religion it was believed that, after his earthly death, such a desperate being may be 'torn to pieces' in Hades (something equivalent to purgatory or even hell) by ferocious devils, which had been awaiting him long before his advent into their realm.

While not ascribing any actual value to such beliefs in explanation of the idea of eternal damnation, I give them merely as a matter of interest, to show that such things were known even in the pre-Christian era.

## CHAPTER XIII

# THE LAST SUPPER WORSHIP

To Thy Last Supper let me be allowed today as a participant, O Son of God!
For neither will I betray any secret to Thine enemies,
Nor will I give Thee a kiss like Judas,
But like the thief I pray unto Thee:
Remember me, O Lord, when coming into Thy Kingdom!

This is the most mystical prayer known to theurgy. It aims directly at the last, intimate and mysterious union of the human soul with its rightful Lord and Master. Short as it is, it contains a world of final achievement, for which—consciously or unconsciously—every living being longs, through the aeons of time and infinities of space.

A formidable task now confronts the aspirant: to understand these deep words of the invocation properly: to make his heart acquainted with the spirit and concept of that symbolical *Last Supper*, and to obtain the inexpressible, immeasurable grace of being admitted to the final union with Him. It is not the task for a limited period of time, as you will certainly realize in a flash of intuition, when meditating upon Him in admiration and surrender. If anyone knows when a man will reach the great aim, it can be only the Master Himself.

But a true aspirant does not bother about it: the *certainty* that flows from the spiritual experience of being present at the Last Supper, dwarfs all anxiety in a man. His duty is to do the best possible and to lay everything at the feet of the central Figure, who presides over the Lord's table.

Now, in order to facilitate your reaching of the right spiritual attitude, the prayer will be explained and analyzed in detail, as has been done with others in previous chapters. And it must be meditated upon and accepted, as only then can the operation start.

1. *To Thy Last Supper*

Here we have a detailed description of that last act of the Redeeming Teacher on this earth, before His final sacrifice on Golgotha. But theurgy does not limit this great happening to time and space: our teaching is, that the mysterious *supper* of the Master, at which selection of His disciples was made in order to separate the wheat from the chaff (remember the dismissal of the traitor Judas?) *lasts forever*. Every son of man must pass through it, before he enters the mansion of the Father, no matter how many lives might be necessary for it. During the supper the Lord gave his faithful disciples the final initiation and admitted them in His communion forever. Presiding at the traditional paschal table, He blessed the food and wine, using them as visible symbols of spiritual unity among the ripe human beings around Him. He called the bread, which He broke for them, His flesh and the wine He gave, His blood. Matter, the vehicle of the spirit through its wandering in manifestation, is an exact analogy of the true relationship between physical man and his spiritual immortal self. In it lies the ultimate truth of being.

In deep inner silence merge into this truth through His grace.

2. *Let me be allowed today as a participant*

This prayer for admission (that is, spiritual enlightenment) belongs to our '*today*', to our present, and not to any unknown and indefinite *future*. This is an important point that shows us, that efforts for our spiritual resurrection should be started immediately we realize its meaning for us.

What does *adjournment* mean, even the shortest one, in the spiritual realm, as in theurgy? Simply that you actually prefer other things, that something else attracts you *now* and therefore you give a priority to the perishable which should be offered to the eternal living in your hidden depths. Therefore in delaying the most essential problems by placing perishable and mortal aims before them, you prevent your admission to the supper. Be your own judge in this matter, but an impartial and *just* judge!

3. *O Son of God!*

This is a well-known term used to define the great Beings

who have united their consciousness with that of the Father, and thereby become His emanation, descendants, to whom the term 'Son' is applicable, perhaps the closest in the limited language of the human mind.

All mystical realities achieved along the way of theurgic prayer belong to the spiritual realm, to the holiest interior of the human soul. Only there can eternity dwell, and only from those depths is the spectre of death truly banned.

Inspired Thomas à Kempis, when speaking about the kingdom of God in his 'Imitation of Christ' tells us that the whole of its beauty is *interior*, that is, independent and beyond the visible shell of this world. The repentant thief also knew that the kingdom lies in the realm that is free from earthly life. After he had been initiated through his suffering and by his faith, he said to Christ: '. . . Lord, remember me when thou shalt come into thy kingdom'.

After having performed the first ritual of Holy Communion, which was the symbol of the basic unity of the universe, the Teacher separated—as has already been mentioned—the wheat from the chaff. Then, with His powerful and tragic words he said: '. . . That which thou dost, do quickly'. He thus expelled the traitor, in whom—as the Evangelists say—the Devil entered immediately he received the salted bread from the Master. He fled to finalize his betrayal, as he could not endure the presence of the Master and his saintly disciples any more.

This brief reminder of the great story has been given here so as to refresh it in your minds and tune you towards its inexpressible, initiatory inner sense, and thus prepare you for the performance of the prayer.

It was not without deep insight that the genius of Leonardo da Vinci chose this final initiation of the Last Supper as the theme for the masterpiece he painted in a Milanese monastery refectory. To be admitted into the presence of the Spiritual Master means enlightenment of the highest degree. The disciple should know this and we can see the fact from the assurance he gives in the next line.

4. *For neither will I betray any secret to Thine enemies*

This is the first vow of the worship. No initiation can ever be predestined for all and sundry. In the mass, the cruel world is far from being ripe enough to accept that which only advanced and chosen disciples can realize. The innermost mysteries of spiritual life should not and cannot be divulged.

5. *Nor will I give Thee a kiss like Judas*

Another vow, to reject the monstrosity of hypocrisy and lies, while having as deterrent the tragic example of the archetype of all traitors—the luckless Judas. You must fully grasp the significance of these two aspects of attitude, forbidden for the initiate, and upon freedom from which you can build your *hope* of being accepted at the *supper.*

6. *But like the thief I pray unto Thee:*

In facing the supreme suffering (the prolonged agony and death on the cross is one of the most painful penalties ever inflicted on a human body) on Golgotha, three condemned men behaved themselves differently. The words of Christ are recorded in the gospels and are well known.

One of the thieves crucified beside the Redeemer—in his despair, torture and fury of the deadly frustration of the lost life—started to insult the Man on the middle cross. But the other thief stopped him. He pointed out that the punishment was rightly deserved by both of them, but the saint between them was innocent. Then, turning to Jesus he prayed to Him.

Parts 5 and 6 of our theurgic formula remind us that we should have a just attitude towards all suffering and injustice inflicted on us. The suddenly converted thief is given as an everlasting example. This lesson must always stand before you when you prepare yourself to perform the great prayer of the *Last Supper.* Every human being born into this world has to bear its self-made and hence deserved *cross,* called 'karma' by our Eastern brothers and the law of cause and effect in occultism. It is only the way in which you solve this problem that matters. The living example of a right solution has been given in this chapter. Meditate about it.

We now come to the conclusion of the prayer:

7. *Remember me, O Lord, when coming into Thy Kingdom!*

Here lies the true hope and solution—the Great Teacher's *grace.* That was the last cry to come from a human being tortured to death. And it is the right final request: not for delivery from the cross (physical desire), but a *spiritual* request, from a man who suddenly matured to the intuitive realization of truth (he recognized who Jesus was); to initiation into the life beyond the grave (hence his prayer for the care of his soul); repentance (the burning off of karma), and realization of the ultimate destiny of a human being (the Kingdom of God).

This is the material upon which you have to meditate in order to be able to perform the worship of the Last Supper with full understanding and a right attitude. This prayer is recommended for use against all inner troubles, painful experiences, attacks of despair, temptations; fear of death and frustration.

It is a very personal formula and in theurgic tradition I could not find any example of the 'Last Supper' being performed by a group or aloud. It is a far too intimate and inner worship, requiring so much intense insight and melting of the hard shell of egoism and indifference, that it seems to be impractical to use it apart from individual action.

Further, we should know that despair is one of the deadliest evils, if not the worst, because its results are so terrible. The examples that follow highlight this. One of the thieves on Golgotha was a prey to despair and as a result he insulted the Christ, for he was completely blinded by his destructive vice. The Church agrees that the cause of damnation of the traitor Judas was not just the fact of betraying and selling his master. The infinite compassion of the Lord is always greater than even the heaviest crime a man can commit and on the way of repentance every sin can be washed away, if a man only takes this step towards the Lord.

But despair efficiently excludes such regeneration, for it is like the hopeless, icy breath of death. Accordingly, Judas found only one solution: elimination through wilful destruction of his body and self-annihilation of spirit (see Chapter XII—'Invocation to the Holy Spirit').

I have known of advanced theurgists who preferred to perform such a sublime spiritual flight, as is the prayer of the *Last Supper*, in the quietness of an empty church or chapel, when the pews were unoccupied and silence and peace reigned supreme in the house dedicated to the Lord.

When praying at home you must ensure that you have conditions in which there will be no disturbances or interruptions caused by the outer world.

# CHAPTER XIV

# THE LORD'S PRAYER

The prayer given to us by the Great Teacher forms one of the chief pillars of theurgy. In Hermetism, the Lord's prayer is used and analyzed with the help of the Kabbalah and in Chapter X of *The Tarot* (pages 203-208) we can find its unfolding done through the classical system of the Sephiroth, which explains its esoteric and initiatory meaning.

Neither hermetists nor theurgists make any claim to a complete unveiling of the mysteries of the gospels, for they all recognize that, in the unsurpassed words of wisdom of Christ, there are depths, unfathomable for the ordinary human mind. These words belong to the eternity and infinity of the universe. So, in the following method of adaptation of the Lord's Prayer for theurgic operations, the writer does not attempt to present his version as a unique or complete one. In any case, this unfolding of the prayer is in accordance with the best theurgic traditions, as it is based on comments by eminent theurgic masters as well as on personal experience, which gives unshakable certainty in interpretation. The reader is supposed to be well acquainted with the text of the Lord's Prayer, so it will not be given here first as a whole, but each part of it will be treated separately.[1]

The prayer is considered to a most powerful means for contacting the Father, to whom it is expressly directed. You should use it before every major theurgic activity, as this will add sanctity and a greater chance of success to your operations.

*Invocation: Our Father who art in heaven . . .*

Here our relation to the Supreme Creative Power is firmly established: it is as intimate as that between an earthly father

[1] **The version of the Lord's Prayer which is used in this chapter has been taken from the Vulgata bearing the imprimatur of Cardinal Francis J. Spellman, D.D., August 15, 1945, U.S.A. This applies to all other references from gospels used in this book.**

and his child. This is most reassuring for every faithful soul. But, the Father is the Supreme Being, who generated and rules every form of life including our own. He is the ultimate *cause* of everything which was, is and will be in the unending eternity of life. He is the only one over whom the universal law of cause and effect has no power. This state of absolute freedom is called Heaven in this invocation.

*First Request: Hallowed be Thy name . . .*

This is instruction on how the holy name of the Father should be respected and pronounced, while on the other hand, the meaning is much deeper and points out that the Great Name should be placed upon the altar of the temple of our souls. There is not and cannot be anything more holy and perfect than is our Father in heaven.

*Second Request: Thy kingdom come . . .*

Can we say that at the present time under today's condition the kingdom of God is flourishing on our little planet? That everything is *perfect* and *good*, and that we also possess these two qualities, which must manifest themselves when the kingdom is ripe within us? The true answer can be only in the negative; but we should desire and expect the coming of the final perfection and Christ reminds us about it. This desire is innate in the developed human consciousness; but not being in a position to attain and practise perfect justice (also one of the attributes of the kingdom), men create their own code of laws, which attempts to reach as much impartiality and give as much support for justice as is possible in the given epoch.

The same applies to the idea of peace and other positive factors of planetary life. Find and meditate about them for yourself on the basis of what has just been said. It may be easier than you think.

*Third Request: Thy will be done on earth as it is in heaven . . .*

God is omnipotent, there is nothing which can resist His will. And this is the axiom of theurgy as well as of many religions. This will must be realized in establishing His kingdom everywhere (as in the second request), but first of all in everyone of us. Only then is fulfilment possible. The great mystery arising from the problem as to why His will is not realized here and now, is not as unanswerable as it seems. However, the answer lies inside and not outside us and this is the cardinal thing which you have to recognize, if you really want to 'know'.

A contemporary Indian sage and saint (Ramana Maharshi, 1879-1950) stated: 'You are in the world—you are the world.' Now, why does not everyone of us, who are the components of the world, arrange the kingdom of God within him—or herself? Why are we not absolutely good, wise, just, and so on? That is WHY the world is also not perfect. The true answer lies within you, and nothing will change this fact.

But in our striving towards Him, in our love for Him and in our hope in Him lies the whole solution, as has always been used by advanced human beings and advocated by the Great Teacher. He is in us and it seems that the part of His will which may be realized through us, is not yet fulfilled.

The Lord teaches us *to strive and to pray* for this ultimate realization, which is already achieved in Heaven, that is, in the realm which is immaterial and independent of matter—Spirit.

*Fourth Request: Give us this day our supersubstantial bread . . .*

This can be understood as a request for conditions, suitable for our life and the development of its purpose in us. This 'bread' is asked for only for our daily needs: we should not look too far forward in our material conditions, for they will come in due time, according to our destiny, which we created in aeons of our existences as separate beings. Now we are returning to the Father's mansions, which is the main aim for a theurgist.

*Fifth Request: And forgive us our debts, as we also forgive our debtors . . .*

Here is the expression of a great spiritual law, which rules over our evolution through existence in forms. The annihilation of our 'karmas' (debts) is dependent upon the way in which we resolve and liquidate the karmas of our neighbours, which is in our power.

This means that there is not a one-sided (and therefore unjust) forgiveness of transgressions. We can expect from the

Supreme the justice that we practise towards our fellow men.

If men only realized this law, the fate of humanity would assume a much better shape. So then it is your personal duty and right to satisfy this law of forgiveness. Remember, upon you depends the fate of the world!

*Sixth Request: And lead us not into temptation . . .*

Until we are perfect, two forces will always fight in us: that of light (spiritual progress) and that of darkness (the reverse, the attraction of matter). In other words these are two poles, positive and negative, good and evil, construction and destruction, love and hatred, and so on. In the case of a confrontation of such opposing forces, man undergoes 'temptation' or a trial. Which way will he choose? These are painful and dangerous experiences, and the Lord teaches us to pray so that we will be spared them if possible.

The more we advance spiritually, the more numerous become our victories (right choices) and the less our defeats (wrong solutions).

*Seventh Request: But deliver us from evil . . .*

We pray for delivery from the onset of the evil forces, opposed and hostile to human liberation from the miseries of life in dense matter. It can also be generalized as a request for freedom from every danger and subterfuge, which sometimes face men. Do not give much thought to enumerating the evils you want to avoid; but simply pray as the Lord taught, and He will know what you really need.

*Conclusion: For Thine is the kingdom, and the power, and the glory, for ever and ever. Amen.*

This is a final confirmation of our faith in God and our glorification of Him.

The Lord's Prayer is seldom used in theurgy as a separate worship. It usually precedes a main operation, or concludes it. Sometimes (see Part II of this book) it forms part of an especially important invocation or exorcism.

Tradition recommends the joining together of hands during the invocation and the conclusion of the prayer, while leaving the use of genuflections during the pronunciation of the seven requests to the operator himself.

## CHAPTER XV

# ACTION FOR LIBERATION FROM INNER TROUBLES

There is no better formula for the purpose than the famous spiritual prayer of St Ephraem the Syrian. It is short (which is most important for a brief and positive action) and concentrated to the utmost, while being expressed in simple words, full of inspired sanctity.

It is invaluable for all cases of inner unbalance, grief, fear and similar sufferings. Our method of analysis will be as usual.

*Firstly:* To give the full text of the theurgic prayer, and then to explain it in detail, so that the aspirant is enabled to realize the spiritual current flowing through every part of it.

*Secondly:* Only when this work has been performed can the final operation take place, with the full use of preliminaries as given in the preceding chapter (see No. XIV).

### FORMULA II

O LORD AND DISPENSER OF MY LIFE,
SAVE ME FROM THE SPIRIT OF FRUSTRATION, DEJECTION, LUST AND PRATING.
BUT GRANT TO ME, THY SERVANT, THE SPIRIT OF PURITY, HUMILITY IN WISDOM, PATIENCE AND LOVE.
O MY LORD AND MASTER! ENABLE ME TO SEE MY OWN INIQUITIES
AND NOT TO JUDGE MY BROTHER!
FOR BLESSED ART THOU FOREVER. AMEN.

### ANALYSIS

a. *O Lord and dispenser of my life*

This is the invocation preceding the contents of the prayer. You recognize the Lord as power upon which your present life depends. If we look deeper into it we will find that our life and its cause is a continuing mystery for us. We are ignorant of so many things which are the results of causes unknown to us. We cannot say for how long we will wear this body, nor what will happen tomorrow: no, not even an hour hence. We cannot get or give any assurance of what will happen for even the shortest period of that subdivision of time which we call the 'future'. The best we can do is to more or less guess; but no certainty can be built upon guesswork. However on seeing the laws of nature, which are so strict and unavoidable in their essence, we cannot but accept that a manifestation which we call 'our life in forms' is also subject to laws, which must have a dispenser, in whose power are included the sparks of our own lives.

And it is He, to whom the *invocation* is dedicated.

Now comes the requests themselves:

b. *Save me from the spirit of frustration . . .*

Some occult philosophers are of the opinion that the feeling of *frustration* is just that of the invisible and inexhaustible *'fire'* which burns people, when they realize the errors and evils they have committed, and when they are able to *foresee* the results of their deeds. It normally happens after the discarding of the physical body, whose gross matter can then no longer dim our finer senses of the other world. Exoteric religions, without any exception, warn their faithful while they are still living, that this 'fire' is a consequence of improper activities and call that deplorable state different kinds of hells, purgatories, and so on. Apart from the perhaps too picturesque descriptions and imaginative details, such as in Dante's *Divine Comedy*, we can see that the basis of the idea of retribution is not a wrong one. The indisputable law of cause and effect supports this idea.

Now you may realize the weight behind the first request in the prayer of St Ephraem, that great theurgist of early Christian times.

If we have a feeling of frustration here and now, it is our natural duty to fight and destroy it, as an evil which spreads for which we are then equally responsible. We pray the Lord to be saved from this evil.

c. [*And from*] *dejection . . .*

If frustration is like fire, dejection is like an icy stream freezing everything it touches. And similarly in order to be liberated from it, we have to suppress any approaching feelings of dejection for the same reasons as we did with frustration. What does dejection mean if not a dimming, or even a dying within us of the inner flame of hope, without which there is no evolutionary life? Dejection is a graveyard of the soul! In this request we pray that the Almighty Lord will allow us to transform the graveyard into a flourishing garden of hope. How well the saints knew about the inner, most mysterious and deeply hidden gardens within us.

d. [*And from*] *lust . . .*

This vice spoils every spiritual aspiration and I hope you will readily agree with this statement. Lust is directed to the most perishable, unstable and therefore unreal form of man—his gross body. Men then identify themselves—albeit unconsciously but nevertheless wrongly—with their physical counterparts, forgetting about their higher being and about the basic *freedom* of man, realizable only in the realm higher than the physical. This means an involutionary trend and no advancement or enlightenment of consciousness. One simply sells one's great inheritance for a miserable 'pottage of lentils', as was described in the Old Testament. But the inner, soundless voice in us speaks for itself. No sane person would suppose that the great Teachers of humanity were slaves to lust. Look into your own consciousness and test this statement, here and now. May the Lord fulfil this request for you.

The normal relations between man and woman, as in marriage, do not enter into this category of evil in us. After all, humanity is still on the level of physical existence, and there is a necessity to incarnate for the overwhelming majority of people. So, new bodies have to be provided and those who are still on the level of individual (that is, separate) existence, have to create more bodies just as their forbears did for them.

That is why a normal sex life has always been accepted by all exoteric religions in the form of marriage, sanctified by the churches. It is necessary concession for the present epoch. Lust appears when sex becomes an aim and an obsession, overpowering everything else in a man.

On the higher level, that, say, of a saint or sage, who has left the rest of humanity far behind him, this concession, of course, becomes meaningless, simply because he no longer needs or wishes any further participation in the providing of new bodies for men. Also, many sensible people would be offended by the thought, that, for example, Christ could be married and have children. In this case, subconscious wisdom is speaking to us.

e. *And [from] prating . . .*

This is another destructive vice, having its roots in weak will-power and mind in the person concerned. A man who likes to prate seems to have little 'inside' and everything 'outside'— on his tongue. There is no depth in him, merely shallow water. It is a serious obstacle to every spiritual achievement. And it is quite a formidable vice, since St Ephraem the Syrian sets it among others in his prayer, and freedom from which he asks for in his inspired formula. So, let us join with him in our own effort.

Now comes the third part requesting not only freedom from sin, but also for the granting of positive virtues.

f. *But grant to me, Thy servant . . .*

Here our true rôle is clearly defined: a theurgist has to be a servant of the Supreme and not of his own mortal will. It is an intimate spiritual relation between the *emanation* (man) and the Great Source (God). The idea of service is basic and one of the oldest in theurgy. Among others we find a statement such as: 'Who serves men will be served by angels.'

Master Andréas, as quoted by Paul Sédir, repeatedly said this. So think deeply of how many evils you will be spared if you will only consider your activities as a service to the Lord. And upon the relative amount of such service in a man's everyday life will depend his position in evolution. A primitive tribesman knows only one way: to serve his body, to feed and defend it. Next come similar duties towards those nearest to him, his wife and offspring. But even most animals do exactly the same and are often ready to sacrifice their lives for their young, when the latter are endangered. The higher our position the wider is the circle of our service. One then advances from, say, feeding the poor, to the bringing of spiritual (that is, imperishable) food to the masses. For Christ said: Not by bread alone . . .'

The highest degree of service for a theurgist is a selfless one without expecting any reward, a service for the whole.

Those interested in a further development of the principles of service will find this in the XIIth Chapter of *The Tarot*.

It is now easy to recognize that the idea of service is the basis of collective theurgic action.

g. *The Spirit of purity . . .*

Here we are praying for a positive and cardinal virtue, which replaces impurity (such as lust, and so on) *leaving no place* for vices in us. What use and realizable power could be found in a theurgic action formally performed by a man, whose whole consciousness is constantly merged in the ocean of passions and lust? We already know that the virtue of any prayer is measured, not by its mere pronouncement, but by the inner force put into the words by us. As Christ said: 'For every tree is known by its fruit. . . .' If impurity prevails in an operator for most of his conscious life and during the actual time of an action, what chance will there be for him to overcome the spoiled current of feelings and thoughts, even when he recites what otherwise would be most potent formulas? There is quite a real and direct danger in doing so, and you will find the reason given in Chapter IX where operators are introduced to collective action.

h. *Humility in Wisdom . . .*

This request is directed against that notorious enemy of any spiritual attainment—pride, and especially the pride a man feels when he apparently has some 'good reasons' for it: if there can ever be any 'good reason' for a vice, which pride undoubtedly is.

We can see that here we have a prayer (by St Ephraem), which is performed not by a beginner, but by an aspirant who has already reached a certain point and achieved the knowledge still lacking in an average man. And here lies the danger. One can easily overlook the nothingness of one's amount of knowledge in comparison with the Lord's wisdom. That is why, in this part of the prayer, the request is just for 'humility in wisdom'. Perhaps 'humility in knowledge' would be more appropriate and logical, fitting the idea better, but I am adhering strictly to the old texts and hence do not feel myself entitled to change their exact meaning for some other approximate version.

When we are possessed by pride, no matter how 'justified' it might appear to be to our mind, we are building a wall, which then separates us from the illimitable freedom of spiritual flight, that is, a supramental experience. Our consciousness then becomes as if rigid, thus preventing subtle intuition from penetrating our awareness.

These are the facts which cannot be changed and we have to either accept or leave them. In the latter event your prayer will remain earth-bound, that is, devoid of effectiveness. It will not have any wings. Moreover, we know that all spiritually developed men like the saints and sages, were pre-eminently modest and humble men. The true value of theurgic methods and their difference from any exoteric religious practices lies just in rather a scientific and psychological approach to an action. This can be achieved only because the great theurgists of the past possessed deep knowledge of the human psyche, and they taught from their own experience.

Thefore let us follow them with confidence, knowing that all the truths which we may now necessarily accept as *theorems,* will later become *axioms* for us, to the measure of our advancement and deepening knowledge, leading us on to wisdom.

In our everyday life we have repeatedly to trust to the experience of other people, using it *ad libitum,* so there is nothing illogical or wrong when we do the same with spiritual wisdom, and take full advantage of it. Providing, of course, that we already have an innate inclination towards and belief in the inner reality in us. If only mental doubts and uncertainty exist in us, we should first weed our garden, until such time as good seeds can be sown it it.

To doubt everything and repulse any constructive effort to really 'KNOW' leads nowhere, except to a cold and fruitless aloofness in a man, for which he has to pay dearly when the hour of his reckoning comes.

It is only the maliciousness of our unsubdued mind which tries to prevent us from sailing on the illimitable ocean that extends far beyond the mind's realm, that is, that of spirit.

But to accept all nonsense and superstition proffered by the ignorant and deceivers—which unfortunately is far too often in this period—would be going to the other extreme and equally harmful and delaying for our progress (see *Ways to Self-Realization,* Chapters XXX and XLIV).

Discrimination was, is and always will be the foremost virtue leading to the path, like a bright lighthouse in the darkness of a stormy night, saving ships from treacherous reefs and rocks.

i. *Patience . . .*

There is not much need to underline the importance of this virtue. Impatience is only a proof that man is unable to control his emotions and mental processes. Little spiritual progress can be expected from such an individual. Patience means that a man has already subdued his primitive egoism, and is able to recognize reason in another's person's position. Impatient people are usually also unbalanced nervously, which cannot positively contribute in forming them into theurgists. That is why the request for patience has been included in this theurgic prayer.

j. *And love . . .*

Chapter X of this book gave a detailed definition and explanation of love, so it would be superfluous to repeat it here. It remains only to stress the compelling importance of love, so beautifully expressed by St Paul who said: 'And if I should have prophecy and should know all mysteries, and all knowledge, and if I should have all faith, so that I could remove mountains, and have not charity, I am nothing.'

The three cardinal spiritual virtues are faith, hope and charity (or love). Finally, if one has no love for the Lord, how can one address one's most intimate prayers to Him?

Now we come to the second invocation, being an introduction to the last request of this prayer.

k. *O my Lord and Master . . .*

This is another devotional way of addressing the Supreme, the first having been made at the beginning of the formula. It again arouses devotion and love for Him.

Do not fail to merge deeply into it when passing through the different stages of this theurgic prayer. It will richly repay you as, upon your attitude and fervent surrender, depends the whole success of the action. The more you are with the Lord, the closer He comes to you, leading on to that mysterious union, which is the immense reward of those who succeed.

1. *Enable me to see my own iniquities*
*And not to judge my brother! . . .*

To those acquainted with occult philosophy this request is clear: it aims at the annihilation in us of that archenemy of Spirit—human egoism. Here the great theurgist of the past is directly on target. We have to see our own vices and shortcomings for ourselves, as only then can the task of removing them be started. But this does not mean that one should constantly meditate about one's faults: that would merely lead to diametrically opposite results, with the strengthening of vices insead of their disappearance. We should substitute virtues for vices and not create any clichés around the latter.

The spiritually blind ego tries to delay the process of inner purification in us, thus preventing progress, and it uses quite a treacherous method. It shows us the errors and evil in others! 'Well, I may be wrong but look at this man or that man; are there not others still worse than me?'

If you really possess some power of discrimination, you will immediately see through the subterfuge. Does it help a sick man to know that other people are also sick, even more so than himself? Does it alleviate his own sufferings? Can the presence of a malady in his neighbour cure his own ailment?

Think deeply about these examples and see just how illogical is the attitude of the deceiver—the ego in man.

What chance have you of improving others while you yourself are merged in iniquities? Every vice is nonsensical when seen through the eyes of truth. But here you have a very strong proof of how the human mind, when led by egoism, can arrive at illogical and harmful conclusions.

Only sixteen years ago some visitors to the great Indian saint and sage (Ramana Maharshi, 1879-1950) remarked, that upon their arrival at the Rishi's abode, lusty emotions and stormy thoughts seemed to increase in them, instead of being quelled. 'It is only natural,' said the sage, 'that the rubbish in us has to come to the surface. Otherwise how can it be destroyed?'

The judging of others is also a striking antithesis of the

cardinal spiritual rule of *unity.* By condemning and destructively criticizing others we only underline our inner separateness. This is not to say, that if we see real harm being done, we should praise it. It would be very wrong. If you can preserve your brothers from harm, it is your duty to show it to them and so, if possible, prevent the evil.

m. *For blessed art Thou forever.*

This thanksgiving and devotional invocation closes the magic circle of your prayer. The operation ends with due obeisance before the Almighty. The invocation must be pronounced with the utmost concentration and deepest feeling, slowly and repeatedly, according to your intuition at this moment.

Now you can use the whole of Formula II in a theurgic manner, that is, *with knowledge and understanding in the way as shown by the great theurgic tradition of Christian saints and eminent occultists.*

Those acquainted with Hindu Yoga may say that there is a strong resemblance to the ancient Bhakti Yoga of Vedantic lore. This is not wrong, but theurgy is more scientific and operates with knowledge of the human psyche, giving more exact methods than the Eastern tradition. It is true that some devotional Vedantic hymns are very elevating, and if the aspirant does not require anything more than emotional bliss, he may be happy enough with them.

In the bibliography of this book I have listed several works on theurgy in different languages and from different periods. The amount of literature on the subject is quite formidable, although in only a fraction of it can one find practical methods appropriate for twentieth century man to follow. Moreover, in some works there is considerable deviation from the general line of traditional theurgy, which is supported by the authority of the true masters of this spiritual art. So, although I have included these books as a matter of course, I am not always in full agreement with them. If we wish to give certain practical knowledge, we also have to use practical methods. In spiritual operations the number of words used is of far less importance than that of the attitude and wisdom, with which the prayer is performed. Hence I have limited the number of theurgic themes to the bare minimum and placed stress on their explanation and correct use. As you will develop in knowledge and practice of the subject, you will see that the shorter a formula is the better you will be able to cope with it, and the greater the concentration that will then be attained. And this means success. This manual is *not* meant for reading, but for studying and practical use. A hundred formulas would only create confusion, but, say, three carefully selected and well explained ones may lead the aspirant to attainment of considerable results, and give him independence and clear insight into the matter. This has been my aim.

### WORSHIP FOR AN EMERGENCY

Sometimes conditions surround us, where it is not possible to perform an elaborate operation, and in which a sudden emergency requires a decisive and highly concentrated action. So here I am giving formulas, traditionally ascribed to great theurgists, some of whom are considered to be saints.

Because of their power and inherent concentration, these formulas should be used with due solemnity and faith, just as was done by the saints. These texts were never given to a wider public. But I believe that the time is approaching of which the Great Teacher of Humanity spoke, when He said: *'Then every secret thing will become open and known'*, and therefore I am taking the responsibility for making them available.

From these formulas everyone will be able to find what he needs for a given moment, choosing the one most suited to his particular emergency.

a. *O Lord, who art the illimitable, eternal joy,*
*Graciously grant me Thy consolation in my sadness!*

b. *O Thou, who art the wholeness of omniscient wisdom,*
*Deign to send me a ray of Thy light to dispel the darkness of my ignorance and doubts!*

c. *Infinite Lord, before whom the whole universe is like a drop of water,*
*Who possessest all the treasures of the world,*
*Grant me relief in my poverty, give me the means to live and to fulfil my duties towards Thee and my fellow men!*

d. *Thou the perfect eternal justice, O Lord, help me against those who try to wrong me, although I did and do not offend them in any way!*

(This formula must be used very cautiously, and only when we are sure that we have not provoked the hostility of our 'enemies' in any way. Otherwise the trouble we are experiencing may be only the repercussion of our own wrongdoing, and the *true justice of God* may then be turned against us.)

e. *O Merciful Lord, my sufferings seem to transcend my ability to bear them. Grant me alleviation or an alteration of the way in which I have now to pay for my transgressions.*

(This worship also should be used only in exceptional circumstances and with great discrimination.)

f. *O Lord, remove this chalice of coming danger and suffering from me! Have mercy upon me, O Lord, my only hope is in Thee!*

(This form of prayer should be used in an emergency, only when every possibility of human assistance has already been ruled out.)

In the most critical cases, when time is short, danger is due within seconds and the mind is already unable to perform anything except a single invocation, the following formulas may be used:

g. *Lord have mercy! Lord have mercy! Lord have mercy!* and so on.

h. *O Lord, help me! O Lord, help me! O Lord, help me!* and so on.

When you see that the end is approaching despite your prayers (as just given), and it is clear that your last moment has come, use the powerful formula of surrender to Him, which is the best possible action for a man in the last seconds of life in his body:

i. *Thy Justice is done, O Lord,*
*Hallowed be Thy Name forever!*

You may also use the last prayer of Jesus, if your feel that you dare to do so:

j. *'Father, into thy hands I commend my spirit.'*

All these prayers must be repeated incessantly with the utmost possible concentration until the emergency passes, or you see that because of circumstances such as g., h. or i., you have to change the formula for one more suited to your immediate position. The prayers under a., b., c. and d. have no application to *exceptional* emergencies and should be used systematically, as the required relief may take longer. It is incredible how much help can be obtained from sincere and solemn use of theurgic worship as given in this chapter. Confidence in the Lord's power and mercy is the deciding factor here. Repetition of formulas without the participation of your heart and merely as just another attempt to escape cheaply from trouble or danger, or worse still, as a kind of 'experiment' (and a more foolish attitude cannot be imagined), will not only bring no relief, but a most positive increase of trouble or suffering. I am obliged to mention this truth and to underline it with all possible gravity.

I do not see any purpose in making a secret of what are sometimes unpleasant truths. There is a set of circumstances where no known activity, not even theurgy can help a man—at least in the present incarnation—and that is when he has committed some extreme foolishness against himself. I am referring to the results of occult bungling, that is, the performance of some practices, which may lead to undue contact with the worlds which are, and must normally be, beyond the reach of an average man who is not especially trained, or personally guided by a true spiritual Master.

Unfortunately, we now hear of many people, and even associations trying to lead their undiscriminating and duped adherents to the 'development of superior powers' in the latter. Practically, this means only one thing—THEIR SUBMISSION TO THE DARK FORCES ON THE OTHER SIDE. This, of course, is done mostly for money, sometimes collected in a cleverly disguised form. All the 'awakening of Kundalini' and other such nonsense belongs in this category. The only result of such 'development' is, and always will be, a great harm to a man's mind and psyche. A mere instruction on how to breathe and 'concentrate' on crudely selected ideas, does not make anyone a superman. The law of gradual evolution cannot be cheated. Unhealthy curiosity is always punished, as it is no substitute for true spiritual and normal progress.

In the last forty odd years I have known of many cases of such inner disaster, which followed on after illicit occult bungling. Some people have terrible visions, from which they cannot free themselves; some are harmed mentally and nervously, and many suffer physical disasters. Families are sometimes broken and permanent or a mild form of idiocy was (and is) the cheapest known price for ill-fated curiosity. Why is it so? Because without due moral and mental preparation, the position of a man who peeps into the 'other side' is just like a swimmer thrown into a bay full of sharks: he has no chance of remaining unharmed. The forces on the 'other side' which alone are contacted by occult bunglers, *are far from angelic. They are definitely evil and eager to harm human beings,* and if the opportunity is given to them they indulge themselves to the full. No assistance from our side is able to make good such illicit contact with the astral demons. Perhaps this is because it then *becomes a man's karma, created by his own efforts.* Although theurgic rites can expel *unwelcome* obsessors they can do little when a man himself wanted to invite these monsters.

I felt it was my duty also to mention these facts in my other works.

## CHAPTER XVI

# ATTAINMENT OF THE FINAL UNION

In theurgy relationship with the Supreme (God) has rather a personal aspect. In our prayers and invocations we often find the pronoun 'Thou'. From other sources of initiation, like hermetic occultism in the West (the Tarot's system of philosophy) and Vedanta and Buddhism in the East, the conception of God, in its highest degrees, is impersonal, absolute, beyond all anthropomorphic colouring.

In general this conception is considered to be the closest to the inexpressible in speech—the real truth of the Supreme. The peaks of Vedantic initiation recognize as the only reality, the great universal consciousness—the SELF, a reflection of which is man's self. Buddha went still further, declining all discussion or building of mental conceptions about that supreme state of liberated consciousness, simply saying: 'Reach Nirvana and then all questions will be solved of themselves.' It is useless to speak about and discuss the THING, which is beyond all speech and thought. Undoubtedly this is a very sober and realistic teaching, but not for all and sundry: to the majority of people abstract ideas are too unreal and aloof.

So, when comparing the theurgic attitude of the Father in heaven, and so on, a problem may arise. Does theurgy really believe in and teach about a *personal God* as the ultimate truth? And if there is some personal conception, is it utterly wrong and impracticable?

The answer is not so simple, and needs a full understanding of the human psyche. Here I will quote only a few essential points, for entering into details would lead us far beyond the purpose of this book. The foremost thing you have to realize and meditate about is, that a 'large circle can contain all smaller ones.' This is a useful simile. Personality and individuality are only limitations of the absolute conception of the universal, or the Whole. Just as the solar systems are very limited in space and mass in comparison with, say, the galaxies to which they belong, and which contain millions of such systems, together with all their suns, planets and satellites, on different degrees of evolution.

But this truth does not deny or invalidate the existence of the smaller units in relation to the incomparably greater ones. Of course, it is not easy for an average mind, untrained in mathematics and the theories of space, to realize the limitless, infinite universe. And so it is with our problem: the conception of the God-Absolute, which being far beyond any of the limitations of personal existence, does not convey much to an average man.

They want something 'closer', more understandable, more 'real' so to speak. In ancient times human beings used very primitive vehicles and other means of transportation, for they had nothing better. In spite of that, they were much better off with those primitive conveyances than without them, although, from the point of view of our present epoch and its achievements, with its surface, air and space speeds hundreds of times greater, there is no comparison.

In due time our inventions and technical achievements of the twentieth century will also appear as child's play to future generations. But does this necessarily make us wrong here and now? Of course not, for our actual *present* is merely a cradle in which the future will be born. And so it is just the same with conceptions about God.

Theurgy offers a workable image of God, while taking into consideration our frailty, which does not allow all of us to raise our awareness to the snowy peaks of the Absolute. But this is by no means an obstacle to our relations with the Supreme. If only we could express and understand the reasons given for the theurgic attitude towards God! After all, do you think that He is unable to realize our limitations at the present time, and therefore will be any the less gracious when He sees sincere efforts, even though imperfect from the absolute point of view? Do even earthly parents love their babies and children less because of the latter's weakness and imperfections, when compared with adults? Involutarily the great words of a Teacher come to mind: 'And other sheep I have, that are not of this fold: them also I must bring, and they shall hear my voice, and there shall be one fold and one shepherd.'

If you are able to realize within yourself the ultimate truth of the real Self, do not think that your adoration of the Whole is essentially different in its way and consequently, in the *result,* from the worship of a man, praying in all the sincerity of his heart to the Father in heaven. Moreover, Christ even told us: '. . . unless you be converted, and become as little children, you shall not enter the kingdom of heaven.' Think for yourself, which quality that is usually present in a child but often lacking in an adult, is essential for attainment of the union?

Theurgic invocations and prayers do not offer any 'high philosophy' (that is, only products of someone's mind), but they are certainly effective if used as intended and furthermore, they are 'workable material' in the realm where they are supposed to be applied: that is, as requests for help, healing, deliverance from troubles and other human sufferings, as has been explained in other chapters.

But there is also something much higher and more real to be attained along the way of proper worship: it is the *experience* of union with the Spirit (God). I say, experience and not 'merging forever'. It was deliberate, because a permanent 'dwelling' in the kingdom means nothing less than final Liberation, or, as religions say—'salvation'. It is a long way that leads to this glorious end and we have to deal with our present position and not with future aeons. *The purpose of this chapter is to show the way to such an experience, based on theurgic science and Tradition.*

In the East they use the practice of Samadhi for the same purpose. Theurgy advises the realization of union with the *Father,* in whose home there are 'many mansions'.

The difference between the methods of Buddhism (esoteric of course), Eastern Yoga and theurgy is now explained. In the first two currents attainment can be a pursuit without any clear idea of a Deity or Supreme Lord of Being, but in the third (theurgy of the nineteenth and twentieth centuries) God is the 'corner-stone' of the whole system. In exoteric Hinduism the conception of God is clearly expressed accompanied by the idea of 'delegation' of His powers to numerous lower deities, who then fulfil the task of ruling the gross, material universe.

Representatives of the esoteric Hindu philosophical thought are much less (if at all) concerned with all these gods, and concentrate on promoting the lofty idea of the 'ultimate truth' or 'reality' in place of the Hindu pantheon. Therefore we are entitled to say that Eastern theurgy still operates on a level comparable to that of the pre-Christian era, because they still worship numerous personifications of the powers which act in this world.

After taking into consideration all that has been said in the preceding chapters and after having successfully practised the recommended prayers and invocations, we may now come to the final attempt at actual *experience* of the *Father's* presence in our own consciouness.

I feel that there is no further need to emphasize the greatness of such a task. Therefore it is better for us to be silent about it and pass on to the work itself.

What we can still mention is the method used by theurgists, who have successfully achieved the goal, and thereby found absolute corroboration of their faith in the Lord.

We cannot enter into any academic discussions here as to why *this* method and not another is recommended for use, and so on. Such deliberations are only a loss of time and opportunity for a seeker. The best possible answer to all such 'whys' and 'hows' would be: *because this method has been experienced, checked and found to work,* which is not necessarily the case with other systems. Those who only want to talk may talk, but those who want to realize will act instead. That is the difference between the two main categories of men and accordingly, each will collect its reward, be it Attainment or—frustration.

There are two main obstacles which prevent us having spiritual experiences:

1. The BODY-AM-I idea and,
2. The disorderly activities of our mind.

We can deal with the *second* obstacle by passing through a practical course of concentration, and because this has been given in Part II of my trilogy, we will not discuss it again here. The *first* obstacle will now be explained.

Find a suitable room and set an appropriate time, where and when no one is likely to disturb you for a couple of hours. Prepare a couch or bed, a table, writing pad and pen, and some incense sticks (if you feel it will be good for your psychic atmosphere). Type or write down, as prescribed, the texts for the operation, that will be given presently, so that you will have them ready to use at any moment. The second, and probably the best method would be to memorize the invocations and prayers beforehand and use them without looking at your notes.

It is possible to perform the operation in a seated (or even kneeling) position, for those who so prefer, but I am still of the opinion that a better elimination of the body's influence can be achieved, when it is in its most inactive, that is, lying position.

When everything is ready proceed as follows:

1. Safely lock the door(s).
2. Place the ends of the incense sticks into a small vessel containing dry sand and light them.
3. Do several cycles of pranayama, as mentioned in foregoing chapter (see *Concentration*, Chapter XV).
4. Perform the invocation to the Holy Spirit (Chapter XII) three times slowly, while standing upright or kneeling.
5. Lie down on your back with a small pillow under your head, relaxing all muscles and crossing the hands over your chest. The body must be comfortable and no pressure felt from any tight clothing. Loose garments like pyjamas and so on, are recommended.

Now repeat the following texts mentally, concentrating carefully on their contents, and AGREE with their conclusions every time you meditate on them. If you disagree or have a doubt, even about one of them, the operation will be invalid, because it will then be devoid of the necessary *power of faith*. Therefore it is better to delay it until you receive more enlightenment.

6. THIS BODY NOW LYING IMMOBILIZED IS ONLY MY MATERIAL SHELL IN WHICH I AM TEMPORARILY DWELLING. I AM NOT IT, AND I WILL LEAVE IT TO DECAY AT THE MOMENT OF MY PHYSICAL DEATH.

Do I agree with this? Yes! Because it is the truth.

7. The whole material world in which I am temporarily living will have no meaning for me at the moment of my death. My family, property, the whole of my environment, my earthly aims, attachments and expectations are all quite VOID,

and I cannot take them beyond the grave. Is this so? Yes! It is the truth!

Live this by realistically imagining yourself leaving everything. *It is a condition for further success.* If you cannot perform it, better to abandon the attempt.

8. In order to be free for union with the Lord in spirit, I am now discarding all my bondage:

a. *My body:* I no longer care about it. It will be a dead thing in due time. I am detaching myself from it and now it has become a foreign thing to me.

b. *My fellow men:* I see only their mortal bodies through the mortal eyes of my own body. When my body is discarded, all of these people will disappear into unreality for me. I realize this! It is the actual truth!

9. Because I cannot find reality and bliss in the visible and sensible world around me, I must seek for both beyond the conditions of this planetary life. They can be found only in Him, who penetrates everything and in whom I live. He is omnipresent like infinite space, and yet beyond all space. My purpose is to feel, to realize his presence.

This is the truth!

This formula must be slowly and fully absorbed sentence by sentence into your awareness, and the final statement, confirming its truth felt to the utmost. This is a condition for a chance to succeed in your attempt at real spiritual merging.

10. I am no longer interested nor affected by any material factors in my environment, my body and everything connected with it. Death, which will annihilate the body and with it all my contacts with life on this planet, may come at any moment, even now. I do not care about it. I want solely to live a pure, independent existence in Him. I am ready.

This is truth for me!

11. O Lord and my Father, I have now abandoned all illusion of separate dwelling in the body. Let me enter into Thy mansion, where there is no darkness, destruction, nor death, but only Thy light and life. For such is Thy promise for those who choose the path of truth.

All this should again be meditated through until every thought disappears except a wordless one about the Infinite Eternal Lord. Only after having done this can one dare to approach the final invocation, which may give you the actual *experience* of union with the Supreme. You should not be surprised or disappointed at the method and its means: it has been tested, and has been found to work fully. The words and statements may appear strange to you and unusually sharp for your mind; but in order to gain supermental experiences one has to resign the worshipping of one's mind. For the mind cannot lead you higher than it is, and the Lord is beyond mind and all matter.

Now you practically do not feel your body. Your consciousness is turned inwards, eyes closed, and eyeballs firmly fixed upwards as if constantly looking at your eyebrows. This cannot be interrupted, or the whole operation will become nullified and you will be thrown back into your body. No thought except the prescribed meditation and invocation can enter your awareness.

As a most suitable preparation for this stage, the last chapters (XXIInd) in both of the books—*Concentration* and *Samadhi* should be studied thoroughly before starting the operation.

12. I see infinite space penetrated by the eternal, unchangeable spirit of our Father in Heaven. O Lord, grant me the grace of entering Thy kingdom. I have left all behind me and now stand naked before Thee!

Now eliminate every thought and start to repeat slowly in the mind:

Oh, LORD, LORD, LORD . . .

merging in the very word until IT comes.

What will then happen only you can know and live through. It is indescribable. One of the infallible signs that you are nearing the verge of success and are ready for the ultimate merging, will be automatic, *rhythmical* breathing, which sometimes commences with the performance of 12, or with the final invocation to the Lord. But do not think about this, even if you feel that your breath is stopping: no harm will come to you in this state. Remain in deep, blissful peace.

Otherwise, the *ladder* will be thrown down and you will fall back to earth.

The first merging may take only a fraction of a minute; but your aim is to make it last for as long as possible. What do you have to do in order to achieve that aim? Not to deviate, not to allow any thought to enter your mind and to encourage (by an indescribable but completely effective inner effort, as given in Chapter XXII of *Concentration*) the feeling of being dissolved into the infinite space around you. It is, of course, no longer any material space, and the foregoing is only an analogy, an attempt to put into words what is far beyond all speech. Nevertheless, IT WORKS, if properly used. And this is all that matters.

After 'coming back' and when your breath begins to return to normality, remain in the same position for a few minutes longer. Try not to think about any trivial (that is, earthly) things and mentally pronounce several times, with full understanding and concentration the invocation of the Last Supper. Then quietly rise, arrange your room in its normal way and return to your everyday life, but try to remember what happened to you during the operation.

As in every theurgic action, this operation had to be thoroughly prepared in advance, the meditation texts typed or written on separate sheets and, as far as possible, memorized so that only in an exceptional case would you have to refer to them as they lie beside you on the table or chair. This is because every time you look at them there is some new distraction, which is dangerous for the success of the operation. You should never mention about your study and exercises to anyone: you must keep them absolutely to yourself. If you divulge them you will thereby create new difficulties not only in the theurgic operations, but *even in your outer, personal life*.

I have seen several examples of how talkative people ruined their own chances of success by speaking to their relatives or friends, who were *not* engaged in the same way. It is the *ego* which likes to boast and prate, even when nothing important has yet been achieved. It is essential to understand that people who, like yourself, are not striving towards some higher goals, will invariably be hostile to your endeavours, and perhaps, even to you, if they know that you are engaged in something 'mysterious' (only to them of course). The cruel world tries to pull down every climber who attempts to reach some higher realm. No whys and hows will help here: you have to recognize this and act wisely and carefully. Such are the hard facts, and we must be acquainted with them.

On a very high degree of development the Lord will give you full knowledge of the laws ruling life, material as well as spiritual, for then you will be ripe for His initiation, so theurgy teaches us.

It is therefore useless and frustrating to strive after details, which are still unattainable and thereby lose the whole. And it must be realized that there is no exception for anyone: we cannot cheat the eternal laws, imposed by the Power which is absolutely beyond all our imagination and intellectual conceptions, that Power which is responsible only to Itself, and not to you.

This wisdom will give you peace even amongst the strongest possible outer disturbances.

Can you desire anything more?

## CHAPTER XVII

# MYSTICAL VISITS

Thomas à Kempis in his unsurpassed *Imitation of Christ* says that 'The whole beauty of the kingdom of God is *interior*'. In this short sentence he succeeds in defining the real relationship and properties of communion with the Supreme, which we call God.

Strangely enough, men often want objective proofs of His existence, in the basically invisible realm of feelings and thoughts, that is, in the realm *within us*. This striking lack of logic becomes still more astonishing, when we take another example of the impossibility of certain objective proofs even in cases concerning purely physical matter.

Can anyone else give you a proof of the taste of food by anything except your own direct experience? You can hear the most convincing and elaborate descriptions of a substance and you will still have no experimental judgment about it, until you taste it with your own tongue. Nothing else will do.

In the spiritual realm this rule is even more compelling. No description can substitute for the real contact with the Lord, as theurgy and its methods teach us, and which you will find in this work. Theurgy has only one aim: to show the way and to create the channels for realization of contact with Him.

But the actual 'movement' in your efforts belongs to you:

1. You walk along the *way*.
2. You fill the *channels* with your energy.

And thus you may attain the final aim.

The descriptions of the experiences following 1 and 2 do not absolve you from individual effort. So why do you find them in this book? The answer is, that the experiences of other successful seekers may touch the sensitive strings in you, tuning them to a similar frequency, attracting you and awakening in you the desire to live through those experiences for yourself.

Among the most magnificent and unforgettable milestones

on the road of theurgic achievement, are the living contacts with the Supreme Power, which some eminent mystics, including Thomas à Kempis, term the Visits of God. In the previous Chapter XVI, I spoke of the attainment of the final spiritual (although only temporary) union with the Consciousness of the Supreme. And here I will attempt to describe the indescribable, the reflection of the Lord in the awareness of the faithful soul, who has opened his whole heart, without any reservations to—Him.

The first experience, which leads to others, is the realization of His existence, and it comes from individual contact (if we dare say so) with Him, thereby becoming a corner-stone of the whole temple of the Great Presence, which is gradually built up in a man.

Then he KNOWS! He IS, at every moment, in every place and what is most tangible in us. It is then as if our individuality had receded on to the second plane, without being dimmed or completely obliterated, and the great wave of the *universal life* fills everything and tells us the truth about Him.

These words, of course, do not reflect the fullness of the spiritual experience, but at least an approximate idea can be formed from them, by those who sincerely want to find the inner temple and its true God. And that is all I can say.

Thinking is then left far below, the mind itself has been abandoned behind the limitation of its own fences, and the eternal bird becomes free for a while.

Then He comes through the wide open gates of the heart and utters the soundless speech into the invisible ears of the awakened soul. Only one who has once experienced this mystical (but how real!) *visit* can feel the sublime closeness of the Infinite and Omnipotent to himself. The background of this confrontation is love: He is infinitely kind and gracious, the all-understanding *friend*, the all-forgiving *father*, the all-knowing *teacher*. One feels that in Him and with Him one cannot have any anxiety or fear any more. The tremendous—almost impossible to imagine—reality of His kindness is beyond any mental level of consciousness. And still, man does not lose his life, for then he—IS. As never before—he lives! Our prayers are then answered in a way that transcends all our most daring expectancy.

At the same time, the cause of such an influx of grace becomes clear. It is a due reward for the opening of the most secret gate of our soul with the unique key of *perfect sincerity.* This should be understood literally: for at this time nothing remains hidden or selfish, everything is surrendered to the Lord.

This key will be at your disposal, if you do not allow it to rust in attachment to, and in the illusion of the outer world of egoism and the *fata morgana* of earthly life.

At this stage it is not wise to look ahead, or to guess about the 'future' for it would simply be falling back into the old destructive chains of the ego-mind. But the awareness of the Presence (or His visit) must not be allowed to be eradicated from you, if it so happens that you do not experience a further visit. You will need It's reflection when you leave your body for travel to the 'other side'. How can this be done?

Several years ago in India, when a devotee asked a spiritual master of this epoch—Bhagavan (divine) Maharshi, 'not to forget him', that is, not to let him lose the master's grace, the sage answered: 'If you will not forget Bhagavan, Bhagavan will not forget you.' One of the secrets concerning the earning of the Lord's grace is the constant inward turning to Him, the thinking about Him, so as not to let the mind be constantly attached to the temporal and evanescent.

How clear and realistic are these spiritual rules in His presence, but how easily they can be exchanged for trivial attachments to material things! The Lord is always ready to listen to the sincere speech of our hearts; but how seldom we allow them to speak! How seldom are we our better, real Self, instead of being fully enveloped in the shroud of this illusory, separate 'life'!

When we are worthy to be allowed into the great Presence of the Lord, this invariably has an ineffable influence even on our 'personal' life, taking over our awareness, when the stream of that life again becomes diverted to the outer world.

Often our prayers, uttered in that period of spiritual lucidity, which accompanies the outpouring of grace, are fulfilled; our conditions improve, and happiness—silent, limpid and full of peace, inner certainty and faith, become our lot for a long time.

It will not be written on your forehead and therefore the outer world may be utterly ignorant of the inner changes which are occurring in you. But what really matters to the man: his real and actual state, which is his true life, or the attitude of the outer, illusory world? True, this becomes clear to us only after we have once experienced the Presence and not before.

The very word 'presence of God' has been borrowed by theurgic science from the Church's arsenal, but philosophically, it is not a very exact term. Theurgy teaches, just as religions do, that God is omnipresent, penetrating everything, material and spiritual alike. So we cannot ever 'escape' Him. But, unfortunately, uninitiated men simply are not aware of this, and do not know anything about the Presence, being wholly absorbed by temporal, physical activities.

Anything beyond these activities lies outside their consciousness. This is the real cause of the world's misery.

That is why theurgy occupies itself but little with philosophy or theology. Its adepts know from their own experience, that no theory will help much and even the best reasoning may still not be followed by the best attitude and deeds. And it is because of this that this book gives, in the first instance, the means for obtaining the right attitude, enlightenment and grace from the Supreme Power, which lead to individual spiritual achievement, after which there are no more doubts.

If children need something, they ask their parents for it: when a conscious man needs assistance and light, to whom should he turn, if not the *Father of every thing*? But His visits, which in their spiritual beauty, are the most mystical events accessible to human beings, require our *free and sincere invitation*. Are you ready for them?

A friend, who had studied both aspects of theurgy as expounded in Parts I and II of this book, once put an interesting question to me: *'What do you consider to be the most essential manifestation of a visit from Him?'*

As I mentioned shortly before, the boons which the *Presence* brings with It are manifold, if our mind tries to enumerate them. But this is unnecessary. When changed into small pieces of currency, a gold coin loses its identity, and when dissected by the mind's efforts—which are always unsuccessful—the spiritual splendour becomes mere triviality. Lord Buddha knew very well about this fact when he taught as expressed by Sir Edwin Arnold:

> 'Om, Amitaya! measure not with words
>   Th' Immeasurable; nor sink the string of thought
> Into the Fathomless. Who asks doth err,
>   Who answers, errs. Say nought!'

The attempts in this chapter to account for spiritual visits are being made in order to assist other seekers of the eternal fatherland of the Lord's kingdom. The spiritual ecstasy of the great Presence is like a closed circuit, like a circle: without beginning or end.

One should be careful not to exchange the inexpressible Presence for a series of mental pictures, in which there will be but little of the original truth of experience. Every vision is inevitably a derivative of the mind's activities, but mind cannot, and did not take any part in His visit.

There is one definition which seems to have the bare minimum of the fallacy inherent in the thinking process, and reflecting as close as possible the impressions, which remain in our consciousness after the experience of the Presence: *It is the state of absolute inner peace, connected with the outer and inner silence.*

Anxiety, fear, expectancy, pleasure, pain, and so on, belong to the misty clouds of the past's phantom. If one is dissolved in His omnipresence one is lost as an individual, but remains as a drop in the ocean. Nothing then is of any interest, except Him. For—HE KNOWS, and you know with Him. This is not the cognition of someone 'being apart' and observing, but it is the wholeness of knowledge, when subject and object are ONE: both are melted together in the mysterious process of His Presence.

But the awareness of the outer world is not completely lost as in Samadhi, and no trance occurs. In Him we find the eternal fulcrum which is, and will be for ever our true identity. That is what Christ meant when He said: 'Come to me, all you that labour, and are burdened, and I will refresh you.'

When He comes to you or, as some say, you enter into Him, the result is infallible: YOU GAIN PEACE.

And that is all the answer that I could give to my questioner.

Forgive me if it is too little; but it is best for you to know, that if anything more is added it will only be diluted truth, lacking conviction in the search. Adding words of the mind to spiritual truth is like that terrible 'blasphemy of the Holy Spirit', which, as Christ told us: '... shall not be forgiven ... neither in this world, nor in the world to come.'

Now you will be able to realize the final aim of true theurgy. It is: TO LEAD MEN BACK TO HIM, INTO THE HIGHEST PRESENCE OF HIM WHO WAS, IS, AND WILL BE FOREVER.

Therefore, do not mix it with any occult or magic teachings. In Chapter X, page 208 of *The Tarot,* concluding the theurgic analysis of the Lord's Prayer, you will find the statement that: '. . . *there are many more magicians than true theurgists, but before them every magician bows his head in adoration and humility.*'

## CHAPTER XVIII

# THEURGIC GROUPS

While there are some who prefer to train individually, as was mentioned in an earlier chapter (VIII 'Personal Action'), collective operations can also be performed (see also Chapter IX 'Ritual for Collective Operation'). Such a group would be much stronger and capable of achieving far greater results than any personal effort by a lone theurgist.

However, collective work is more complicated and depends upon many factors, which is only natural. Any co-ordination among several human beings always necessitates quite a lot of organization and special conditions, and it is not otherwise with theurgic activities.

In this chapter we will study the action of collective theurgic work in its general form, which will fit every circumstance and need. Tradition tells us that it is not advisable to ask for help in detail and in all cases. Why is this so? Because we can assume that the power which is able to help in conditions that are beyond any human possibility, will certainly know the true cause of troubles and their best remedy. We cannot attempt to teach the Supreme, if we wish to consider ourselves to be reasonable and sane men. We also have to be aware, that there must be cases where even the strongest and most devoted collective organization will not obtain the desired results, and we should already know about this from former chapters. There are *irrevocable* things and events, where nothing can change their course.

Two things are necessary for the formation of a theurgic group of helpers:

1. willing members and
2. an able leader.

Without members there will not be any group at all and someone must take the responsibility and toil of leading.

What is required of a prospective leader of a theurgic group? Of course, he must have some personal experience, firstly from his training in individual action (see Chapter VIII 'Personal Action' and Chapter V 'Instructions for Action'). He must believe in his work and be devoted to it. Then he should study the way of collective work, and be well acquainted with the simple ritual, designed for the group, which he will find in this and following chapters. The formal part, that is, the texts for use and the proceedings to be followed must be written down by the prospective leader on separate pieces of paper in a strict sequence of the activities and sermons required, without leaving anything to the last moment or to his memory. This is because there have been quite a number of cases where the leader has lost the thread of his duties during a meeting and thereby brought confusion and disappointment to those present at the session.

It is the accepted thing in theurgic groups, that each of the members can assume leadership of an operation in an emergency, and usually a group of good standing has more than one member able to lead the session. Such an arrangement is highly recommended.

The general ritual for action by a theurgic group is composed of five parts, which consist of five verses of worship and related requests and the final conjuration And all of it must be fully understood and agreed with before any meeting can start.

To begin with I will give the 'verses' separately, together with explanations and reasons for them, as these are things which a prospective leader must know thoroughly.

The principal condition for any theurgic work is the *proper tuning* of the operator's consciousness, which thus allows him to attract the superior powers and benefit by their grace and assistance. The traditional way for that attainment is by the use of suitable texts, which may bring the same blessed results to you, that they brought to your predecessors. Moreover, in any theurgic action one has to establish one's own position, that is, to know where one stands and what one wants.

At this point, Chapter IV 'Faith in the Supreme' should be recapitulated before you read any further.

Presuming that this has been done, we will proceed.

Once while strolling among some sand dunes at the seaside, my attention was caught by a large type of ant, about half an inch long, running among the blades of sun-scorched grass.

When I stopped for a moment and slightly bent my head in order to see the little creatures better, they stood on their hind legs, watched me intently and menacingly opened their large jaws. Their limited consciousness was unable to comprehend the true relationship of the forces involved. The ants could not see that a slight movement of the human foot would squeeze every scrap of life from their bodies, in spite of all their 'courage' and daring threats.

While driving his car, with passengers in the back seat, a man was involved in an accident as his vehicle climbed a steep mountain road. On one side there was a drop of about 3,000 feet down the side of the mountain, which was covered with a few trees and bushes. The narrow road had been under repair and the edges were lined with a large amount of loose gravel, which gave the impression that there was firm ground beneath it; but such was not the case. Then at a certain moment as the car moved over towards the edge to allow another to pass, it lost its grip of the road and rolled down the steep slope. It seemed that there was no hope that the car and its occupants would not be smashed to pieces at the foot of the mountain so far below.

Then suddenly, after rolling over several times, the car came to standstill, and the uninjured occupants looked at one another, as if unable to believe that they were still alive and not crushed to pulp.

When the driver carefully left the car, which was standing upright on its four wheels, facing back towards the road over fifty feet above, he saw the cause of salvation. Across the path that the rolling vehicle had been taking lay an enormous old log, parallel to the road, and half-rotted away by decay. It had caught and held the rear wheels of the car, thus preventing any further movement. Yet a few feet either to the left or right meant a free fall to the bottom.

On a hot summer day a young man was swimming in the sea with other people, while sunbathers lined the beach. Suddenly there was an agonized cry of pain and despair. Then just a few reddish coloured waves that closed over the fin of the shark as it disappeared into the depths.

At the turn of this century a French theurgist remarked that: 'Man is not aware that he is brushing with death several times daily, but remains unharmed until his hour comes.

There are powers guarding everyone, and without their mysterious co-operation nothing can happen to a man.'

So, the poor ants did not know that their little lives were at the mercy of the towering monster; the driver of the car had no hope of being saved, and the swimmer did not sense how close his end was. People do not know the power which causes them to live, suffer, rejoice or die, except that this by far exceeds the relationship between man and ant. But theurgy knows! It teaches us that this irresistible, absolute power is HIM, the source of every beginning and every end (see Chapter III 'God in Theurgy'). To realize the proper relation of that spark of consciousness which we are, to that of the *Whole*—is wisdom, attainable for some of us, here and now. Theurgy states that these relations can be discovered and cognized, enlightening our lives forever. But it does not come of itself until a man starts to co-operate with the movement of discovery within himself. Theurgy gives methods for this task.

After this brief explanation, helping us as it may to gain a *true attitude*, upon which all our success depends in the spiritual realm, it is now time to give the actual formulas for the operation. When the circle is ready (see Chapters V, IX and X) we can start.

I. *I know that a sincere prayer is a blessing from the Almighty, but a negligent invocation of the Lord falls as a damnation on a foolish man.*

Only absolute sincerity towards God is good enough for Him. Since we are infinitely less in comparison with Him than an ant is to a man, we dare not adopt an improper attitude (that is, one devoid of respect and admiration or is defiant) towards Him, if we do not wish to bear the inevitable consequences, no matter in what period of time or space they will come. It is along these lines that this verse must be meditated upon and absorbed.

II. *There is no man born who has not committed a sin: so, before I turn to Thee, O Lord with my prayer, I beseech Thee to be gracious to me, a sinner, who, with head humbled deep in the dust before Thee, is sorry for all his iniquities.*

We cannot spend our lives without committing errors and offences, commonly called—sins. Here we must sincerely recognize this fact, otherwise we are not worthy to face the

Lord, as we would be only hypocrites. His infinite Grace may accept our humility and genuine sorrow for the iniquities committed, and only from this position can man approach the the Supreme. In this state of Grace we are better able to help others.

III. *I pray, O Lord for my brother/sister (give full name) who is in distress because of errors committed against Thy goodness and wisdom, but Thou who art the whole of grace and compassion, may lighten the burden of my brother/sister (again give the name) if Thou hearest my prayer for him/her.*

The actual action for the distressed person starts at this point. We recognize and realize that suffering of every kind is only a result of a man's own errors against the laws of the Supreme, who is the ultimate wisdom and goodness. Our misdeeds offend both. We then appeal to His grace and compassion and not just to rigid justice, which would surely condemn us. It is a mystery to us how the Lord is, at one and the same time, supremely just, compassionate and gracious. Meditate immediately about these attributes of God and an understanding may grow in your heart.

Because of their limited vision, the tiny white or red corpuscles in our blood stream surely know little, if anything at all, of what a man is thinking. Their consciousness does not reach far enough to understand why a man is acting in one way and not another, and so on. Perhaps this simple analogy will be of some use to your minds.

In this part of the worship we pray for a lightening of the karmic burden, which is oppressing our suffering brother or sister. This is because He knows better, what can be done within the limits of justice and law. Leave everything to Him, asking only that our prayer will be heard. That is the best that we can do in this spiritual operation. And it is undoubtedly a spiritual one, because it is an unselfish and not an egoistic request. The lack of that 'tiger of egoism' (the words used by the famous Indian sage—Shankaracharya) refers to the spiritual realm within us.

IV. *May help and solace be given to you, brother/sister (give name) and may Grace flow through my hands into you. Let the Lord's will be done!*

This is the culminating point of the whole operation. And if one has been provided, members perform the imposition of hands upon the photograph of the person concerned. They should try to memorize his or her face beforehand. The name should be repeated three times, slowly and loudly and the members also repeat the words of the leader.

Now we can see what realms are contacted during this operation:

a. The *spiritual,* in the form of pure prayer with an intention to help.

b. The *imposition of hands,* sending additional astral current flowing through the bodies of the members, joined together by the cord. If it is a purely physical sickness we are trying to cure, we may fortify the immediate result by contracting all the muscles in our bodies when the prayer starts and remaining so until the name of the patient is said and then gradually releasing the tension. Anyway, this is a well-known occult method for quick assistance.

c. Finally, we place everything in the hands of the Lord, thereby purifying the whole operation, and so gaining a chance for its success. It is only His will which can produce results, unobtainable in any other way. Usually, people turn to theurgic methods of cure only when official medicine has showed itself to be powerless.

The fifth verse which follows, is a thanksgiving to the Lord. Speech can never describe the perfection of the Lord and our blessings directed to Him are certainly inadequate, but we do our best. There is also the request, that our prayers be allowed to join the worship of the saints.

V. *Blessed be Thou, O Lord, enlighten me through Thy initiation! Let my prayer join the unceasing current of worship of Thy saints, and rise to Thee as the smoke of incense.*

In theurgy it is accepted that the prayers and admiration of the saints (living as well as departed) for God, rise like streams of spiritual aroma to His throne, in the symbolic language of the Church. They are then closer to truth and to Him. And in theurgic tradition there is mention of a spiritual vision of an occultist, who saw the whole of our planet as a dark globe, except for the brilliant streams of light, similar to living columns, ascending from the darkness of earth to heaven, which had been created by the holiness in the hearts of the saints.

This symbolism is so obvious that we do not need any explanation. Saints, unlike ordinary men, spend their days and nights in constant contact with the Lord through their love, humility, devotion and endurance. They are also called the 'flowers of humanity', and the hope that an erring planet may be spared because of the presence of the few saints on it, is well known in the scriptures. The conceptions of the saints transcend all religions and limited dogmas and creeds.

Preparation for any collective theurgic operation calls for a complete assimilation of these few ideas and the explanations of the texts used. Primarily all of this refers to the leader of an operation and his assistants, who stand in for him when necessary. Photographs of 'patients' which are used during meetings may be returned to them afterwards, so as to form a visible link with the group of helpers.

When the operation is performed by a large group, and the object of its attention is another group of men or an organization, the invocation to the Holy Spirit (Chapter XII) may be added before the usual ritual.

The group's work influences its members, promoting their inner enlightenment and raising their moral and mental standards. The first signs of enlightenment come in the form of inner peace, serenity, lack of fear of death or relapses into the limitations of personal life. Mental anxiety fades away, and with it the thirst for putting innumerable questions, which, after all, belong purely to the realm of the mind. This is because *intuition*, so far superior to any mental cognition, gradually takes the place of mental deliberations and thoughts.

This attitude can be expressed by having full confidence in the Almighty, and certainty of the fact that—HE KNOWS! What more can be said?

# CHAPTER XIX

# ASSISTANCE FOR THE DEPARTED

In theurgy, as in the majority of exoteric religions, we have an elaborate ritual for those who have left the physical world and are living in the in-between-incarnations period on the astral plane, and subsequently the mental one. Basically the form of help is similar to those already described in earlier chapters. But in some details there is a considerable difference in conditions on the physical and astro-mental levels. When living in our physical bodies here, on this earth, we are repaying and building our karmas. The whole of earthly life consists of an uninterrupted stream of actions, the variety of which is almost infinite.

The average man can enjoy the fullness of his awareness of life only in the physical world, which is the sole reality for him. He cannot see much (if anything) of the connections with his far distant past and cannot foresee the future. The results of his good or bad deeds, if they are not circumscribed by man-made laws, that is, his feelings and thoughts, which he incessantly radiates into the astro-mental atmosphere, are usually unperceivable for him, and the inexorable law of cause and effect does not show itself in immediate retribution or reward. Our 'debit' and 'credit' accounts arise and grow without our knowledge. Under such conditions, theurgy has definite methods and means for intervention, as you can see from some former chapters, so there is no need to repeat them again.

But things are utterly different for disincarnate beings. After having discarded their physical bodies, they start to 'see' more in the realm, normally closed to any physical means of cognition.

Tradition tells us that immediately after death a man faces his 'first trial'. What is it?

In the moment of separation from the body the consciousness of the dying man has a short period of lucidity, which is very rich in consequences: he sees the whole of his former existences, the life which just passed away, and the future wanderings through different worlds. He now sees, and this is a deciding factor for his peace or torment, the casual links between all he did during his incarnations, as well as his imminent conditions, which are the outcome of his past.

Why is it called the 'first judgment' in occultism and also in some great religions? And who is the 'judge'?

Tragically, in this case the judge is the man himself, for he sees his errors and what awaits him as retribution, balancing them against each other in his account.

Because he sees and knows all this, he can neither ask for, nor give himself absolution which theoretically, would still be possible on the earth where others judge us. But here, there is no more illusion or deceipt.

Because, generally speaking, humanity is still attached more to the involutionary (evil) 'pleasures' of the flesh, than to the evolutionary (good) paths of sacrifice and sainthood, the pictures seen by the dying (and subsequently the dead person) are rather grim. From his realization of a wrongly spent incarnation—if such is the fact, as in the majority of cases—and the consequent suffering ahead, grows the 'fire' which some religions call *hellish*.

This fire is invisible and promotes internal rather than external suffering. Nobody needs to imagine the traditional boilers of melted tar, horned and tailed 'executioners' and other figments of the imagination. However, this inner fire, which cannot be extinguished like a physical fire, has a name. It is—*frustration,* raised to an immense intensity, unknown on the earth where there are thick veils of matter and the possibility to forget inner troubles, even for a short time, through activities on the physical plane. So what help can theurgic methods give in such a desperate situation where nothing can be changed in the 'life of results'? Very much indeed, as we will soon see.

The fuel which enhances and feeds this 'hellish fire' of frustration beyond any hope (for then the man does not know the extent of time in his new conditions), is based on ignorance, in which the majority of people are merged while on earth, and in which they die.

This ignorance is the direct result of egoism and materialism, like a black veil which envelopes the spiritual consciousness, present in the depths of every being, but which cannot manifest itself when dimmed by that veil. On the 'other side', arising from ignorance, there is a lack of right understanding of one's true position, of the temporary character of one's suffering and torment, of the loneliness in that suffering and the lack of hope for all future improvement and redemption of created evils. Of course, all of this is only a brief outline. Do not forget that *death does not add any wisdom* beyond that which was already possessed in the earthly lifetime, and the dead person does not know or 'see' any more about the Supreme than he knew or saw when still alive in his physical body.

Now you can probably guess how incarnate theurgists can help their departed, suffering brothers. Very good and wise men do not depend much on help from the earth. A theurgist can create positive forces by the power of well-directed prayers and invocations, sending them forth on behalf of the departed, to the source of all grace and compassion. Usually, we refer to certain forms of spiritual energy emitted by theurgic groups, or in the operations of a single person as:

a. The LIGHT OF HOPE, so that a disincarnate person begins to realize the temporary character of his suffering.

b. The leading of his emotions and thoughts to the vision of the Merciful Lord, whose grace is always ready to pour into a heart, sincerely sorry for its former errors and misdeeds.

c. The creation of an atmosphere of healing peace around the one who has trespassed, which will act just as a soothing, cooling stream of water does for a tired and thirsty man.

d. Finally, and it is the most powerful kind of operation, to direct our prayers, filled with love and compassion for the dead brother, to the Lord, as He alone knows the best way of transforming the spiritual energy—created by the prayers of worshippers—into solace and boons. This is the fulcrum of every theurgic action, for the living and dead alike, and a full understanding of it is the condition of effectiveness of your spiritual assistance.

In theurgic tradition there is a special form of prayer for departed people. It is based on a deep knowledge of the human psyche. The gnawing fire of frustration can be abated only when a man feels right justification for his past misdeeds. It seems, perhaps, to be a wrong conception. It may be so for human justice, but not for the absolute justice, which is in the illimitable wisdom of the Lord. For He alone knows all, as to why we transgress His laws of righteousness and love. So, who apart from Him can perform what is impossible for men, and justify what, from the limited human point of view would seem to be utterly unjustified?

When, by our imploring, the grace of the Lord descends upon the suffering person, in the fire of hopeless frustration, it may take a most effective form of 'justification', as given in the following formula:

BLESSED BE THOU, O LORD!
TEACH HIM THY JUSTIFICATION.

This is used as an introduction to the actual prayers for the dead. Christ told us that the *Father* does not judge anyone. But the living laws He has formulated automatically bring retribution, just as a stone, when thrown upwards, must fall back to earth. So, in this indirect way the Supreme can be conceived of as a *judge*. And now, the suffering spark of consciousness (that is, the man) aware of its errors, begs the Judge Himself to teach it His absolute, perfect justification. This is the final surrender of a suffering human to Him, and a tragic, but spiritually beautiful impulse: it is the efficient way to His grace.

The Lord's justification of a man is supreme. Although it is not conceivable that the finite means of cognition, which are at the disposal of man, will ever comprehend the wisdom and purpose of the actions of the infinite Lord, the results can be assured.

We have only to realize that, when the earthly life creates the causes of future experiences, the departed human being faces a life of results, and cannot change anything in them. That is why our departed brothers and sisters are in such great need of assistance. And it is a truly noble action on our part, when we bring help and solace to them. A detailed account of this matter (that is, life after death and the happenings in it) is given in Chapter XIII of The Tarot.

It is good to know, that if one dies without much time to prepare oneself for the passage to the 'other side', the same powerful, short and easy to remember invocation can be mentally repeated during the time of agony, so that it becomes the *last thought*, which is of overwhelming importance to a man's posthumous fate. For, after leaving the body, everyone faces the same danger from the fire of frustration, unless one has been a saint or a prominent white occultist.

Of course there are numerous useful and effective *last thoughts*, with which a man can safely perform his 'change of planes', and these have been given in my *Trilogy* as well as in *The Tarot*. But as this book deals with theurgy, theurgic formulas have to be given.

After the basic invocation, subsequent action on behalf of the departed follows the same lines as for living persons, but with a few necessary alterations. For the convenience of the reader I am giving it in full:

I. *I (we) know that a sincere prayer is a blessing from the Almighty, but a negligent invocation of the Lord falls as a damnation on a foolish man.*

II. *There is no man born who has not committed a sin: so, before I (we) turn to Thee, O Lord, with my (our) prayer, I (we) beseech Thee to be gracious to me (us) a sinner(s), who, with head(s) humbled deep in the dust before Thee, is (are) sorry for all his (their) iniquities.*

III. *I (we) pray O Lord for my (our) departed brother/sister (give name . . .) who is in distress because of errors committed against Thy goodness and wisdom, but Thou who art the whole of grace and compassion, may lighten the burden of my (our) brother/sister (give name . . .) if Thou hearest my (our) prayer for him/her.*

IV. *Blessed be Thou, O Lord, teach him/her Thy justification!* (Chant slowly three times.)

V. *The imposition of hands* (on the photograph of the deceased, if provided):

*May help and solace be given to you, departed brother/sister (give name . . .) and may grace flow through my (our) hands into you. Let the Lord's will be done!*

VI. *Blessed be Thou, O Lord, teach him/her Thy justification!* (Chanting as before.)

VII. *Blessed be Thou, O Lord, enlighten me (us) through Thy initiation! Let my (our) prayer join the unceasing current of worship of Thy saints, and rise to Thee from my (our) heart(s).*

The whole of this action can be conducted either by a single operator or by a theurgic group, which latter case is much more effective, except when the lone operator is a really strong and experienced person, devoted to the cause of assistance to his fellow men, and possessing a high degree of spiritual initiation. After this prayer is performed, the operator, or group leader pronounces the classical formula of the final absolution (three times) as follows:

VIII. *O Lord, grant him/her eternal peace,*
*And may perpetual light shine on him/her forever.*

The spiritual tuning and understanding of the weight and sanctity of our service for the departed are of equal value in any theurgic operation, fortified as it is with the authority and power of the formulas used. If you decide to act, be fully aware that some day you too will be in the same position as will every human being, which has to abandon its physical body and then face the painful and difficult phases of transition into the other worlds and forms of existence.

So, perform your spiritual task (which is a duty for everyone who is advanced and intelligent enough for it) just as you would like it performed for yourself, when your turn comes. Never forget the infallible truth, that you MUST die, like those who went before and those who will come after you.

Do not give much thought to the masses who boast of their alleged 'enlightened agnosticism'. It is only their ignorance and hiding of heads in the sand, as a stupid African bird is supposed to do.

This ignorance stems from materialism, which can be translated into a lower degree of development, no matter how mentally clever such types may appear to be. For knowledge of perishable things, and of certain limited fields of cognition is a very different thing from wisdom.

After what has been described in former chapters, there is no need to discuss here the importance of a funeral mass, said for a departed human being. Occultists know that there is no necessity for an officiating minister to be a saint, although such a fact is of very great importance, because the ritual alone has liaison with the powerful egregor of the religion, and it attracts the attention of this spirit to the advantage of the deceased.

The stronger the devotion and concentration of the participants in every theurgic operation (the mass included), and the more pure are their everyday lives, the more powerful are the forces of the invisible world influenced and made ready to co-operate with us.

For those who are keen to penetrate deeper into the mysteries of the 'after death' life, the XIIIth Arcanum of *The Tarot* can be recommended.

## CHAPTER XX

# INVOCATION OF THE FOUR SPIRITS OF NATURE

As you know from previous chapters, the chief receiver of theurgic prayers and invocations is God Himself, and worship of Him suffices for all our purposes and needs. But there are also certain subordinate powers, which fulfil the Lord's will and designs throughout the different realms of the infinity of creation. And this is parallel to ordinary human existence, where there are those who command and those who have to obey the ruling man or sovereign above them.

Theurgic tradition recognizes, that by invoking the powers that direct the life-processes and care for the destinies of humans, man can obtain some assistance from them, which, although limited, is very important to him at certain times.

Therefore it is my duty here to give the proper formulas and invocations for each of the four great powers.

### INVOCATION OF THE SPIRITS OF THE AIR (SYLPHS)

Spirit of light, Spirit of wisdom, whose breath gives and takes away the form of everything; thou, before whom the life of beings is like an unsteady shadow and quickly passing vapour; thou who raises the clouds and who marches on the wings of the wind. Thou exhales, and infinite space becomes inhabited. Thou inhales, and everything which has issued from thee returns to thee. Be blessed eternally! The infinite movement in the eternal stability! We glorify thee and we bless thee in the changing kingdom of created light, shadows, reflections and images, and we incessantly aspire to thy immovable and imperishable light.

Penetrate into us a ray of thy intelligence and warmth of thy love: then what moves will be fixed, shadow will become body, spirit of the air become soul, dream become a thought. And we will no more be carried away by storms, but will hold the bridle of the winged horses of dawn and will direct the course of the winds of evening, to fly before thee.

O spirit of spirits, O eternal soul of souls, O imperishable breath of life, O sigh creative, O mouth which exhales and inhales the existence of every being in the ebb and flow of thy eternal word, which is the divine ocean of movement and truth. Amen.

### INVOCATION OF THE SPIRITS OF FIRE (SALAMANDERS)

O immortal, eternal, uncreated, father of everything, who flies in the ever-rolling chariot of worlds, which always revolve! Dominator of ethereal immensities, where rises the throne of thy power, from whose height thy all-embracing eyes see everything, and thy beautiful and holy ears harken to everything, hear thy children, whom thou hast loved since the birth of the ages! For thy gilded, great and eternal majesty is resplendent beyond the world and heaven of stars; thou art risen upon them, O sparkling fire! There thou firest and entertainth thyself through thine own splendour, which, from thy essence, emits the inexhaustible streams of light which feed the infinite spirit.

This infinite spirit feeds everything and makes this inexhaustible treasure of the substance, ever ready for generation, which produces and adapts the forms thou has impregnated with the principles.

It is from this spirit that those most holy kings who surround thy throne and form thy court, have obtained their origin, O universal father; O unique! O blessed father of mortals and immortals!

Thou hast created powers which are wonderfully similar to thy eternal thought and thy adorable essence; thou hast established them as superior over the angels, who announce thy will to the world; finally thou hast created us, as the third rank in our element's empire. There, our continued exercise is in praising thee and adoring thy desires; there, we are incessantly burning and aspiring to possess thyself; O father, O mother, the most tender of all mothers! O admirable archetype of maternity and pure love! O son, the flower of all sons! O form of all forms, soul, spirit, harmony and number of all things! Amen.

### INVOCATION OF THE SPIRITS OF WATER (ONDINES)

O terrible king of the sea, who holds the keys of the heavenly cataracts, and who locks the subterranean waters in the caves of the earth; king of the deluge and the spring rains; thou who openest the sources of rivers and fountains; thou who commandest the humidity, which is like blood of the earth, to become the sap of plants, we adore thee and we invoke thee, thy mobile and changeable creatures!

Speak to us in the great movements of the ocean, and we will tremble before thee. Speak to us in the whisper of the limpid waters, and we will then desire thy love.

O immensity, in which all rivers of being, which is renascent in thee, are themselves lost! O ocean of infinite perfection! O height which thou reflectest in the depths! Depths which thou exhalest into height, lead us to true life through intelligence and love!

Lead us to immortality through sacrifice, so that some day we will be found worthy to offer the water, blood and tears, for remission of errors. Amen.

### INVOCATION OF THE SPIRITS OF EARTH (GNOMES)

O invisible king, who took the earth as thy fulcrum, and who dug in its abysses, in order to fill them with thy omnipotence; thou whose name makes the archways of the world tremble; who makest seven metals to flow in stony veins, O monarch of seven lights, remuneration of subterranean workers, lead us to the desired air and the kingdom of light! We wake and work incessantly, we seek and hope, through the twelve stones of the Holy City, through the buried talismans, through the magnetic axis, which passes through the centre of the world; O Lord, Lord, Lord, have mercy on those who suffer, widen our chests, loosen our heads, enlarge us! O stability and movement, O day enveloped by night, O darkness veiled by light! O master who never keeps back the salary of thy workers! O silvery whiteness, O golden splendour! O crown of living and melodious diamonds! Thou who bearest heaven on thy finger like a ring of sapphire, who hidest beneath the earth, in a kingdom of precious stones, the marvellous seeds of stars!

Live, reign, and be the eternal dispenser of riches, whose guardians we have been made by thee! Amen.

These strange and beautiful prayers, dedicated to the non-human beings, the so-called spirits of nature, should be incorporated in any ritual where we seek assistance in one of those kingdoms, that is, air, fire, water and earth. How may this be done? Actually, the aspirant's own intuition must tell him. Nevertheless theurgic tradition recommends the use of these prayers under appropriate circumstances. For example, if you have to fly and are anxious for your safety, use the invocation to the sylphs; if in danger from fire in any form, use that to the salamanders; if you are travelling by sea use the one for the ondines, or if visiting dangerous caves, that for the gnomes.

Of course, these invocations do not dispense with the special formulas or prayers, as given in this book, and directed to the Supreme Power. They are merely a kind of useful supplement to be used as, and when needed by the operator.

# PART II

# THE RELIGIOUS TRADITION IN THEURGY

And everything you ask the Father for in My Name with faith, will be given to you.

RITUAL ACCESSORIES

# CHAPTER XXI

# INTRODUCTION

We have now finished with the first part of this work belonging to the general theurgic system, that can be studied and practised by anyone who recognizes the existence of the Supreme Power, in which the whole of the visible and invisible universe has its beginning and existence in time, and in which the allness of manifestation finds its final rest. Briefly, this amounts to absolute faith in the deity.

This aspect of theurgic science may appeal best to those who are not interested in, or associated with, any particular religious currents, and can manage without them.

But the majority of people are attached emotionally, mentally and spiritually to the powerful egregor of Christianity, and for them theurgy has a definite religious aspect, which has been well elaborated and has a tradition of long and good standing. For the majority of us, *Faith* is connected with this tradition, and the part of theurgy dealing with it is a powerful factor in our relations with God.

The following chapters will be dedicated to this matter.

Actually, the Christian mass is of purely theurgic origin, and so are its purposes: to worship God and to obtain from Him boons and spiritual salvation, as promised by its founder —Christ, Who is recognized as the immanent second person of the Holy Trinity, that triple reflection of the manifested deity: so far, the only one which man has been able to conceive and realize.

Why then did Christian theurgy come into existence, and what are the reasons for this fact? The answer is not very difficult to find.

The mass, as God's service, is an institution of a general character, having very definite and inflexible forms, and not necessarily answering all the needs of everyday life. Moreover, the mass can be said only by a man specially trained and entitled to perform it, who is called a priest or minister. This leaves only one way open to the faithful: to limit themselves in their spiritual life to patterns which are fixed in advance and do not allow of any special variations in respect of the human heart, mind and problems of life. Priests and ministers form only a small percentage of the population and cannot always be readily available to meet the needs of each member of their flocks. And, apart from this, men often feel themselves entitled to act directly, by turning to God according to their desires, needs and inspiration, which do not always fit in with the mediation of an average priest.

The mass would be an ideal means for leading men to their Lord if every minister was a saint, and his parishioners educated to the fulness of real *faith* and submission to the Highest Will. And there have been some splendid examples where such has been the case, among them being St Vincent de Paul and the famous St John Vianney, the 'Curé of Ars', who transformed the life of a backward French village of dubious morality and devoid of religious fervor, into a much better Christian community. By his mysterious spiritual magnetism he attracted wandering and erring souls from afar, bringing them to the light of higher life (see *Concentration,* Chapter XX).

But, unfortunately, present-day humanity cannot as yet afford to produce a saint for every few hundred men, so things must remain as they are.

Of course, the Christian aspect of theurgy, based as it is on religious beliefs, does not oppose religion itself, but merely tries to make it more active and closer to men in their need. All this you will undoubtedly recognize for yourself when you study the following chapters, which describe this tradition and the methods inherent in *operational Christian theurgy,* through the printed words you read, thereby connecting yourself with the *current flowing through them.*

That is all that can be done, but it will suffice for those who are ripe enough and willing to replenish their lives with the regenerating stream of spiritual adventure.

In order to assist such people I have collected, selected, arranged and translated from the original languages, the best and most powerful texts available for safe use. The majority of the prayers and conjurations were composed by saints, who knew human nature and its weaknesses and needs very well.

The remainder have come from occultists who, at the same time, have been ministers of the Church. As you may see, these formulas are not as concise as those in Part I of this book. But it is the reader-aspirant himself, who has to make his choice between the two methods, and to decide, which of them suits him the best. A warning must be given here: it is a very serious matter and making a joke or only a 'test' of theurgy will bring *severe retaliation from the side of the forces, which are far superior to any human strength.*

In the Christian version of theurgy, apart from the verbal ritual, there also exist certain material symbols, with which you will have to operate. So before giving the actual formulas, it may be useful to list what should be provided for operations.

a. It is desirable for the operator to have a long white garment with sleeves, which can be slipped over his usual clothing during the time of worship, and he can then discard his jacket or coat. Other rules governing dress are given in Chapter VI.

b. Two identical glass or porcelain vessels with covers, will be required, something like those used for sugar. One will be for the blessed water and the other for the salt.

c. A small jug or similar container with a cover will also be needed to hold the blessed oil.

d. A dish will be required to use for the blessing of bread and other food-stuffs.

e. A small wooden table that is not too low (a *round* one is perferable, but not essential), and a white table-cloth to cover it, reaching down to about six inches from the floor.

f. A round shaped brush with a wooden or metal handle, for the sprinkling of blessed water.

g. A wooden crucifix about ten inches high, with the figure of the Crucified One fixed to it (the latter being obtainable from any shop handling devotional accessories). It should be mounted on a base so as to allow it to stand upright. If a good hanging crucifix can be found, a simple round base cut from plywood can be glued and tacked to it by a handyman and then varnished, together with the whole cross.

h. The texts for worship and the operational formulas for blessings, and so on can be used directly from this book, with markers in the required pages, so that no searching will be necessary. Alternatively, the operator can write or type out the required texts.

i. A double candle-stick and an incense burner.

Some operations, such as lengthy worship, exorcisms, and so on, allow for the participation of an assistant operator, who, in collaboration with the leader, recites certain parts of the ritual, usually the final ones. Such an attendant should have his own texts for the ritual and watch the leader for a sign when to read them.

The use of prayers for every need and in every circumstance finds a firm foundation in the Gospels of Christ. Here I will mention only a few excerpts, which vividly illustrate this statement:

'He that believeth and is baptized, shall be saved: but he that believeth not shall be condemned.

'And these signs shall follow them that believe: In my name they shall cast out devils: they shall speak with new tongues.

'They shall take up serpents; and if they shall drink any deadly thing, it shall not hurt them: they shall lay their hands upon the sick, and they shall recover.'

ST MARK, 16:16-18

'. . . Amen, amen I say to you, he that believeth in me, the works that I do, he also shall do; and greater than these shall he do.'

ST JOHN, 14:12

'. . . all things are possible to him that believeth.'

ST MARK, 9:22

The greatness of the healing power's obtaining of grace is the direct cause of the degree of our faith.

The Great Teacher mentioned, that everything we ask for in His Name will be granted by the Father. *You can easily note the spirit of this statement when going through all the theurgic formulas,* as given in the subsequent chapters. *Prayer can do everything* is the motto of theurgy. But what really is prayer? Certainly not an occasional turning to God, merely when we are assaulted by a variety of miseries or disasters, or even in the case of lesser needs. Such behaviour would only indicate the absence of the basic qualities so necessary for positive results in every turning to the Supreme Power for help and grace.

I would like to quote a brilliant comment on prayer taken from the works of the famous French theurgist—Abbé Julio:

'What really is prayer? For a rationalist it is an incomprehensible thing; for a mystic—it is the simplest thing in the world to realize, because prayer is a mystical act *"par excellence"*.

'Prayer, that is, true prayer, is an elation of the heart through which one raises oneself to God with love. This does not require any effort. When a mystic thinks about God, he cannot suppress his emotion and his confidence, just as a child on seeing its mother again after a short separation, cannot restrain itself from rushing into her arms.

'And then something happens that is very little known.

'Just as the mother opens her arms and runs ahead to embrace her child, so God comes to meet the one who turns to Him with love, as if to enfold him in His arms, if I am permitted to speak about the "arms of God". But this anthropomorphism is necessary in order to be understood. Actually, prayer suffices for everything: so what do we still have to ask for from our Heavenly Father? Did not Christ tell us that the Father knows all our needs, and that there is no necessity to ask Him about anything?'

It is the truth. But all men cannot be mystics and they are unable to abandon everything with full faith and certainty into the hands of Providence. Therefore we are also compelled to consider prayer from another point of view. Even a mystic able to perform the spiritual leap, often feels an urge to ask God about something he particularly desires. *It is not forbidden.* Moreover, the Lord likes us to turn to Him with all our confidence and faith, and beg Him even about the simplest things, no matter whether they are temporal or spiritual. Many people think that one should not ask God about any temporal advantage or assistance. This is an error. There is no offence in such prayers, in so far as one does not fall into the grip of materialism. We cannot adhere to and admire both God and mammon at one and the same time. If I ask God to cure me, or to provide me with the means to meet my obligations, I may or may not obtain them. If I get what I prayed for, I may find it very convenient, and so develop the tendency to demand more and more. On the other hand, if I did not obtain anything, I may become discouraged and start to think: I have been praying my best and there is no result. What is the use of all such efforts?

To speak in such a way is a *grave offence* against the wisdom and infinite goodness of God, who knows better than we do, how to display His justice towards every man.

In every prayer the greatest force lies in the lack of selfishness on the part of the worshipper. That is why our prayers are most effective when we act for others. Love and compassion are then the motive powers and they are the reflection of the Almighty's relationship to us. But when we pray for something for ourselves which is not granted, we should say: 'My God, I would have liked to have had this thing, but Thou didst not grant it to me: Thou has reasons of which I do not know. *Fiat!*

If you have such a spiritual attitude you can ask for anything, because you will then be agreeable to God and will not offend Him. A spontaneous prayer is the one which comes suddenly from the heart, fortified by a firm confidence in God's goodness and wisdom, and the knowledge that He does not want anything except our happiness; but that He does require His creature to become perfect. A spontaneous prayer is one where we speak to Him as to a person for whom we have the greatest affection.

In such a prayer one confesses to God one's most secret things, asks Him for advice, spiritual grace and even temporal advantages, and lets Him know one's smallest joys and troubles, while thanking Him for what has already been obtained. Even without our confessions God has perfect knowledge of the most intimate corners of the human heart, but it is just that *effort of opening* up our most hidden inner life to Him that counts. This process is extremely beneficial, because it purifies a man and makes offences against God less probable.

Good prayers are always like a sowing of valuable seeds: they will grow, but the time they take is dependent upon circumstances too numerous to mention since they are connected with a man's inner contents, which differ in every human being. Some plants grow quickly, but, for example, fruit trees which produce the most valuable crops usually require a longer period for growth and bearing.

Happiness lies only in God, and no prayer is ever made in vain. A man who fears God will do good deeds, and whoever is established in justice will possess wisdom.

Some readers, who are familiar with my former works on Oriental Yoga, Self-Realization, concentration and meditation, as well as the Hermetic Philosophy of the Tarot, may ask themselves: What has the present book about theurgy as the art of effective prayer in common with the author's former ideas, and does not this book contradict all or most of them?

The answer is most emphatically in the negative. This book does not refute any of my previous writings. It is the duty of the attentive student to discover this for himself. However, I will make a few comparisons. The contemporary spiritual master, Sri Ramana Maharshi, who was born in India and who is often classed as an example of a Jnani, that is, one who has followed the path of wisdom through self-realization, was actually not interested in exoteric religions as such, but he never denied the existence of the Supreme Power, or God, calling It the Central, Spiritual Consciousness, or Great SELF, which is the final aim of attainment for every being. In his sayings we find passages of unequalled beauty and power, when this sage speaks about God, worship and even Christ:

'A Master is one who has meditated solely on God, has flung his whole personality into the sea of God . . . he becomes only the instrument of God; and when his mouth opens it speaks God's words without effort or forethought; and when he raises a hand, God flows again through that, to work a miracle.

'That one point where all religions meet is the realization . . . of the fact that GOD IS EVERY THING, AND EVERY THING IS GOD.

'Realization is nothing but seeing God literally.

*'Jesus, the man, was utterly unconscious [of being a separate personality] when he worked his miracles and spoke his wonderful words. It was* WHITE LIGHT, *the* LIFE, *which is the cause and effect, acting in perfect concert. "My Father and I are one".'*

To me, these words of the modern Indian sage about Christ are of unsurpassed beauty and spiritual light, and perhaps you will now understand, why I was able to remain a Christian (if this label must still be used) while being an admirer and follower of the Maharshi, at whose feet I spent the most significant period of my whole life.

And what of the sage's ideas about worship? Are they different from those of Christian saints or of Theurgy? Judge for yourself, as this will be best. The Maharshi says:

*'How can you best worship God? Why, by not trying to worship him (but) by giving up your* WHOLE SELF *to Him and showing that every thought, every action, is only a working of that* ONE LIFE *(God)—more or less perfect according as it is conscious or unconscious.'*

All saints had their own techniques for praying, and they used the basic power to enable them to raise their prayers far beyond the level of the average man. This power is the ability to CONCENTRATE, without which there can be no saint, theurgist or true yogi. That is why I dedicated one of my books to *Concentration.* On the other hand, theurgy is one of the corner-stones of hermetic philosophy, as expounded in my *Tarot.* So even in this case there is no contradiction, but rather one work supporting and enlarging the reach of another.

There is no occultist, truly religious man, or theurgist who would not accede to the idea of the ONE Supreme Power or God. But ways to attainment (in hermetism—'reintegration', in Hinduism—'liberation', or 'mukta', in Christianity—'salvation', and so on) are different, which is the cause of the differing attitudes of seekers of the final truth—God. It is only a normal law of manifestation, acting through variety towards the union.

I feel obliged to mention, that in our present epoch of rampant materialism, which is the result of putting mortal mind on the throne rightfully belonging to the Immortal Spirit—God, even this evident truth has been tentatively undermined by some 'amateur', pseudo-spiritual writers, who have expressed the idea of the possibility of the existence of as many gods as there may be galaxies in the universe.

For people with such aberrations theurgic methods of communication with the source of all life, as is taught in theurgy, cannot be utterly incomprehensible and inaccessible (see Chapter XII 'Invocation to the Holy Spirit', para. 9).

The simple ritual and other paraphernalia as recommended here are, of course, only a means of assistance in order to create the desired solemn attitude and concentration, necessary for operations. But there is also another factor which speaks on behalf of the use of our ritual. Everything that happens in the physical world has its unavoidable repercussion on the invisible part of the universe, in this case, the astral counterpart of the earth, which has its own population and forces acting in it. Both are closely connected at every moment and in every place. Our activities attract or repel the desirable or undesirable beings from the 'other side'. Now you will understand the aim and purpose of the ritual. If you are so strong that you can omit it, it is your own business.

The wise person takes every opportunity to get the necessary assistance in order to reach the aim with more certainty.

In certain prayers and exorcisms you will find the sign ✠ (cross) inserted between some words and sentences. This means that, if these crosses belong to an action not involving another person, or external objects, and refers to the operator himself, *he has to put the usual sign of the cross* on himself, just as is done in church.

For theurgic purposes there is no essential difference as to whether you put your hand first on the right or left shoulder (eastern Orthodox and western Roman Catholic traditions respectively). But it is accepted that you bow slightly every time you cross yourself.

Now, when another person or some object is to be blessed in your operation, the cross must be made twice, every time you see it in the text for prayers or invocations. This means, that first you proceed as explained in the previous paragraph, that is, making the sign of the cross on your chest, and likewise *over the person to be blessed* or the object(s) to be sanctified, or in the air in their direction at the height of your face.

It is clear, that such a procedure relates to all subsequent chapters dealing with the exorcising of water, oil, salt, ill people, plants, dwellings, and so on.

In all cases the sign must be made rather slowly, with the dignity inherent in this powerful theurgic means, using a broad movement of the right hand, as if in a square with eighteen-inch sides.

The sprinkling with blessed water, which you will find is

largely used in this kind of theurgic action, should be done in the likeness of the cross with an energetic, fast movement of the hand, so that the water from the saturated brush will reach its aim.

The reserve of blessed water and oil can be stored in bottles and poured into the special containers on the table during the operation. The relative positions of the objects on the table used during operations can be seen from the picture preceding this introduction to Part II of this book.

It is useful to have a small cupboard (about 2 feet x 1½ feet x 1 foot on a table in the room where you intend to operate, which can be used for storing these few ritual accessories. Many theurgists paint such cupboards white or cream.

The ritual items are (full list completing items a. to i. at the beginning of this chapter):

1. Standing crucifix (about 9 inches x 6 inches).
2. Two glass containers with lids, one for water and the other for salt, each about 6 inches high.
3. Two candlesticks with candles.
4. A small burner for incense.
5. A box of incense.
6. A brush (bristle or artificial fibre) for sprinkling blessed water.
7. A small brush for blessed oil.
8. Two small bottles for oil and water (for transport purposes).
9. A white table-cloth (new).
10. Your white garment, socks and cord (if you decide to use them).
11. A magic sword (if desired).
12. Your book (the present one) containing the texts for operations. The Book of Psalms for use in Part II should also be provided.

All of these items must be exorcized and blessed before starting the first operation. The ritual for each object is given in the following chapters. In the initial ceremony you begin with the blessing of salt, then comes water, as it is necessary for many operations concerning worship and exorcizing. The blessing of the remaining items can proceed in the order that you require them. But usually a theurgist performs the blessing of ALL objects in the prescribed ritual, one after another. This will take longer and you should be prepared for it.

Items such as vessels, burner, candlesticks, and so on, are blessed according to the same ritual, only their names are mentioned separately (see 'The Basic Blessings and Invocations', 'Blessing of Clothes', and so on).

If you feel a desire to add more solemnity and power to your action, perform the 'Great Invocation to God' (Chapter XI) once, just before starting the particular operations of blessing. Besides starting every personal operation with this important prayer, it is also recommended that due use be made of genuflection and incense.

Persons who are not initiated and who do not belong to your theurgic group *should not be admitted to any intimate operation,* that is, one that does not affect them directly, such as the blessing of ritual items, and personal worship, but they can be present at the blessing of the sick and prayers for the benefit of others, providing they are not cynically disposed or of a derogatory attitude, which may adversely affect you and the others present ('Do not cast your pearls before swine' as Christ told us).

# CHAPTER XXII

# BASIC BLESSINGS AND INVOCATIONS

Every operation starts with the general invocation, which precedes all prayers no matter what their purpose. It may be said up to three times before you pass on to the theme proper for the action.

a. OUR DEFENCE IS IN THE LORD'S NAME,
WHO CREATED HEAVEN AND EARTH.
LORD, HEAR MY PRAYER,
AND LET MY CRY ASCEND TO THEE!

## b. THE GENERAL BLESSING

O God, in whose light all our actions and even the smallest thoughts are sanctified! We beseech Thee to extend Thy blessing on this creature (give the names of things and persons) and make (name . . .) use it with thoughtfulness, according to Thy will and Thy law, who alone, in Thy goodness, can grant it. Through the invocation of Thy most holy name, grant health of body, salvation of soul, and everything necessary for this life, which we beseech with devotion and faith. THROUGH JESUS CHRIST, OUR LORD! Amen.

*This formula is sufficient for any ordinary purpose,* but if it is necessary to display more powerful forces against evil influences or the spirits of damnation, hatred and malice, the following conjuration should be added:

c. Bless, O Lord, this creature (name . . .) so that Thy blessing becomes a remedy for Thy creature (name . . .) redeemed through Thy precious blood; and grant, that through the invocation of Thy holy name and all Thy saints (or here a special saint can be chosen), Thy servant (name . . .) who will use it, will receive blessing, health, protection against all ailments and the snares of demons and other enemies. That is why I, the servant of God, acting in Thy name, and the name of saint (give the single name or all saints) am blessing and sanctifying ✠ this creature (name . . .) in order that it (he or she) will be a defence for Thy servants, like a devouring fire against evil spirits, and destruction, expulsion and annihilation of all demonic deeds as well as the demons themselves. In the name ✠ of the Father ✠, and Son, ✠ and ✠ Holy Ghost. Amen.

### d. BLESSING OF THE WATER

I exorcise thee, creature of water, ✠ in the name of God the Father, omnipotent, in the name of Jesus Christ ✠ Thy Son and our Lord, and through the virtue of the ✠ Holy Ghost, in order that thou become exorcised and blessed *water*, which will disperse all the enemy's forces, and in order that thou will extract and eradicate the enemy himself, together with his apostate angels.

Through the power of our Lord ✠ Jesus Christ, Who will come to judge the living and the dead, and to destroy the world by fire! Amen.

*Let us pray:*

My God, who has established for the benefit of human beings the greatest sacraments with the substance of *water*, be pleased with our prayers and with this element of water, which must serve for purification; shed the boon of Thy ✠ blessing so that Thy creature used in Thy mysteries, will serve through divine grace, for defeating the demons, and the expulsion of sickness; let every place where it may be sprinkled, such as the dwellings of the faithful and everywhere else, become free from all impurity and harmful matter. May there never remain any pest or contamination of the air, and let all hidden snares of the enemy be dispersed.

And if there is anything which could harm the health or peace of the inhabitants of these places, let the sprinkling with this water dissipate all these influences. Let all health asked for and invoked in Thy holy name remain beyond the reach of all attacks. Through our Lord Jesus Christ. Amen.

Throw some salt into the water three times while making the sign of the cross, and say;

May this mixture of salt and water become union, in the name ✠ of the Father, ✠ and Son, ✠ and Holy Spirit. Amen.

✠ O Lord listen to my prayer
And let my cry ascend to Thee!

*Let us pray:*

O God, the maker of all invincible power, king of the indestructible empire, ever triumphant and magnificent: Thou who defeats the forces of the opposing power, who tames the fury of the raging enemy, who victoriously foils Thy hostile detractors: We beseech Thee, O Lord, trembling in humility, and we ask Thee to look favourably on this creature of salt and water and honour it in Thy goodness, and sanctify it by the dew of Thy mercy, so that everywhere that it is shed with the invocation of Thy holy name, all infestation of the impure spirit will be removed, the terror of the poisonous Serpent be rejected, and let the presence of the Holy Ghost deign to be felt everywhere among us. Thus we implore Thy mercy.

Through our Lord Jesus Christ, who lives and reigns with Thee, our God, in union with the same Holy Ghost through the ages of ages. Amen.

Sanctify, O Lord, this water: give it power to relieve us and to expel every malady, to put all demons to flight and to preserve us from their snares. ✠ In the name of the Father, and Son, and Holy Spirit. Amen.

It is recommended that theurgists always have some blessed water with them, with which, in case of need, to sprinkle the sick, their houses, land and animals and also the food of the sick people and that of their animals.

### e. BLESSING OF THE SALT

Take some pure salt, in a saucer or a special vessel provided with a cover, as was done with the blessed water, make the sign of the cross ✠ and chant:

Our defence lies in the Lord's name,
Who created heaven and earth.
Lord, listen to my prayer,
And let my cry ascend to Thee!

I exorcize thee, creature of *salt* ✠, through the living God, through the true God, through the Holy God, who ordered that thou will be thrown into water by Elisha the prophet, in order to cure the sterility of water; in order that thou become the *exorcized salt*, for the benefit of the faithful, and that thou bring to all who partake of thee, health of body and soul, and in order that from every place where thou may be spread, all illusion and evil will disappear along with the maliciousness or subterfuge of every devil. I also conjure every impure spirit in the name of Him, who will come to judge the living and the dead, annihilating the world by fire. Amen.

*Let us pray:*

O God eternal and omnipotent, we implore Thy infinite clemency, so that in Thy compassion, Thou will grant ✠ blessing and ✠ sanctifying of this creature of salt, which Thou hast created for human use; so that all who will use it will receive salvation of soul and health of body, and everything touched or saturated by thee will be purified from all uncleanliness and the invasion of the evil spirit. Through Jesus Christ, Our Lord. Amen.

### f. BLESSING OF THE CROSS

This operation is valid for every kind of cross, small or large, metal or wooden. The cross should be placed on the table on which there is the vessel containing the blessed water and salt. The operator kneels and says the Lord's Prayer and then proceeds as follows:

✠ Our aid is in the Lord's name,
Who created heaven and earth.
O Lord, hear my prayer,
And let my voice ascend unto Thee!

O Lord Jesus Christ, bless this cross through which Thou hast wrenched the world from the power of demons, enduring Thy suffering of Thy holy passion, and thereby triumphing over the inventor of sin, who boasted of having made the first man fall by tempting him to take the fruit of the forbidden tree. Thou, O Lord, who lives and reigns forever.

*Let us pray:*

We implore Thee, O Holy Lord, omnipotent Father, eternal God, to deign to bless this sign of the cross, so that it becomes a salutary remedy for the human species, to fortify our faith, to make us progress in the doing of good deeds, and become the redemption of our souls, our consolation, protection and defence against the cruel attacks of our enemies.

Through our Lord Jesus Christ, who lives and reigns with Thee, my God, in the unity of the Holy Ghost! Amen.

Through the ages of ages!

(If present, one of the assistant's answers:)

So may it be!

Lord be with you!

And with thy spirit.

Raise your hearts!

To Thee, O Lord.

Render grace to our Lord—God!

This is the only just and worthy deed.

*Let us pray:*

O God, who has made this patibulary tree of the blessed cross, which was once a means of punishment for criminals, an instrument of life and redemption, grant that everyone of Thy people who is armed with this standard of existence, will be powerfully taken under Thy aegis. Through Jesus Christ, our Lord. Amen.

May this cross be for us a strong foundation of faith, certitude of hope, defence against unhappiness, help in prosperity, victory over all enemies, sure guard for our cities, protection for our lands, and a true pillar of our houses. Through this cross may the shepherd preserve intact the herds, ✠ which the victorious lamb gave to us to lead to the eternal salvation! Through our Lord, Jesus Christ. Amen.

✠ Sanctify, Lord Jesus Christ, this holy sign of Thy passion let it always serve as a rampart against Thy enemies, as well as being a standard of victory for those who believe in it.

Now put the incense on the charcoal and say the following prayer:

O God the omnipotent Lord, in the midst of Thy trembling armies of angels, of spirits more pure and ardent than fire: deign ✠ to look ✠ to bless ✠ and to sanctify this incense; so that its perfume disperses and removes from Thy creatures every disease, infirmity and snare of the enemy, and that they will not be wounded by the teeth of the ancient serpent, for Thou hast redeemed Thy creatures with Thy precious blood. Through Jesus Christ, our Lord. Amen.

Now sprinkle the cross with blessed water and incense it.

O God of Glory, great God of armies, most potent Emmanuel, God the Father of truth, God the Father of wisdom, God the Father of beauty, God the Father of every light and vigilance over us, Who reigns over the worlds,. disposes of kingdoms, is the giver of rewards and distributor of everything good; to Whom every race, nation, tribe and language is obedient, and to Whom serve the infinite legions of the Angels.

We beseech Thy goodness so merciful, to sanctify ✠ this sign of the cross, to bless it, this trophy of Thy victory and Thy redemption. Look at this invincible sign, through which every satanic power is annihilated; before it was a mark of infamy, now it is the sign of honour and grace; it was a terrible punishment, now it is a means to pay all the debts of our sins.

May this cross be sanctified in the name of ✠ the Father, ✠ the Son and ✠ the Holy Spirit; may the ✠ blessing of that cross on which the hands and feet of the Saviour were nailed, descend on this cross and may all who pray and bend before it in order to honour Jesus Christ, find in this cross health for their souls and bodies, Through Jesus Christ, our Lord. Amen.

The operator kneels and bends deeply before the cross, then kisses it with humility and piety. Those present do the same.

### g. GENERAL BLESSING OF THE OIL

✠ Our refuge lies in the Lord's name,
Who created heaven and earth.
O Lord, listen to my prayer,
And let my cry ascend to Thee!

I exorcize thee, creature of oil, through God the omnipotent Father, who created heaven and earth, oceans and everything in them. Let the power of the enemy, the whole army of the devil, and every invasion and deception of satan, be eradicated and put to flight from this creature of oil, in order that all who use it shall obtain salvation of soul and health of body, in the name of God ✠ the Father omnipotent, and ✠ Jesus Christ His Son, our Lord, ✠ and the Holy Ghost, the consoler, and let them remain forever in Their love, and of our Lord Jesus Christ, who will come to judge the living and the dead, purifying the world by fire. Amen.

✠ O Lord, hear my prayer,
Asst.—And let my cry rise to Thee!

*Let us pray:*

O Lord, God the omnipotent, before Whom stand the whole army of angels well known to us through the spiritual service which they bring to us; deign to bless and sanctify this creature of *oil,* which Thou hast provided from the juice of the olive, and with which the sick are anointed, according to Thy commandments, so that they may recover their health and be able to give thanksgiving to Thee, O God the true and living.

We beseech Thee, to make it so that all who will serve with this oil which we ✠ bless in Thy name, will be delivered from all langour and sickness, and all snares of the enemy.

Let all adversaries be removed from your creature, which Thou hast redeemed with the precious blood of Thy only Son, so that it never will be wounded by the sting of the ancient serpent. Through Jesus Christ, our Lord, Thy Son, who lives and reigns with Thee, my God, in unity of the Holy Spirit, during all the ages of ages. Amen.

Sprinkle with blessed water.

### h. FORMULAS FOR UNCTION TO BE PERFORMED ON SICK PERSONS WITH BLESSED OIL

As usual, burn two candles on the round table and use some good incense. Mentally say 'Our Father' with the utmost concentration. In the left hand take the vessel containing the blessed oil and then pronounce:

May God Himself make perfect this unction of health!

In the ✠ name of the Father, and ✠ Son, and ✠ the Holy Spirit. Amen.

(Touch the breast, forehead and hand of the sick person with the oil.)

May the Holy Cross be your ✠ Light, ✠ health and blessing, according to the will of our Lord Jesus Christ. Amen.

May the Holy names of Jesus, Mary and Joseph be ✠ known, ✠ blessed, ✠ and glorified throughout the whole of Earth! Amen.

### i. GENERAL BLESSING OF BREAD, WHEAT, FLOUR, VEGETABLES, AND SO ON

✠ Our help lies in the Lord's name,
Who created heaven and earth.

O Lord, hear my prayer,
And let my cry rise to Thy throne!

*Let us pray:*

Lord Jesus Christ, bread of angels, bread of the living, bread of eternal life, deign to bless this our bread (or give the names of any other substances to be blessed) as Thou blessed the five loaves in the desert; may all those who taste it receive health of body and soul; and may this bread (give other names if necessary) serve against all ailments and other snares of the demon. That is why I (name . . .) Thy servant, am blessing, in Thy name ✠, am ✠ sanctifying and exorcizing this bread (or other substances) just as before Elias had blessed the flour in the dough-trough, and blessed the bread cut under the ashes. Elias, who, thanks to the power of that food, then walked during forty days and forty nights to God's hill, Mount Horeb.

So, in the same way ✠ do I bless, ✠ sanctify and give this bread to Thy creature, so that it can receive and eat it, in order to exterminate from its body all evil, incantation or bond, sign or deed of the devil, as well as demons themselves, and every fever and malady. O Lord Jesus Christ, Thou who Thyself art the bread of life, born in Bethlehem, ✠ bless ✠ and sanctify this bread here, in Thy name (and in the name of a saint if one is chosen) ✠ I bless ✠ and sanctify it, through the same name, which is Thine and terrible in Its power; and with it I destroy every spell. Yes! Through Thy holy name, O Lord Jesus, I bless this bread ✠ and sanctify it, ✠ and I infuse into it the whole virtue of that name, so holy, in order that every diabolic vexation will be destroyed.

Be ✠ blessed, be ✠ sanctified, and may the Lord always be with thee, O blessed bread: extinguish the power of every poison, arrest everything which can harm, remove every adversity, destroy every spell, expel demons far from (name . . .), creature of God, as well as from all creatures.

O Saint Michael, through thy holy goodness, ✠ bless this bread. O Saint (give whichever name you prefer) extend over this food (name . . .) your holy blessing, so that it becomes an ardent fire against demons, and destroys every enterprise and deed satanic. Amen.

*Let us pray:*

Most Holy Lord, God the omnipotent, God the eternal, ✠,

deign to bless this bread (or name of the food) with Thy holy and spiritual blessing, so that it becomes salvation for the soul and body of all those who partake of it, and protects against the snares of the enemy.

Through our Lord Jesus Christ, Thy Son, the living bread, descending from heaven, who gives to the world life and salvation, and who lives and reigns with Thee, my God, in the union of the Holy Ghost, through the ages of ages. Amen.

Sprinkle with blessed water.

### j. A SHORT BLESSING OF BREAD FOR USE OF A SICK PERSON

✠ Our aid is in the Lord's name,
Who created heaven and earth,
Lord, hear my prayer,
And let my cry ascend to Thee!

*Let us pray:*

O Lord omnipotent, who sends the blessing ✠ of the Father, ✠, and of the Son, ✠, and of the Holy Spirit, on this creature of bread in order that everyone who partakes of it receives health of spirit, protection of the body, certitude of salvation, firmness in faith, consolation in hope, the wholeness of charity, the power of perseverance, and the call of the Holy Ghost. Through our Lord Jesus Christ. Amen.

### k. BLESSING OF TREES, SOIL, VINEYARD, GARDEN, CROPS AND SOWING

(Must be made in the place which has to be blessed.)

✠ Our aid is in the Lord's name,
Who created heaven and earth,
O Lord, hear my prayer,
And let my voice ascend to Thee!

May God, our Master, bless ✠ us, and grant our soil and land fertility, so that it fructifies a hundred times, and that, full of life and happiness, we will be able to collect the fruit of it. Deign, O Lord, to bless this land, in order that, in due time, it will give an abundant and salutary return. That is because I (name . . .), Thy servant, in Thy name and in the name of Saint (give name of preferred saint), I ✠ bless it and I ✠ sanctify it, so that no evil spirit can bring any trouble here. In the name ✠ of the Father, ✠, of the Son, ✠, and of ✠ the Holy Ghost. Amen.

O Holy Lord, omnipotent Father, eternal God, we humbly beseech Thee to let us collect a crop, sufficient for our needs and abundant in all the fruit. Let our vineyards be heavy with grapes, our trees with fruit, and our crops abundant: deign that storms will be spared us, as well as the tumult of hail, and everything that can poison or spoil the crops. I beg you, Saint (give the desired name) ✠, to bless ✠ and sanctify ✠ this soil and land, ✠, these crops, ✠, these trees, ✠, these vineyards, ✠, these fruits, ✠, these vegetables, ✠, these grasses, ✠, which are food for our animals, and everything made free from any demon's power or interference. In the name ✠ of the Father, ✠, of the Son, ✠, and the Holy Spirit ✠. Amen.

O Lord, multiply your goodness to us, and let the over abundance of Thy blessings, so desired by us, extend over all these products of the earth, over our crops, grapes and fruit, giving them perfect maturity and fertility. Through Jesus and ✠ Son, and ✠ Holy Ghost. Amen.

*Let us pray:*

O Lord Jesus Christ, send the Holy Spirit, together with Thy holy angels, to defend and protect our crops and fruit against harmful worms, ravaging birds, and against demons, and let them be blessed, as well as myself, who am blessing ✠ them, these fruit or sowings, crops, wheat, barley, oats, grapes, apple trees, cheese, and so on. In the name of ✠ the Father, and ✠ Son, and ✠ Holy Ghost. Amen.

# CHAPTER XXIII

# SPECIAL BLESSINGS

## 1. BLESSING OF LANDS AND FIELDS

✠ O Lord, dispenser of all goodness, necessary for human existence, we beseech Thee to look on these lands and fields with Thy gracious eye! Deign to give and to preserve the fertility of the soil, we implore Thee to listen to our prayer:

*(Now say the Lord's Prayer loudly, and then Psalm 84)*

*Let us pray:*

Thou will bless us during this year of mercy!
And our fields will be filled with an abundance of fruit.
The eyes of all men turn to Thee, O Lord, with hope
And, in due time, Thou gives them their daily food.
✠ O Lord hear my prayer,
And let my cry rise unto Thee!

*Let us pray:*

O God, our refuge and our strength, since Thou are the very creator of piety heed the pious prayers of Thy children, and permit that we obtain in full what we beg from Thee. God, clement and good, who through Thy infinite power is present everywhere.

We implore Thee to listen to us and grant us grace so that ✠ the blessing of these fields becomes permanent for the future and remains inviolable; that all these faithful people who pray unto Thee, will be worthy to obtain the boon of Thy support and grace!

We implore Thy goodness, O God the Omnipotent, so that Thou extend the rain of Thy blessings on the fruits of this earth, that Thou grant to them a just distribution of air and rain, and allow Thy children, united here before Thee, to thank Thee for all Thy beneficence shown through the abundance of all the good things from the fields and the fertility of the soil. Let all those who are suffering from hunger be consoled; and let poor and abandoned people praise Thy glorious name. ✠ Through Jesus Christ, our Lord. Amen.

May the blessing ✠ of the omnipotent God ✠ the Father, the Son ✠ and the ✠ Holy Spirit descend in abundance on these fields and on all the goods in this place, remaining here with us for ever. Amen.

Sprinkle with blessed water saying:

ASPERGES MY HYSSOPO—ET MUNDABOR;
LAVABIS ME AQUA—ET SUPER NIVEM DEALBABOR!

## m. BLESSING FOR EVERY REMEDY

✠ Our aid is in the Lord's name,
Who created heaven and earth.
O Lord, hear my prayer,
And let my cry ascend unto Thee!

*Let us pray:*

✠ O God who created man in such an admirable way, and who has reformed him in a still more admirable way, Thou, who deigns to come to his aid in so many different ailments, against which our mortal humanity fights and suffers. Be gracious to our prayer and extend from heaven Thy celestial ✠ blessings upon this remedy so that everyone who will partake of it, will be able to recover health of soul and body. Through Jesus Christ, our Lord. Amen.

*Let us pray:*

We implore Thy goodness, O eternal God, so that this medicine made to expel diseases, devilish forces, infestation of evil spells and devils themselves, far from the human body, which I ✠ bless, ✠ and sanctify in Thy name and in the name of Saint (give the name . . .) will also be blessed by Thee, God the omnipotent and merciful, God full of goodness ✠.

Extinguish in (name . . .), who has partaken of this remedy, all the fire of fever, troubles of the intestines, headaches, ailments of the heart, and so on; dispel all his (her) sufferings, and remove the crushing weight of sins. Remove every infestation from each part of his (her) body, be present in the face of the phantom's dangers and suppress all tumours. May this medicine expel the present sickness: let demons flee together with their associates, their deeds and means of aggression.

In ✠ the name of Jesus ✠ I exorcize thee, this remedy, to preserve all thy natural force and I conjure thee—in the name of Christ, to obtain supernatural powers. Bless ✠ O Lord this remedy and infuse into it the virtue of Thy Holy Ghost in order that it can serve to eject, destroy, annihilate and exterminate from the human body all evil spells and the demons themselves. Therefore I (name . . .), Thy servant, ✠ I bless thee, ✠ I exorcize thee, I ✠ sanctify thee, and I call all the blessings of God's servants upon thee, O remedy. May you have every power necessary to defeat all demons and their deeds along with their devilish armies.

Finally, let the blessing of Saint (name . . .) descend upon this remedy in the name ✠ of the Father, of the ✠ Son, and of the ✠ Holy Spirit. Amen.

Sprinkle the medicine with blessed water.

### n. BLESSING OF THE CHALK

With this blessed chalk inscriptions may be made on doors, while mentioning the names of the three magi who came to greet the child Jesus after His birth at Bethlehem. This is done to remove every invisible, hostile influence from the home or site.

✠ Our aid is in the Lord's name,
Who created heaven and earth.
O Lord, listen to my prayer,
And let my voice ascend unto Thee!

*Let us pray:*

✠ O Lord, my God, bless this creature of chalk: let it be salutary to humans; make it so that through the invocation of Thy holy name, everyone who will take up this chalk and write with it on the doors of his home the names of the saints, Casper, Melchoir and Balthasar, will receive through their virtues, health of body and salvation of the soul.

✠ Through our Lord, Jesus Christ. Amen.

Sprinkle with blessed water.

### o. BLESSING OF CANDLES

✠ Our aid is in the Lord's name,
Who created heaven and earth.
O Lord, listen to my prayer,
And let my cry ascend to Thee!

*Let us pray:*

O Lord Jesus, Son of the Living God, ✠ bless these candles for every moment of our prayers: extend Thy heavenly blessing to them, O Lord, through the virtue ✠ of Thy Holy Cross; Thou who gave this cross ✠ to the human species in order to dispel every darkness. Let these candles, through the sign ✠ of the Holy Cross on them ✠ when they are lit, dispel and dissipate every power of darkness, so that they may be frightened and confused, fleeing far from our homes, and never again to have the courage to approach or molest Thy humble servants, O God the omnipotent, who lives and reigns through all the ages ✠ Amen.

### p. BLESSING OF THE SALT AND WAX

✠ Our aid is in the Lord's name,
Who created heaven and earth.
O Lord, listen to my prayer,
And let my voice rise unto Thee!

✠ O Lord, God the omnipotent, who grants the blessings of ✠ the Father, and ✠ of the Son, and of ✠ the Holy Ghost, to this creature of salt (or wax) let him who will take it or wear it on himself, be delivered from all spells, illusions, fears, temptations, discordance, hostility, pusillanimity, troubles of the soul, all traps of the devil and his servants, in brief, from every danger of body and soul, and of enemies visible as well as invisible. Let him obtain health of spirit, protection for the body, certainty of salvation, firmness in faith, consolation in hope, fulness of charity, and indeed—in his hour of death—the virtue of endurance and the visitation of the Holy Ghost.

✠ Through Jesus Christ, our Lord. Amen.

Sprinkle with blessed water.

### q. BLESSING OF CLOTHES

✠ Our aid is in the Lord's name,
Who created heaven and earth.
Lord, hear my prayer,
And let my cry ascend unto Thee!

I exorcize you, clothes, which are lying here before me, in the name of Him, who gave you the purpose to protect and cover human beings, as well as for their embellishment.

Be ✠ blessed clothes, ✠ pure ✠, beyond all the powers of the demon and his servants, beyond all his traps and witchcraft, no matter of what kind they might be. Do not hold any devilish force in you, but clothes, in the ✠ name of the Lord and His Saint (give name . . .) be ✠ pure, ✠ blessed and ✠ sanctified: we implore Thee, O Lord, deign to ✠ purify, to ✠ bless, and to ✠ sanctify these garments.

That is why I, Thy humble servant, in Thy name and in the name of Saint (name . . .), I ✠ bless, ✠ purify and ✠ sanctify these clothes. Make it so, O Lord, that all those who will use them will receive Thy grace and an abundance of Thy blessings, and that every demon and his actions will be excluded from the person wearing these clothes, being a weapon against the enemy. In the name ✠ of the Father, of the ✠ Son, and of the Holy Ghost. Amen.

Sprinkle with blessed water.

# CHAPTER XXIV

# VARIOUS FORMULAS

### r. BLESSING OF LINEN

✠ Our aid is in the Lord's name,
Who created heaven and earth.
O Lord, hear my prayer,
And let my cry ascend unto Thee!

*Let us pray:*

O Lord Jesus Christ, who through the simple touch of the edge of Thy garment deigned to cure a woman affected by bleeding; and who in the same way through the touch of the belt and other clothes of Thy apostle Paul, expelled diseases of every kind, and all evil spirits! We implore Thee, to let those who will be dressed in or covered by these clothes, or use these linen and veils ✠ which we now are blessing in Thy name, be worthy to preserve and recover health of soul and body.

Through Jesus Christ, our Lord. Amen.

Sprinkle with blessed water.

### s. BLESSING OF WINE

✠ Our aid is in the Lord's name,
Who created heaven and earth.
O Lord listen to my prayer,
And let my cry ascend unto Thee!

O Lord, be gracious; O Christ have mercy, O Lord, have mercy! (Now read the Lord's Prayer aloud.)

Lord, save Thy servants,
Who put their hope in Thee, O Lord!
Send them help from heaven,
And protect them from Thy Mt Sion,
So that the enemy will get no profit from them,
And the son of evil will be unable to harm them,
May it do them no harm!
O Lord, listen to my prayer,
And let my voice ascend unto Thee!

*Let us pray:*

O most Holy Lord, Father omnipotent, eternal God, who wanted Thy Son, co-eternal and co-substantial, to descend from heaven and at the time fixed by Thee, temporarily incarnate in the bosom of the most holy Virgin Mary, so that lost, errant sheep will be found and brought back on His shoulders, and to cure those who fall into the hands of thieves, by alleviating their wounds and cruel pains, while pouring oil and wine on them.

✠ Bless and sanctify this wine, which Thou has produced from the vineyards, in order to serve as a drink for men. Let everyone who takes this wine and drinks it, receive salvation of body and soul. If he travels, may he be fortified, until his journey ends in full peace and happiness.

*Let us pray:*

O Lord Jesus Christ, who is called a true grape and who called Thy apostles branches of that grape; Thou who has formed a choice vineyard from all who love Thee: ✠ Bless this wine and infuse into it the virtue of Thy blessing, so that everyone who will take and drink it, shall be able, through the intercession of Thy beloved disciple St John the apostle and evangelist to escape all ailments and the most harmful passions. In drinking this wine may he recover health of soul and body. Though Jesus Christ, our Lord. Amen.

*Let us pray:*

O God, who made bread to be our food, to satisfy our bodies, and wine to gladden the heart of man, let all who drink this wine be worthy of spiritual joys in the eternal life! Through Jesus Christ, our Lord. Amen.

✠ Bless, O Lord, this drink, in order that it will become a salutary remedy to all who partake of it; and, through the invocation of Thy holy name, let everyone who tastes this wine, obtain health of body and soul, through Thy grace!

And may the blessing of the omnipotent God ✠ the Father, the ✠ Son and the ✠ Holy Ghost descend upon this wine and remain there forever. Amen.

Sprinkle with blessed water.

*If the wine is to be used for a sick person, add the following formulas:*

O God, eternal and omnipotent, the eternal salvation of

those who believe in Thee, hear our prayer for Thy servant (name . . .) for whom we implore the assistance of Thy mercy. Give him (her) back his (her) health so that he (she) will be able to give thanksgiving to Thee in Thy church! Through Jesus Christ, our Lord. Amen.

EXORCISM FOLLOWS:

I exorcize thee, substance of wine, in the name of ✠ the Father of the ✠ Son and of the ✠ Holy Ghost, that you will not be spoiled by any impure spirit, and that all such spirits and their deeds will be compelled to fly from you. Therefore I exorcize thee, I ✠ bless thee, wine, in the name of Jesus Christ and Saint (name . . .). Deign to bless and sanctify this wine, as in Cana of Galilee Thou changed water into wine, blessing it for the benefit of men. So may it be!

Through Jesus Christ, our Lord. Amen.

Sprinkle with blessed water.

If desired additional prayers may be used:

I ✠ bless this wine and ✠ sanctify it, so that it becomes similar to the wine, which Christ poured for His faithful at His spiritual feast.

O good Jesus again say a word:

✠ Bless ✠ sanctify this wine as ✠ if I bless it myself: and through this sanctified wine I destroy all evil spells, I defeat and put the demons to flight, in the name of Him, Who alone fills the press. Amen.

Sprinkle with blessed water.

### t. BLESSING OF TREES

✠ Our aid is in the Lord's name,
Who created heaven and earth.
O Lord, listen to my prayer,
And let my voice ascend unto Thee!

O God, who has deigned to bless with Thy protection, providence and visit to the plantation of these trees, again be gracious to maintain ✠ it, to ✠ bless it and to ✠ sanctify it.

We implore Thee that everyone who tastes the fruit of these trees, obtains health and will be protected from every evil.

Through Jesus Christ, our Lord. Amen.

Sprinkle with blessed water.

### U. BLESSING OF A SPRING

✠ Our aid is in the Lord's name,
Who created heaven and earth.
O Lord, listen to my prayer,
And let my cry ascend unto Thee!

We humbly beseech Thee, O Lord, in Thy sweet mercy, to ✠ sanctify with heavenly blessing the water from this spring, and to make it healthy for general use.

Also deign to make every invasion and temptation of the devil disappear, so that all who will carry, drink or use this water for any other purpose necessary for life, will enjoy the grace of robust health, and be able to give Thee thanks a thousand times: Thee, O Lord, sanctifier and saviour of every being.

Through Jesus Christ, our Lord. Amen.

Sprinkle with blessed water.

### V. BLESSING OF A RING, FLAG, AND ALL OTHER OBJECTS

✠ Our aid is in the Lord's name,
Who created heaven and earth.
O Lord, hear my cry,
And let my prayer ascend unto Thee!

✠ Lord the omnipotent, look on Thy people who are praying to Thee, and deign them the grace of the blessing they implore from Thee: may this object (give its name . . .) be purified through Thy gracious will, let it become a symbol of our good intentions; let it remain unspoiled by any impurities, and let it dispel all inimical influences. May it bring happiness to those who wear or use it, like a sure anchor, holding the ship of our life in the secure harbour of salvation.

✠ Through Jesus Christ, our Lord. Amen.

Sprinkle the object with blessed water, incense it and make three signs of the holy cross over it.

### W. BLESSING OF A SEPULCHRE

✠ Our aid is in the Lord's name,
Who created heaven and earth.
O Lord, hear my prayer,
And let my cry ascend unto Thee!

*Let us pray:*

God the omnipotent, who guards souls, who is the certainty of our salvation and the confidence of those who believe in Thee, deign to look with a gracious eye upon our service at this moment ✠ and deign to purify ✠ bless ✠ and ✠ sanctify this place destined for burials. Let all the human bodies which are brought here for their eternal rest, be worthy on the great day of judgment of a place on Thy right and thus enjoy the eternal life.

Kneel before the cross just erected and say:

May all the faithful dead be granted eternal rest, we beseech Thee O Lord, to hear our prayer!

The operator rises and while making the sign of the cross on all four sides of the world, says clearly in a loud voice:

*Invocation:*

May Thou, O Lord, purify ✠, bless and ✠ sanctify this sepulchre. We implore Thee to hear our prayer!

Kneeling:

> Asperges me, Domine, hyssopo—mundabor:
> Lavabis me aqua et super nivem dealbabor!

Incense the crucifix, going around it and bowing to the east, west, south and north.

*Let us pray:*

My God, who is the creator of the whole universe, redeemer of the human species, perfect ordainer of every creature, visible as well as invisible: with imploring voices and pure hearts we beseech Thee to deign ✠ to purify, ✠ to bless and ✠ to sanctify this place of burial where some of Thy servants will have their bodies placed, when the course of life will be finished for them.

It is only Thou, in whom they put all their confidence, that Thy infinite mercy will allow them full remission of their sins. And to every body which lies or will lie here, awaiting the sound of the trumpet of the chief archangel, grant them Thy eternal consolation.

Through our Lord Jesus Christ. Amen.

# CHAPTER XXV

# EXORCISMS

### A POTENT EXORCISM AGAINST ALL EVIL SPIRITS AND FORCES ON THE EARTH AND FROM THE 'OTHER SIDE'

This powerful invocation has a widespread use, not only against evil influences, but also against imminent dangers, such as fire, natural catastrophies, enemy action, and so on.

It should be performed with a lighted candle (preferably two) on the table used for theurgic operations and placed before the crucifix, between the vessels containing the blessed water and salt. The incense is placed before the candle (or candles), which must be blessed in a separate ceremony, as given in Chapter XXIII.

It would be best if you could procure candles used during the midnight Easter Resurrection service.

It is also desirable for the operator to wear his white garment and white socks and shoes, as is done in all important exorcisms and prayers.

O ✠ Logos, who became flesh and was nailed to the cross, who sits on the right of God the Father! I conjure Thee through Thy holy name, on the pronouncing of which bends every knee in heaven, on earth and in hell; grant fulfilment of the prayers of those who put their faith and confidence in Thee.

Deign *to preserve* this creature (name . . .), through Thy holy name, through the virtues of the holy Virgin, Thy mother, through the prayers of all Thy saints, against all the oppressions and evil spells of demons and evil spirits, Thou, who lives and reigns with God the Father and in union with the Holy Spirit. Amen.

✠ HERE IS THE CROSS of our Lord Jesus Christ, upon whom depends our salvation, our life, our spiritual resurrection; it is confusion for all demons and evil spirits.

So fly and disappear from here demons, sworn enemies of

the human race, because I conjure you, hellish demons, malicious spirits, no matter who you are, present or absent, or under which pretext you might be invited, conjured or sent for: by your own will, or forced by threats or by the cunning of evil men or women, in order to torment persons or to dwell in this place.

Therefore ✠ I can conjure you now, no matter how stubborn you may be, to leave this creature (name . . .). I order ✠ you through the great living God, ✠, through the true God, ✠, through the Holy God, ✠ through God the Father, ✠ through God the Son, ✠, through God the Holy Ghost ✠ and especially through Him ✠ who was sacrificed in Isaac, ✠ who was sold in Joseph, ✠ who being man was crucified ✠ through whose blood St Michael, fighting against you, demons, defeated you, made you fly and finally threw you into the abyss.

I forbid you, in His name and His authority not to do any evil to this creature (name . . .) under any pretext; neither in his (her) body nor outside that body; neither by vision, nor by fear nor confusion; neither by day, nor by night; no matter whether he (she) sleeps or wakes, eats or prays, or acts physically or spiritually.

If you are disobedient to my will, I will throw upon you all curses and excommunications and condemn you, in the name of the most Holy Trinity, to go into the sea of fire and burning sulphur, where you will be led by the blessed St Michael. If you have been invoked by some powerful and positive order; if some cult of admiration and incense has been used on you; if you were brought here by speech or the magic of herbs, stones or air; if this has been done in a natural or mysterious way; if these things are temporal or spiritual; finally, if even the names of the Great God and His angels have been used; if someone has examined minutes, hours, days, months and years; if a pact has been concluded with you, silently or in open speech, or even with a solemn oath: ✠ I AM BREAKING, DESTROYING AND CANCELLING ALL THESE CAUSES AND THINGS ✠ through the power and virtue of God the Father, ✠ through the wisdom of the Son, ✠, the only redeemer of all men, and ✠ through the goodness of the Holy Ghost.

Briefly, through Him ✠ who accomplishes the law in its fulness, ✠ who IS, who WAS ✠ and who WILL BE forever ✠

Omnipotent ✠ Agios ✠ Ischyros ✠ Athanatos ✠ Sother ✠ Tetragrammaton ✠ Jehovah ✠ Alpha and Omega!

So must every hellish force be put to flight and defeated, destroyed through the sign of ✠ the holy cross, made over this creature (name . . .), the cross on which Jesus Christ died, and through the intercession of the blessed virgin Mary, holy angels, archangels, patriarchs, apostles, martyrs, virgins and confessors, and all the saints who eternally enjoy the presence of God, as well as holy souls who still live in God's Church.

So render your homage to the highest, most potent God, and may it reach the throne, like the smoke of that fish from the abyss, which has been burned by order of the Archangel Raphael.

Disappear, as the impure spirit disappeared when it faced the chaste Sarah. May all these blessings expel you and may they not allow you to approach this creature (name . . .) who has the honour to wear on his forehead the sign ✠ of the holy cross: because the orders I am issuing to you are not mine, but His, Who was sent from the bosom of the eternal Father, to annihilate and destroy your evil spells, and Who did so when He suffered death upon the wood of the cross.

He gave us the power to order you in the same way, because of His glory and for the advantage of the faithful. Now we forbid you, because of the power obtained by us from the Lord Jesus Christ, and in His name, to approach this creature (name . . .). Fly and disappear on seeing this ✠ cross (raise the crucifix and make three signs of the cross with it in the air) and in the name of Jesus Christ, our Lord.

✠ HERE IS THE LORD'S CROSS—fly, powerful enemies!
✠ THE LION OF THE TRIBE OF JUDAH, RACE OF DAVID—is triumphant,
✠ Alleluia, Alleluia, Alleluia!
✠ JESUS OF NAZARETH, King of the Jews, protect us from every evil!
✠ CHRISTUS VINCIT! Christ is the Victor!
✠ CHRISTUS REGNAT! Christ reigns!
✠ CHRISTUS IMPERAT! Christ commands!
O my God, purify my heart and efface all my sins!
Jesus, Mary, Joseph, secure and deliver me, I implore you!
FIAT, FIAT, FIAT—Amen.

✠ In the name of the Father, and Son, and Holy Ghost ✠ Amen!

Sprinkle the room and those present in it with blessed water while making the sign of the cross over them with the crucifix.

*N.B.;* If you are absolutely sure that certain people are doing the enemy's work, and if you know that they do not believe in God, nor love Him, or even that they are fighting against religion and devotion to the Supreme, you may include their names in the part of this exorcism, which is directed against the dark forces and evil spirits. Be very careful about such an addition and act only because you sincerely recognize the harm that can be done and the ungodliness of such people; but never because of any *personal* grudge or hatred against them, which may be very dangerous for yourself, as you would not be operating with the correct attitude.

The almighty and most merciful Lord cannot accept prayers that come from an insincere heart filled with hatred. It is the foolish black magician who operates because of hatred and envy. And he always receives his terrible reward.

Therefore, general advice would be: you would be best advised not to use this form of exorcism which directs its force against human beings. Leave their account to be made by their Lord and Creator, who judges the living and the dead.

There are no restrictions as regards action against non-human enemies, such as evil spirits and phantoms, as you can see from the texts of the exorcisms: for theurgy teaches that our Lord did not die in order also to redeem the astral scum, which do evil purely because they like doing evil.

In some occult manuals mostly in French (see: Papus, *Traité Méthodique de la Magie Pratique;* P. V. Piobb, *Formulaire de Haute Magie*), which are still available, the names of the evil spirits can be found, which are responsible for definite troubles against human beings. If, in such a case, you are sure of the origin of the trouble or obsessions, names can be mentioned.

Then the operation should be performed inside a circle, made with the blessed chalk, and the operator should have a magic sword (see *The Tarot,* Chapter III, Lessons 7 to 8) with him.

# CHAPTER XXVI

# SPECIAL INVOCATIONS

## INVOCATION WHEN IN ACUTE DANGER

A controversial paradox was once expressed by an apparently advanced mind, which stated: 'I know that I do not know anything.' Another replied: 'But others do not know even that.' In spite of the seeming progress of knowledge in this century, an earnest thinker must agree that man knows much less about himself, his life, destiny, beginning and end than, say, about a petrol or steam engine, which actually, is under man's real control and whose functioning can be directed and foreseen almost one hundred per cent, thus leaving an insignificant gap for unexpected and uncontrolled factors. But not so with us! The current life teaches us, that many unknown 'x's' are included in its final equation.

No reasonable man can be assured of living a definite number of years, immune from certain diseases, from accidents, and the smiles and reverses of fortune. In brief, no one can guarantee anything about his life. The most that can be done, is a careful use of the theory of probability, which eventually can conjecture to a certain degree, the development of events for an average case.

But for a living and thinking individual all this still remains in the realm of guesswork.

We know that guesswork cannot provide us with any positive statement. Often a sickly child grows into a healthy man and lives to a ripe old age, while someone who is well endowed through heredity, may contract a crippling ailment and thus shorten his apparently excellent life expectancy to the minimum. A newspaper boy may rise to the status of a millionaire, while children of a well-established, rich family may finish in a pauper's home.

These are only a few simple examples, which everyone can add to as much as he wishes, and then reach a certain, inevitable conclusion: *man cannot be called a master of his earthly life, nor can he control it as an engineer does his machinery.*

However, as it is unthinkable that there can be an effect without a cause, there must be powers, ruling over the incalculable and uncontrollable elements in human lives. If we look on theurgic operations from this point of view, we then recognize that ultimately, and in plain language, they are *attempts to influence the deciding factors of human life.* The existence or non-existence of the Supreme factor (often called —God) cannot be proved or disproved with full certainty at the present time, by the highest motive power in an average man—his thinking and reasoning processes of his mind-brain. This is an old truth, which is otherwise well known to us. Similarly, a taxi-driver is not necessarily supposed to possess all the knowledge of the engineers who constructed his vehicle; but he can still fully use it even without much theoretical knowledge.

Theurgy does not claim that it can prove the existence of God. But it teaches us that it can offer means and methods for obtaining what man asks for from that Power. In simple language, is it not again, the *influencing of causes* in order to obtain definite results? One may theoretically agree or disagree with such a conclusion, and it is your own business; but what matters here from the practical point of view is that, *used in the way prescribed and under the right conditions, theurgic operations do work,* and yield clear-cut results. Apparently an intellectual conception of the Supreme power does not play any deciding rôle in the success of theurgic actions. Although a few eminent theurgists undoubtedly possessed quite wide and truly philosophical conceptions of God (Pythagoras, Iamblichus, Plotinus, Paracelsus, Claude de St Martin, Eliphas Lévi, Papus, Philip of Lyons, and so on) as an absolute an impersonal being, the majority had and still have rather anthropomorphic ideas about the Almighty, which were and are *no obstacle to achievement of the aims of their operations —for both types of worshipper* (here I mean the adherents of both aspects of theurgy, as given in Parts I and II of this book).

So a theurgist should not be too proud, if in his imagination, God is an abstract and absolutly perfect and attributeless being, while on the other hand he should not be abashed if he cannot raise his mind beyond the concept of an immensely powerful and merciful Father in heaven, who is full of goodness and who graciously deigns to hear his simple but sincere worship. This is because we do not know which type of believer is able to ensure more boons, grace and help from Him.

In ancient Athens, in about the first century after Christ, there was the cult of the 'Unknown God', and on His altars the usual offerings were made and worship performed. The fact that the human mind by itself cannot enter into any direct contact with the Supreme Being is no obstacle to worshipping It and in obtaining the requested boons or grace and assistance, if the worshipper really believes in It. There have been innumerable cases of evident intervention by the Power, which is beyond all the known forces in the realm of nature, and often seemingly opposed to those natural laws, and hence is frequently called a *supernatural power*. These cases are too well known to be mentioned here; but the reader can find many examples in several books listed in the Bibliography.

Theurgy does not deal with any theoretical deliberations, but with real facts and the use of its methods. I am not trying to convince you of the existence of God—the supreme provider of everything, but only to mark the way in which desired results may be asked for and obtained.

Consequently, non-believers (as has already been mentioned in Part I) cannot take any advantage of, or get any profit from the theurgic method of channelling one's life into a desirable way.

One of the most tragic moments in life is that of real danger, which cannot be avoided by natural means. I am speaking of imminent danger, when apparently nothing can help us to prevent the perilous trend and final catastrophy. You will understand that less serious cases are also within the reach of theurgic operations: whoever can run, can also walk.

What form should our turning to the Lord take in times of acute danger?

*Firstly*, the invocation must be short, for there may be no time for any long litany. The consciousness must be tuned quickly according to circumstances.

*Secondly*, the outer form of the invocation must speak clearly to the mentality and emotions of the operator, dramatically depicting the most eminent spiritual power of the Lord, who has to give us respite.

*Thirdly*, the request must be clear-cut and brief, concentrating on the sole purpose of saving the man from the danger.

The formula recommended below will be well known to many religious people who attend the Catholic or Orthodox church services. It is a very old one, from the days when the saints composed the prayers and masses. But, unfortunately, like many other valuable spiritual weapons, this one is seldom used for the purpose mentioned here.

It can be whispered, said aloud, chanted or sung, depending upon the conditions at the time and the attitude of the operator.

We see, that this prayer is essentially composed of two parts, as is usual in almost every theurgic formula, that is, the *invocation* and the *plea*. Of course, you already know about the third part sometimes included in the worship, that is, a blessing for the Almighty, to start or end the action, which is *praise* of the Lord.[1]

### GREAT INVOCATION

GOD THE HOLY,
HOLY AND MIGHTY,
HOLY AND IMMORTAL,
HAVE MERCY ON ME (OR US)!

It should be repeated with faith and the utmost concentration, allowing us to forget everything except this prayer during the time of need. We should not dare to allow any other thought to intrude into our awareness.

This prayer must *not* be used lightly, especially if we feel that we are able to cope with the dangerous situation in a normal way, such as leaving the dangerous place, or performing a reasonable physical activity in order to avoid the peril. We must *first* try these things, and under no circumstances try to 'tempt the Lord' through our own negligence. To attempt to 'test' Him, by performing a prayer insincerely, merely in order to make an 'experiment' as to whether or not a prayer can be effective, means one of two results: (a) such a

[1] *The usual form of praise added to some invocations is:* 'BLESSED BE THOU O LORD!'

false invocation will *never* be successful, and (b) it might bring swift *punitive* action, which is usually disastrous for the originator of the blasphemy.

How would you react, if someone directed a request to you and you knew that his entreaty was not based on truth? You most certainly would not fulfil such a deceptive request. But the Lord knows human hearts and minds infinitely better than the cleverest man ever could! So now you will realize the tenor of this warning.

Another formula used in similar conditions of grave peril is:

HEAR ME, O LORD!
HEAR ME BECAUSE OF THY GREAT GOODNESS.
I PRAY UNTO THEE:
HEAR ME AND GRANT THY MERCY!

# CHAPTER XXVII

## DEFENCE AGAINST INIMICAL FORCES

Theurgy teaches us, that if we want to secure the assistance of the Supreme Power against those who try to harm, or are already harming us without any valid grounds as justification for such behaviour, we must first submit our own intentions, feelings and deeds to the Supreme Judge, while acting with pure consciousness and full understanding.

For this purpose I have collected some fragments from the inspired psalms of King David, the prophet, which fit perfectly as an introduction to our intimate turning to God for justice and defence.

Here must be given a most earnest warning in this regard: if, after the most sincere and selfless search in your conscience you find that you cannot apply to yourself, the texts given in the 'Introduction' that follows, and that you are not without any conceivable guilt towards your enemies, then do NOT dare to use any theurgic operations under any circumstances, otherwise your activities will then turn against you with the most disastrous results. One cannot mock or lie before the Lord without punishment!

Therefore first carefully meditate on all parts of the Psalm that follows, for the purpose of self-examination, and then decide whether or not you can beseech the highest power to protect you

### INTRODUCTION

*Psalm 25*

Lord, be thou my judge; have I not guided my steps clear of wrong? Have I trusted in the Lord, only to stumble on my path? Test me, Lord, put me to the proof; assay my inmost desires and thoughts. Ever I keep thy mercies in mind, ever the faithfulness bears me company. I have not consorted with false men, or joined in plotting evil; I have shunned the company of the wicked, never sat at my ease with sinners. . . .

Judge me, O Lord, and remove me from iniquitous and deceitful men. Because Thou art my strength. God is our refuge and our power; our help in tribulations which attack us so strongly. That is because we will have no fear if even the earth will be turned over and mountains immersed in the depths of the ocean.[1]

If after this instruction you feel that you are able and justified to implore the Lord for help against your enemies, fast for at least six hours before the operation, take a bath and put on fresh clothes. Place two candles on your round table, which you arranged for all your theurgic operations. The candles may be blessed beforehand in a special operation, just as all the paraphernalia you use in any theurgic action. You dare not use unexorcized items, as otherwise it would be simply opening a door to the uninvited, evil influences, which may prevent any success in your operations.

On the table we should find a vessel containing blessed water and a brush with which to sprinkle it; incense in stick or powder form; a blessed sword (if the action is intended for use against very powerful, invisible, evil forces, a standard magic sword may be used, but an additional theurgic blessing as given in Formula 'V' in Chapter XXIV must be performed, apart from the presumed previous magic consecration); and, finally, and most important of all, your crucifix (see Chapter VII 'Conduct of Operations'). A clean white table-cloth (preferably new, but not made of wool) should be spread over the table. You may also use your white shirt-like garment if you have provided one. Full security against any interruptions or visits must be assured before starting the ritual.

But even after you have definitely decided to operate theurgically against your oppressors, you should also know what you may achieve and what are likely to be the results. If someone is harming you there can be two reasons for the fact:

1. Your troubles come from your past, as a retaliation for your own erroneous deeds, and the present offender is merely a willing instrument of your fate (or karma).

[1] Christ in infinite wisdom gave us another, purely spiritual means to deal with offenders and enemies: '. . . if one strike thee on thy right cheek, turn to him also the other.' Of course, only men who are spiritually ripe enough can afford to practise this.

When making another man suffer, one acquires negative clichés for one's future, which result in inevitable retaliation. If you do intervene in this trouble and finally defeat the offender, two possibilities again arise. *Firstly,* that because of your theurgic action and preparation for it, accompanied by inner enlightening, you simply *redeem* your former 'debts' and thereby remove the enemy from your present life. *Secondly,* if this is not the case, but you still succeeded in satisfactorily repelling the attacks, it would mean only a temporary relief, a delay, in the functioning of the law of cause and effect (karma). In this instance you do not win anything in the long run.

2. If your trouble starts by being a 'new account', and the enemy is only contracting a debt when wronging you, then your successful action is fully justified and good for you both. The offender is thus prevented from committing any further evil, and so burden his own destiny, while you, the victim, are freed from the intended or already developing evil.

It is extremely difficult to see through and to know what is the cause of our troubles with our neighbours, that is, to which of the two categories mentioned above your own case belongs. It requires full spiritual insight, reaching into the past as well as into the future, and the ability to read correctly both sorts of clichés—past and future alike. And this is what you should know before you decide to defeat your enemies in a theurgic way.

All this refers to flesh and blood enemies. When a hostile action against a theurgist comes from the invisible world, and evil forces (demons, larvas, bad elementals, and so on) are suspected, there will be no doubt as regard one's right to act against such interference. It is against the law, that dwellers from other worlds are permitted to engage themselves in harming human beings. If such is your case, you are fully entitled to defend yourself, without any second thoughts.

### PRAYER FOR GENERAL DEFENCE AGAINST EVERY KNOWN ENEMY

✠ O Michael the Archangel, guardian of paradise, come to help God's people, and be pleased to defend us against the demon, and in general against our powerful enemies; come to lead us finally into God's presence, into the abode of the blissful!

My Lord God, I shall sing your glory in the presence of your angels! I will make to Thee my humblest homage in Thy holy temple and I shall proclaim the greatness of Thy name!

*'And Jesus passed between them, and walked away. . . .'*

May Jesus, our Lord, be blessed now, and forever. Because He is our Saviour, He will lead us happily into ways which He has marked for us. O Jesus, may the darkness blind our enemies, so that they cannot use their eyes, and to show their indignity; may they be curbed into the dust of the earth!

Jesus, extend over them the effect of Thy indignation, and may Thy just anger put them into perpetual fear; may horror and dismay destroy their courage, as a result of the realization of Thy power! Jesus, make them immobilized like stones, so that I (name . . .), who am Thy creature, which Thou hast redeemed with Thy precious blood, will be allowed to pass freely.

Jesus, the power of Thy arms is always marked with a miracle, and through this very force exterminate those powerful enemies, abating the pride of these ungodly ones, who have raised themselves against me!

Jesus, guard me from those who raise themselves on all sides, in order to cause me to perish. Jesus, save me from this unjust man (or woman, give the name . . .)! Jesus, deliver me from those who are committing evil, who seek to spill my blood, or who desire to take my life, my honour and my properties!

✠ God is my defence against all sorts of unchained beasts, who fight against me; His hand will serve me as a shield against the arrows of my enemies. I shall be fearless, when I see even a hundred thousand beside me: God has put His arms around me and so I shall not perish or disappear under His guidance!

O great God, cure me (name . . .) (if there is a sickness), deliver me (name . . .) from (if there is is an enemy, give the name . . .) ✠.

Glory to the Father, the Son, and the Holy Ghost, from the beginning and through the whole of eternity, today and forever, through the ages of ages! Amen.

## EXORCISM OF POPE LEO XIIITH AGAINST SATAN AND HIS APOSTATE ANGELS

✠ Our defence is in the name of the Lord,
Who created heaven and earth,
O Lord, listen to my prayer,
And let my cry ascend unto Thee!

## PRAYER TO ST MICHAEL THE ARCHANGEL

O glorious prince of the heavenly army, St Michael the Archangel, defend us in this fight and this ardent combat, which we have to sustain against the powers of this world of darkness, against the spirits of malice, that spread through the air! Come to assist men, whose God created the immortal, and who He has made in His image, and who He has redeemed for the great price from the tyranny of the devil.

Fight God's battles together with the whole army of blessed angels, just as you fought against the prince of pride—Lucifer and all his apostate angels.

And they could not retain any triumph, and there remained no place for them in heaven any more. But it has happened, that the great dragon, that ancient serpent, called the devil and Satan, who sets traps for everyone has fallen. Yes! He has fallen to the earth, and his angels have been sent down together with him. So, here this old enemy, this old homicide, again rises with renewed rage! Disguising himself as an angel of light, he will go around us with his band of evil spirits for a long time, and he invades the earth in order to efface from it the name of God His Christ, to steal the souls, destined to obtain the crowns of glory, to immolate them and to put them to the eternal death. The virus of Satan's perversity, like an immense river of impurities, flows, enhanced by this evil-doing dragon, and infiltrates into men of corrupt spirit and heart. He pours into them his own spirit of lies, ungodliness and blasphemy; he sends them the mortal breath of lust, together with all vices and iniquities. The Church, this bride of the immaculate lamb, is full of bitterness and deceptions created by its enemies, who put their sacrilegious hands on everything the Church holds intact in its heart. Come! Invincible general of heavenly armies, to save God's people against this invasion of perversity, in the realm of spirit, and to bring this people to victory!

The holy Church admires you St Michael, and considers you as its faithful guardian and powerful patron, and is glorified by having such a defender against the nefarious forces of earth and hell. Pray to the God of peace, that He allows us to crush Satan under our feet, so that he can never again hold men prisoners and harm the Church.

Take our prayers to the presence of the Highest, so that the mercy of the Almighty touches us, and you can catch that dragon of evil, that ancient serpent, which is the devil and Satan. And thus you will be able to chain him and cast him into the abyss, and he will never again be able to seduce men.

That is why we lean on you (St Michael the Archangel) for support and protection, while being full of confidence in the power of Jesus Christ's name, our Master and our God; so that is why we fight hard in order to repel the attacks and subterfuges of the demon.

✠ Here is the Lord's CROSS (raise and hold the crucifix above the table)—fly! O perverted enemies! Christ is the victor! Christ alone reigns!

O Lord, let Thy mercy descend upon us,
For Thou art our sole hope.
Lord, hear my prayer,
And let my cry ascend unto Thee!

### THE EXORCISM
### (CONTINUATION OF THE ACTION)

✠ May every impure spirit, every satanic force, every hellish invasion of the enemy, every legion, association and devilish sect be exorcized through us, in the name, and through the power of our Lord, ✠, Jesus Christ!

We conjure all you forces of darkness to go away and fly far from the Church of God, far from the souls made in the image divine, and redeemed by the precious blood of the divine LAMB.

And hence, never again will you dare, O serpent full of lies, to deceive the human race, or persecute Gods' Church, or to shake or riddle the elect of God ✠.

This is the order of God the Highest, to whom you wished

to be equal, in your great vice of pride and ridiculous pretensions, equal to God, who wants all men to be saved and to come to knowledge of the truth!

✠ GOD THE FATHER ✠ IS YOUR MASTER, O SATAN!

✠ GOD THE SON ✠ IS YOUR MASTER!

✠ GOD THE HOLY SPIRIT ✠ IS YOUR MASTER!

Devil, you are under the command of Christ's majesty, who is the eternal Logos, made into flesh, who for the sake of salvation of our human race, imperilled by your cowardly jealousy, humiliated Himself personally unto death itself. He remains with us forever, until the end of the age. He commands the great mystery of the cross (raise the crucifix high) and other Christian sacraments. He commands the great faith of apostles and all the saints, His servants.

Therefore, accursed dragon, and all sorts of diabolic legions, we conjure you through the living ✠ God, through the ✠ true God, through the ✠ holy God, through the God who so much loved the world that He gave to the world His only Son, so that every man who believes in Him will not perish, but will obtain the eternal life: cease therefore to deceive human creatures and to pour on to them streams of the poison of eternal damnation!

Retire Satan! Inventor and teacher of every deceit, enemy of human salvation! (Make a broad sign of the cross in the air with the crucifix.)

Make room for Christ, in which you can find nothing for your deeds. Be humiliated under the powerful hand of God! Tremble and fly before this invocation, which we perform with the holy and terrible name of Jesus, before whom tremble all the hells, to whose virtue heavens, powers and dominations are submitted. Whom cherubim and seraphim glorify incessantly, without ever being fatigued, say:

Holy, holy, holy is the Lord God of Armies! ✠

(Place the crucifix back on to the table.)

*Let us pray:*

God of heaven, God of earth, God of angels, God of archangels, God of patriarchs, God of prophets, God of apostles, God of martyrs, God of confessors, God of virgins, God who has the power to give back life even after death, and rest after labour!

Because there is no other God apart from Thee, and there cannot be any other God but Thou, the creator of the universe, of everything visible and invisible. Now we address to Thy glorious majesty this humble prayer: deign to deliver us, because of Thy power, from every evil influence, trap, deception and perversion of the hellish spirits, and keep us healthy and guard us from every evil. ✠ Through our Lord Jesus Christ ✠. Amen.

Grant that all the enemies of Thy faithful servants be abolished. We beseech Thee, hear our prayer!

Sprinkle blessed water around and on everyone present.

### MEANS OF DISCRIMINATION BETWEEN GOOD AND EVIL SPIRITS

There is no need to emphasize to the earnest reader the importance of right and immediate discrimination, if a theurgist encounters some forces from the invisible worlds. Here I am following the traditional rules and rites, which so far have been held partly in secrecy, and partly forgotten by the Church's organizations. It is time that the formerly hidden knowledge is revealed, at least in the parts which cannot harm even in inexperienced or wrong hands.

Accordingly, the gift of discrimination between good and inimical forces is not a common one, but rather a rare grace, given to only a few. Nevertheless, apart from first-hand knowledge, as mentioned previously, there are certain signs and details of apparitions, which allow us to classify them with the minimum probability of error.

It cannot be denied, that under certain circumstances and with the permission of God the souls of departed human beings can return, that is, find a means of communication with living people and to manifest their presence in many different ways.

There is no doubt about the 'returning' of saintly souls, because of unmistakable statements in the scriptures. We read, for example, that the prophet Samuel appeared to King Saul, while St Gregory gives many proofs of it in his *Dialogues.* It is likewise with angels as the scriptures mention in a number of places.

But, if good beings come from the other side to help and enlighten, evil ones come just in order to test, deceive or to punish us.

Because they are malicious and deceitful, it is necessary to know their type of frauds and methods of conduct, for they often try (and unfortunately often succeed) to assume the appearance of the forces of light in order to deceive and confuse us. But it has been said, that only those who like to be deceived—are deceived. For good spirits, who know very well about the dangers which come from the dark powers, would never try to avoid our measures of control, which every reasonable man cannot dispense with under any conditions.

To begin with, if the apparition produces frightening noises, and is accompanied by various kinds of trouble, and so on, we should be very careful and our suspicions will be justified. Then we have to behave ourselves as if in the presence of a demon, and use the means of self-defence given in this book. An abundant source of useful information can be found in the statements of St Antonin in Chapter XVIII of his work about the life of St Athanase, referring to the recognition of evil spirits (and malicious souls on the other side).

Here are the infallible signs denoting the presence of an evil spirit or the perverted soul of a dead person.

a. If they are frightened and fly when confronted by holy things, or signs made by men: the cross, blessed water, the name of Christ, the Virgin Mary, or any saint, holy relics, Agnus Dei, blessed candles, the stole of a priest, or any other object which the Church uses against demonic maliciousness. Also if such a spirit or apparition mocks at or turns aside from these words and objects.

b. If they give a false or perverted reason for their appearance.

c. If they say anything against the faith or general doctrine of the Church, or advise practices which are opposite to good behaviour and the common sense of honest people.

d. If they try to create in us thoughts of pride, vanity and the desire for homage, egotism, despair and everything that is opposite to the accepted rules of morality and honesty.

e. If they try to prevent us reporting these apparitions to our spiritual guide or confessor.

f. If they appear in the hideous outer form of an inferior being, or disappear in stench, disorder, fear or uproar.

g. If they come again despite the fact that they may have obtained for humans the required assistance or fulfilment of their desires: this is because good spirits and souls, having once helped do not return again to disturb men.

h. If their coming seems to be pleasant, but their departure brings only sadness, desolation, trouble for the soul, darkness in heart and mind, and similar negative impressions: for good spirits and souls bring solace and light, peace and consolation, but never any trouble or evil.

When, in spite of our careful investigation and checking, we are still not in a position to define beyond all reasonable doubt, whether or not the visitors from the other side come for good or evil, it then remains for us to use one of the potent exorcisms given in this book, and await the results. The good ones will not be affected by the formulas or curses against evil spirits but the latter will invariably show their displeasure, anger, fear and then flee.

# CHAPTER XXVIII

# HEALING OPERATIONS

### BLESSING OF A SICK CHILD

✠ Peace be with this home!
And with all its dwellers! (Answers one of those present.)

Sprinkle the sick child, its bed and the whole room with blessed water, saying:

ASPERGES ME HYSSOPO—MUNDABOR!
LAVABIS ME AQUA—ET SUPER NIVEM DEALBABOR!

Lord, have mercy, Christ, have mercy, Lord, have mercy!
(Now say the Lord's Prayer.)

✠ Our God is full of mercy,
The Lord guards the children.
✠ Let those little ones come to Me.
The Kingdom of Heaven belongs to them!
✠ O Lord, hear my prayer,
And let my cry ascend unto Thee!

*Let us pray:*

O God, maker of all that grows, strengthening every growing thing, extend Thy right hand over Thy servant (name . . .), who is sick at such a tender age; make it so that he (she) recovers and gains the fulness of health and reaches a well-ripe age, thanking Thee through all his (her) life and giving to Thee his (her) most grateful homage!

*Let us pray:*

O Father of mercy and God of every consolation, full of compassion for Thy creatures, grant through Thy goodness—the grace of cure not only of the soul, but also of the body of this poor little sick child, and raise it from its sick-bed, giving it back to Thy holy Church and its good parents. Let every day of its life, which Thou will graciously prolong, be filled with grace and wisdom, and that this child grows in Thy holiness and justice, giving thanks to Thy mercy, through good and gracious deeds.

✠ Through Jesus Christ, our Lord. Amen.

*Let us pray:*

O God, who assigns their proper functions in an admirable way to angels and men; grant us this grace, so that the life of this child will be spared and protected on this earth through all those, who serve Thee in Heaven!

✠ Through Jesus Christ, our Lord. Amen.

They will impose their hands on the sick, and the sick will be cured; may Jesus, son of Mary, salvation of the world, our Lord, be gracious to you (name . . .) forever, through the intercession of the Apostles, St Peter and St Paul.

(Now read the beginning of the Gospel of St John, 1: 1-12.)

*St John, 1: 1-12*

'In the beginning was the Word, and the Word was with God, and the Word was God. The same was in the beginning with God. All things were made by him: and without him was made nothing that was made. In him was life, and the life was the light of men. And the light shineth in darkness, and the darkness did not comprehend it. There was a man sent from God, whose name was John. This man came for a witness, to give testimony of the light, that all men might believe through him. He was not the light, but was to give testimony of the light. That was the true light, which enlightened every man that cometh into this world. He was in the world, and the world was made by him, and the world knew him not. He came unto his own, and his own received him not. But as many as received him, he gave them power to be made the sons of God, to them that believe in his name.'

### THE FINAL BLESSING OF THE SICK CHILD

May our ✠ Lord Jesus Christ be beside you to defend you;
May He ✠ be in you—to preserve you;
May He ✠ be before you—to lead you;
May He ✠ be behind you—to guard you;
May He ✠ be above you—to bless you;

Christ, who lives and reigns with the Father and the Holy Ghost—for all eternity, forever.

May the blessing of the omnipotent God ✠ the Father ✠ and the Son, ✠ and the Holy Ghost—descend on you, and remain with you forever! Amen.

Sprinkle with blessed water.

### BLESSING OF A SICK ADULT

If the one officiating and the sick person have faith, a cure or a considerable improvement is assured. This prayer invokes God and His superior spirits (angels and saints) to look towards us and to assist us. Prayer and faith almost enforce the Almighty to descend towards us and then we have the case of a miracle.

✠ Peace be on this home!
And on all its dwellers.
*Asperges me hyssopo et mundabor.*
*Lavabis me aqua et super nivem dealbabor!*
(Now read your choice from Psalms: 6, 31, 37, 50 or 90.)

✠ Lord have mercy on us,
Christ have mercy on us,
Lord have mercy on us!
(Read the Lord's Prayer.)

*Let us pray:*

O Lord, save Thy servant!
Who has his only hope in Thee, O my God!
Come, O Lord, from heaven, Thy sanctuary, to his aid!
And may the Mount of Sion protect him (her) (name . . .).
Let the enemy have no success in harming him (her),
And no son of evil be able to injure him!
Be for him, O Lord, as a powerful fortress,
In the face of the enemy;
May the Lord bring him (her) help, on his bed of suffering.
Lord listen to my prayer,
And let my voice ascend to Thee!

*Let us pray:*

Lord Jesus Christ, let Thy peace and mercy enter into this home together with my humble person; let every malice of demons fly from this place; and let the angels of peace descend here! Let all discordance and prejudice abandon this home! O Lord, make the grandeur and sanctity of Thy name shine for us; Bless our requests: Thou who art holy and merciful, who lives eternally with the Father, and Holy Spirit, through the ages of ages. Amen.

Look, O Lord, at Thy servant (name . . .) who is suffering from bodily infirmities, and renew this soul, which Thou created: make it improve through this trial, and let him (her) feel permanently saved through Thy mercy.

✠ Through Jesus Christ, our Lord! Amen.

*Let us pray:*

O Lord, the merciful consoler of the faithful, we implore Thy immense goodness so that in the moment of the coming of my humble person, Thou also deigns to enter, and to visit—just as Thou visited Simon's mother-in-law—Thy servant (name . . .), prostrated on this bed of suffering; be propitious to him (her), O Lord, so that after having recovered his former health, he (she) will be able to go himself (herself) into Thy Church for thanksgiving to Thee, my God, who lives and reigns through all the ages of ages. Amen.

*Let us pray:*

O God, who alone possesses the wholeness of mercy, accept our prayers: may ourselves and Thy servant (name . . .) bound by the chains of sins, be fully delivered from them through Thy infinite mercy!

Through Jesus Christ, our Lord. Amen.

*Let us pray:*

O God, the only succour in our human infirmities, prove the power of Thy aid in relation to this sick servant of Thine: let him (her) supported by Thy helpful mercy, be able to appear in Thy holy Church, in good health.

✠ Through Jesus Christ, our Lord! Amen.

O Lord God, we implore Thee, grant to Thy servant (name . . .) the joy of permanent health for his (her) soul as well as body: and through the glorious intercession of the Blessed Mary, eternally virgin, deliverance from the present sadness and give him (her) the enjoyment of eternal happiness.

Through Jesus Christ, our Lord. Amen.

Now extend your hands over the sick person, saying the following prayers:

✠ They will impose their hands over the sick,
And they will have their health improved.

May Jesus, the son of Mary, salvation of the world, and our Lord, always be clement and propitious to you (name . . .), through the intercession of the apostles St Peter and St Paul. Amen.

Read the beginning of the Gospel of St John, 1: 1-12, then finish the operation, blessing the sick person thus:

May the Lord, Jesus Christ ✠ be close to you to defend you;
May He ✠ be in you—to preserve you;
May He ✠ be before you—to guide you;
May He ✠ be behind you—to guard you;
May He ✠ be above you—to bless you;

He who lives and reigns with the Father and Holy Ghost, through the ages of ages. Amen.

✠ May the blessing of the omnipotent God ✠ the Father, ✠ the Son and ✠ the Holy Spirit descend upon you and rest with you forever. Amen.

The following part of the operation can be performed additionally, if desired by the sick person and if there is time for it. It constitutes the further strengthening of the effort to assist the ailing one. Anointment with the blessed oil can be performed, using a small, soft brush on the forehead, breast and hands of the sufferer. If a particular part of the body is affected, it too can be anointed. All movements are made in the form of a small cross with the brush, and left, not wiped off during the time of the operation.

### PART II OF THE SERVICE FOR THE SICK

First read Psalm 6 and then the Gospel of St Mathew, 8: 5-13.

*St Matthew, 8: 5-13*

And when he had entered into Capharnaum, there came to him a centurion, beseeching him, and saying: Lord, my servant lieth at home sick of the palsy, and is grievously tormented. And Jesus saith to him: I will come and heal him. And the centurion, making answer, said: Lord, I am not worthy that Thou shouldst enter under my roof; but only say the word, and my servant shall be healed. For I am a man subject to authority, having under me soldiers; and I say to this, Go, and he goeth, and to another, Come, and he cometh, and to my servant, Do this and he doeth it. And Jesus hearing this, marvelled; and said to them that followed him: Amen I say unto you that many shall come from the east and the west, and shall sit down with Abraham, and Isaac, and Jacob in the kingdom of heaven: but the children of the kingdom shall be cast out into the exterior darkness: there shall be weeping and gnashing of teeth. And Jesus said to the centurion: Go, and as thou hast believed, so be it done to thee. And the servant was healed at the same hour.

*Let us pray:*

O God the omnipotent and eternal, the eternal salvation of those who believe in Thee, grant us the fulfilment of our prayers for Thy sick servant (name . . .), for whom we implore the succour of Thy mercy: let his (her) health return again to him (her) so that he may bring his (her) sincere thanksgiving to Thee, O Lord!

✠ Through Jesus Christ, our Lord. Amen.

Read Psalm 15 and then the Gospel of St Mark, 16: 14-18.

*St Mark, 16: 14-18*

'At length he appeared to the eleven as they were at table: and he upbraided them with their incredulity and hardness of heart, because they did not believe them who had seen him after he was risen again. And he said to them: Go ye into the whole world, and preach the gospel to every creature. He that believeth and is baptized, shall be saved: but he that believeth not shall be condemned. And these signs shall follow them that believe: In my name they shall cast out devils: they shall speak with new tongues. They shall take up serpents; and if they shall drink any deadly thing, it shall not hurt them: they shall lay their hands upon the sick, and they shall recover.'

*Let us pray:*

O God of heavenly virtues, who through the power of Thy commandment expels from the human body all langour and every infirmity, be gracious to (name . . .), Thy servant, so that he (she) can be set free from his (her) ailments, recovering his powers and returning to health, blessing Thy holy name.

Through Jesus Christ, our Lord. Amen.

Now read Psalm 19 and then the Gospel of St Luke, 4: 38-41.

*St Luke, 4: 38-41*

'And Jesus rising up out of the synagogue, went into Simon's house. And Simon's wife's mother was taken with a great fever, and they besought him for her. And standing over her, he commanded the fever, and it left her. And, immediately rising, she ministered to them. And when the sun was down, all they that had any sick with divers diseases, brought them to him. But he laying his hands on every one of them, healed them. And devils went out from many, crying out and saying: Thou art the Son of God. And rebuking them, he suffered them not to speak, for they knew that he was Christ.'

*Let us pray:*

Most Holy Lord, Father the omnipotent, eternal God, who through the infusion of Thy powerful virtue deigns to strengthen our poor human constitution, which is so fragile, so that by the most salutary remedy of Thy compassion our souls and bodies are revived; look with a propitious eye on (name . . .) Thy servant, so that this terrific trial of bodily disease may be put away from him (her). Grant him (her) the grace of restoring his (her) former perfect health.

✠ Through Jesus Christ, our Lord. Amen.

Read Psalm 5 and the Gospel of St John, 5: 1-9.

*St John, 5: 1-9*

'After these things was a festival day of the Jews, and Jesus went up to Jerusalem. Now there is at Jerusalem a pond, called Probatica, which in Hebrew is named Bethsaida, having five porches. In these lay a great multitude of sick, of blind, of lame, of withered; waiting for the moving of the water. And an angel of the Lord descended at certain times into the pond; and the water was moved. And he that went down first into the pond after the motion of the water, was made whole, of whatsoever infirmity he lay under. And there was a certain man there, that had been eight and thirty years under his infirmity. Him when Jesus had seen lying, and knew that he had been now a long time, he said to him: Wilt thou be made whole? The infirm man answered him: Sir, I have no man, when the water is troubled, to put me into the pond. For whilst I am coming, another goeth down before me. Jesus said to him: Arise, take up thy bed, and walk. And immediately the man was made whole; and he took up his bed and walked. . . .'

*Let us pray:*

Look, O Lord, on Thy servant (name . . .) crushed in his body by sickness, and warm this soul, which Thou has formed: so that being improved through this hard trial, he (she) will feel himself (herself) saved forever through the remedy, which only Thou can administer. Through Jesus Christ, our Lord. Amen.

Read Psalm 90.

*Let us pray:*

Omnipotent and eternal God, look favourably on the infirmity of Thy servant (name . . .) and extend Thy omnipotent hand over him (her) for his (her) protection.

Make an imposition of hands over the head of the sick person, pronouncing the final prayer of the blessing of the sick child.

Sprinkle with blessed water.

During all healing operations it is accepted that two lighted candles be on the table, visible to the sick person. Incense may also be used during the service.

# CHAPTER XXIX

# BLESSING OF ANIMALS AND FOOD

## BLESSING OF ANIMALS

✠ Our aid is in the Lord's name,
Who created heaven and earth.
O Lord, listen to my prayer,
And let my cry ascend unto Thee!

O Lord my God, king of heaven and earth, Logos of the Father, through whom everything is put at our disposal, for food and other purposes, consider now how small we are when facing Thy greatness: and in the same way that Thou graciously come to aid our works and needs, so deign in Thy infinite goodness ✠ to bless these animals (or animal) (give the name if desired) in their herds, to preserve them, and grant to Thy servants the grace perpetual, as well as temporal prosperity: so that in thanking Thee for such abundant boons, we may incessantly glorify and praise Thy holy name.

In particular bless this creature (name . . .) which Thou gave to us for its and our advantage and common life. Thou who lives and reigns through all the ages of ages. Amen. In the ✠ name of the Father, and ✠ the Son, and ✠ the Holy Ghost. So will it be!

## BLESSING OF SICK ANIMALS

✠ Our aid is in the Lord's name,
Who created heaven and earth.
O Lord, hear my prayer,
And let my cry ascend unto Thee!

O my God, who gives food and care for the life of every creature, men and animals alike, deign to bless these animals (or animal) (give the name) destined to support our lives, do not allow them (it) to perish in our service, we do not want to use them (it) otherwise than for Thy glory and we duly thank Thee for them (it). ✠ Through Jesus Christ, ✠ our Lord. Amen.

If the animals are not used for food, change to the following exorcism:

*Let us pray:*

O Thou, my God, whom everything obeys, and who through Thy wise and sweet attitude wants these poor dumb animals (or animal) to become good servants of men, deign to cure ✠ and to ✠ bless these animals (animal) (give name . . .) so that they (it) will not perish in our hands, but remain safe and sound. We are conscious of Thy mercy towards us, so order Thy ✠ angel-exterminator: 'Do not raise thy hand against them!' In the name ✠ of our Lord Jesus Christ. Amen.

*Another prayer* may be added for the same purpose:

We implore Thee, O Lord, in Thy mercy to remove every kind of evil from Thy faithful servants, and expel from our animals (or animal) the perilous breath of disease which is ravaging them (it), so that after having punished those among them which were misled, Thou mercifully spare those, which still remain with us.

✠ Through Jesus Christ, our Lord. Amen.

*Additional* prayer for the same purpose:

O Lord, we implore Thy infinite goodness towards these (or this) animals (animal), which have succumbed to a grave sickness, so that they (it) will be cured through the power of Thy name and ✠ Thy blessing; extinguish in them (it) every trace of the devilish power, which makes them (it) suffer and be sick, so that they (it) will not ail any more. Thou, O Lord, art the sole defender of them (it): give them (it) back health and life.

Through our Lord Jesus Christ. Amen.

Sprinkle with blessed water; the blessed oil can also be used in cases of extreme distress.

### BLESSING OF BEES

✠ Our aid is in the Lord's name,
Who created heaven and earth.
O Lord, hear my prayer,
And let my cry ascend unto Thee!

*Let us pray:*

O Lord, omnipotent God, who created heaven and earth as well as every living creature in them, for the use of human beings; Thou who ordered that waxen candles, made from the bees' work, may be lit in Thy temples, during the performance of Thy holy sacraments, in which is consumed the most precious flesh and blood of Lord Jesus Christ, Thy Son!

Grant that Thy holy blessing may descend on these bees and their hives, so that they may multiply and become productive, being preserved from every evil, and that the results of their work will serve to praise Thee, to praise of the Son, and of the Holy Spirit.

✠ Through Jesus Christ, our Lord. Amen.

### BLESSING OF BUTTER AND CHEESE

✠ Our aid is in the Lord's name,
Who created heaven and earth.
O Lord, hear my prayer,
And let my cry ascend unto Thee!

*Let us pray:*

Deign, O Lord God, the omnipotent, ✠ to bless and ✠ to sanctify this creature of butter (or cheese) which Thou allows us to extract from the animal substance; let everyone of Thy faithful servants, who eat these products, be provided with Thy heavenly blessings and Thy grace.

✠ Through Jesus Christ, our Lord. Amen.

### GENERAL BLESSING OF ALL FOOD AND DRINK

✠ Our aid is in the Lord's name,
Who created heaven and earth.
O Lord, hear my prayer,
And let my cry ascend unto Thee!

*Let us pray:*

O Lord ✠ bless this creature (name . . .) so that it becomes a salutary remedy, and through the invocation of Thy holy name, let everyone using this food or drink obtain health of body and salvation of soul.

✠ Through Jesus Christ, our Lord. Amen.

Sprinkle with blessed water.

### ANOTHER BLESSING OF FOOD AND DRINK

✠ Our aid is in the Lord's name,
Who created heaven and earth.
O Lord, listen to my prayer,
And let my cry ascend unto Thee!

*Let us pray:*

✠ Bless, O Lord, this creature which Thou gives to us as our food (or drink), let it be, that through the invocation of Thy holy name, everyone using them with thanksgiving and firm faith in the aid he may get from them, will receive health of body and salvation of his soul; and that using this food and drink which comes from Thy generosity and liberality, we may long more ardently after entering into Thy eternal kingdom, where there is no more need of food and drink, but where one rests in the justice, joy and peace of the Holy Spirit.

✠ Through Jesus Christ, our Lord. Amen.

Sprinkle with blessed water.

### BLESSING OF A WELL

✠ Our aid is in the Lord's name,
Who created heaven and earth.
O Lord, listen to my prayer,
And let my cry ascend unto Thee!

*Let us pray:*

Lord God the omnipotent, who ordered the abundance of waters to flow through the smallest clefts of the subterranean channels, into the depths of this well, make it so that through Thy aid and Thy ✠ blessing the evil traps and influences from the other side will be expelled far from this well, and that all devilish ambushes will be annihilated; and the water in this well remain for ever limpid and purified from all soiling.

✠ Through Jesus Christ, our Lord. Amen.

Sprinkle with blessed water.

# CHAPTER XXX

# PRAYERS ON PARCHMENT

A very interesting tradition in theurgy is concerned with 'Prayers on Parchment', recognized as effective when performed strictly in the prescribed manner and in the right attitude.

The text must be very carefully written out in one's own handwriting on genuine parchment, or, in case of difficulty in obtaining it, on a good parchment-paper, of the highest quality obtainable. It must be thick and durable, and capable of being folded without breaking. Instead of ordinary ink, black Indian should be used, the same as for artistic inscriptions and drawings.

On one side of the parchment the operator writes the text in his own language, and then in Latin on the reverse. If he is unable to read properly in Latin, this condition has to be waived.

Cases have been known, where, because of certain difficulties, the Latin texts had to be omitted, and excellent results were still obtained.

When the sheets with their prayers are ready (a separate sheet for each prayer), they should be taken to a Church, and there blessed during the special mass of the Holy Spirit, by a friendly priest.

This performed, the parchment should be recited (one or three times) before bedtime, and then put under one's pillow for that night. The operation can be repeated until the desired results are obtained. In any case, the name and surname of the person who is to benefit from the prayer must be written below the text.

### a. PRAYER FOR WINNING A LARGE PRIZE IN A LOTTERY OR ANY OTHER LEGAL CASH CONSULTATION, OR TO FIND HIDDEN TREASURE, AND SO ON

✠ O Lord, Jesus Christ, Thou who said: I am the path, the

truth and the life! And because Thou lovest truth, in Thy wisdom Thou hast deigned to disclose to me unknown things; grant that these be revealed to me again this night, just as Thou knowest how to recall them to small children, teach me the unknown secrets and things to come in the future, as well as everything else. So that in this way I can know whether or not this thing exists and where. Make it so that death be sweet and beautiful to me, and that everything in life be to me like a beautiful and fragrant garden full of delicious fruit of every kind. Show me everything that can be pleasant to me, and if that hour has not yet come, give to my heart eagerness and ardour like fire, or like the freshness of the springs of the water of life, or any other grace which pleases the Lord.

Finally, may the saint-angels ARIEL, RUBIEL and BARACHIEL be full of love towards me and may they powerfully help me to reach my aim (mention your desire), so that I (name . . .) may foresee, know, see, have and possess it.

I ask this in the name of the Great God, who some day will come to judge the living and the dead, and purify the world through fire! Amen.

Now recite the Lord's Prayer three times, and say three *Ave Marias* for suffering souls *on the other side.*

### b. A PRAYER TO ELIAS AND ELOHIM

This is used in order to be successful in business and for protection against visible and invisible enemies.

✠ ELIE ✠ ELOHIM ✠ ELOA ✠ LION ✠ YA ✠ ESERCHEL ✠ AGLA ✠ SADDAY ✠ ADONAY ✠ AGIOS O THEOS ✠ ISCHYROS ✠ ATHANATOS ✠ ELEISON IMAS: O Lord the Great God, holy, omnipotent, immortal, make me (name . . .) your servant secure, although I unworthy.

Deliver me from all danger, from death of the body and soul, and from the snares of all my enemies visible and invisible.

✠ JEHOVAH ✠ SABBAOTH ✠ EMMANUEL ✠ SOTHER ✠ TETRAGRAMMATON ✠ OMOUSIOS ✠ EHEYE ✠ ALPHA AND OMEGA ✠ VIA ✠ VERRITAS ET VITA ✠ let Thy holy names be profitable and salutary to me (name . . .), who is a servant of God.

For Thou has said: ✠ THIS IS MY BODY—say also: Let Him

love me, and Thy love will do a miracle no less great: the conversion and salvation of a soul, the binding of evil forces, unleashed against myself. In the name ✠ of the Father, and of the ✠ Son, and of the ✠ Holy Ghost. Amen.

### c. PRAYER AGAINST EVERY KIND OF SICKNESS AND EVIL

✠ Through Christ, with Christ, and in Christ, praise, glory and honour through the ages of ages to Thee, Father the omnipotent, in the unity of the Holy Spirit. Amen.

*Let us pray:*

Advised by Thy salutary rules, instructed in Thy divine school, dare we say:

*Recite the Lord's Prayer.*

O Jesus, may the power of the Father, wisdom of the Son, and virtue of the Holy Spirit cure this sickness and expel this evil (name the sickness and the evil) far from me (name . . .).

O Jesus, our Lord Jesus Christ, I believe that in the night of that holy Thursday, on the holy Last Supper, after having washed the feet of Thy disciples, Thou took the bread in Thy most holy hands, blessed it, broke and distributed it among Thy apostles, saying: ACCEPT IT AND EAT, FOR THIS IS MY BODY.

Similarly, Thou took the chalice in Thy most holy hands, rendered thanksgiving and gave it to them saying: ACCEPT IT AND DRINK, FOR IT IS MY BLOOD OF THE NEW ALLIANCE, WHICH WILL BE SHED FOR MANY, FOR THE REMISSION OF SINS: EVERY TIME THAT YOU WILL DO THE SAME, DO IT IN MY MEMORY.

I beg Thee, my Lord Jesus Christ, that through these most saintly words, through their virtue and through the merit of Thy most holy passion, this malady will be cured and this evil depart (name them . . .). O Jesus! In the name ✠ of the Father, the ✠ Son and ✠ the Holy Ghost. Amen.

### d. PRAYERS FOR DELIVERY FROM ALL TROUBLES, PAINFUL IDEAS, EVIL TEMPTATIONS, OBSESSIONS POSSESSIONS AND ALL SUFFERING BROUGHT ABOUT BY EVIL FORCES

✠ In the name of the Father, and ✠ of the Son, and ✠ of the Holy Ghost. Amen.

O

✠ HEL ✠ HELOYM ✠ SOTHER ✠ EMMANUEL ✠ SABBAOTH ✠ AGLA ✠ TETRAGRAMMATION ✠ AGIOS ✠ O THEOS ✠ ISCHYROS ✠ ATHANATOS ✠ JEHOVAH ✠ YA ✠ ADONAY ✠ SADDAY ✠ HOMOUSIOS ✠ MESSIAS ✠ ESERCHEYE ✠ FATHER IS NOT CREATED ✠ SON IS NOT CREATED ✠ HOLY GHOST IS NOT CREATED ✠ JESUS CHRIST IS THE VICTOR ✠ CHRIST REIGNS ✠ CHRIST COMMANDS ✠.

(Raise the crucifix three times, making the sign of the cross on the four sides of the world—east, west, north and south. Sprinkle blessed water around and put incense in the burner and light it.)

It is through the demon's suggestions and deeds that he has tried to bind you (name . . .). It is through the mercy of Jesus Christ, Son of the living God, who descended from Heaven and was incarnate in the womb of the blessed Virgin Mary in order to save the human race, that you may be delivered from every impure spirit and that you may throw the demon and every other evil spirit far from you, into the foremost depths of the hellish abyss.

✠ Here is the cross of the Lord, ✠ flee powers of the enemy ✠ HE IS VICTORIOUS FOREVER, the lion of the tribe of Judah, born of the race of David. Alleluia!

Put the crucifix back on the table.

### e. PRAYER FOR A HAPPY MARRIAGE

✠ O Lord most gracious, who gave Sarah for wife to Thy servant Abraham, and who through an admirable sign, showed Rebecca as spouse to his so obedient son—Isaac: grant also to me, Thy servant, advice as to which person I should marry (give the name of the person if you know it), so that it may be accomplished with the assistance of Thy saint angels: Michael, Raphael and Gabriel. Through Jesus Christ, our Lord. Amen.

(Try to remember your dreams on the following three Fridays.)

### f. PRAYER AGAINST THEFTS AND THIEVES

Three bodies are suspended on three crosses.
But how different are their virtues!
Here is Dysmas and there is Gestas,

Between them is the divine Power. . . .
Dysmas raises his heart to the highest peaks,
But the luckless Gestas falls to the bottom of the abyss!
Deign, O Supreme Power, to preserve us and our goods.

Say this verse often, and you will not suffer any more losses. The parchment with this prayer, duly consecrated, must be placed in the chest, vault or anywhere else you may have your valuables. Sprinkle them with blessed water and make a sign of the cross over them.

## ORIGINAL LATIN TEXTS OF THE PRAYERS ON PARCHMENT

a. *Domine Jesu Christe, qui dixisti: Ego sum Via, Veritas et Vita: Ecce enim veritatem dilexisti, incerta et occulta sapientiae tuae manifestasti: mihi adhuc manifesta quae revelet in hac nocte, sicut ita revelatum fuit parvulis solis; incognita et ventura atque alia me doceas, ut possim omnia cognoscere, si sit et ita sit; monstra mihi mortem ornatam, omni cibo bono pulchrum et gratum pomarium, aut quamdam rem gratam; sin autem, ministra mihi ignem ardentem, aut fontem aquarum currentem, vel aliam quamcumque rem quae Domino placeant; et vel Angeli Ariel, Rubiel et Barachiel sisti mihi multum amatores et factores ad opus istud obtinendum.*

*Quod ego N (nomen) cupio praevidere, cognoscere, scire, videre, habere et possidere, per illum Deum qui venturus est judicare vivos et mortuos, et saeculum per ignem. Amen.*

(Say the Lord's Prayer three times and three Aves for souls suffering after death.)

b. ✠ Elias ✠ Elohim ✠ Eloa ✠ Leo ✠ Ya ✠ Eserchel ✠ Agla ✠ Saddai ✠ Adonai ✠ Agios o Theos ✠ Ischyros ✠ Athanatos ✠ *Eleison imas: Sanctus Deus, Fortis, Immortalis, adjuva me N. famulum tuum* (or: *famulam tuam) indignum* (or: *indignam). Ab omni periculo, a morte aeterna animae et corporis, ab insidiis inimicorum, visibilium seu invisibilium eripe me.*

✠ Jehovah ✠ Sabbaoth ✠ Emmanuel ✠ Sother ✠ Tetragrammaton ✠ Omousios ✠ Eheye ✠ Alpha et Omega ✠ Via ✠ Veritas et Vita ✠ *mihi famulo tuo* (or: *famulae tuae) N., salutaria sint altissima tua Nomina.*

Dixisti: ✠ *Hoc est Corpus meum; dic: Me amet! et Amore tuo majus erit prodigium: Animae conversio et salvatio: pessimas Potestates quae contra me ruunt fortifer constringe.*

*In nomine* ✠ *Patris* ✠*et Filii* ✠ *et Spiritus Sancti. Amen.*

c. ✠ *Per Christum, et cum Christo, et in Christo, tibi Deo Patri omnipotenti, et in unitate Spiritus Sancti, laus honor et gloria!*

*Per omnia saecula saeculorum. Amen.*

*Oremus. Praeceptis salutaribus moniti et divina institutione formati, audemus dicere: Pater Noster, qui es in coelis etc.*

*Jesus! Potentia Patris, sapientia Filii, virtus Spiritus Sancti, sanet hoc vulnus, depellat malum istud . . . a me N. Amen.*

*Jesus! Domine Jesu Christe, credo quod nocte Jovis in Caena, postquam lavasti pedes tuorum, accepisti panem sanctissimum manibus tuis, et benedixisti, et fregisti, et dedisti tuis Apostolis, dicens: Accipite et comedite: hoc est enim corpus meum; similiter accepisti calicem in sanctissimas manus tua and gratias egisti, et tradidisti illis, dicens: Accipite et bibite, quia his est meus sanguis novi testamenti, qui pro multis effundetur in remissionem peccatorum; haec quotiescumque feceretis, facite in meam commemorationem. Obsecro te, mi Domine Jesu Christe, ut per haec sanctissima verba et per virtutem illorum, et per meritum sanctissimae Passionis tuae sanetur hoc vulnus et malum istud. Amen.*

*Jesus! In nomine* ✠ *Patris  et Filii* ✠ *et Spiritus Sancti. Amen.*

d. *In nomine Patris* ✠ *et Filii* ✠ *et Spiritus Sancti. Amen.* ✠ Hel ✠ Heloym ✠ Sother ✠ Emmanuel ✠ Sabbaoth ✠ Agla ✠ Tetragrammaton ✠ Agios ✠ o Theos ✠ Ischyros ✠ Athanatos ✠ Jehovah ✠ Ya ✠ Adonai ✠ Saddai ✠ Omousios ✠ Messias ✠ Eserchel ✠ *Increatus Pater* ✠ *Increatus Filius* ✠ *Increatus Spiritus Sanctus* ✠ *Jesus* ✠ *Christus vincit* ✠ *Christus regnat* ✠ *Christus imperat!*

✠ *Si diabolus ligavit vel tentativit te N. suo effato vel per sua opera, Christus Filius Dei Vivi per suam misericordiam liberet te ab omnibus spiritibus immundis, qui venit de Coelo et incarnatus est in utero beatissimae Virginis Mariae cause humana salutis, et ejiciendi diabolum et omnem malignum spiritum a te in profundum inferni et abyssi.*

✠ *Ecce crucem Domini:* ✠ *fugite, partes adversae* ✠ *vicit Leo de tribu Juda, radix David. Alleluia!*

(When using this prayer, it would be useful to add the first Chapter from the Gospel of St John the Evangelist.)

e. ✠ *Kyrie clementissime, qui Abraham servo tuo, dedisti uxorem Saram, et filio ejus obedientissimo, per admirabile signum, indicasti Rebeccam uxorem: indica mihi* (write your name and surname) *servo tuo quam sim nupturus uxorem* (name) *ancillae tuae quem sim nuptura virum* (name and surname) *per ministerium tuorum spirituum Michael, Raphael et Gabriel. Per Dominum nostrum Jesum Christum, qui vivit et regnat cum Deo Patre in unitate Spiritus Sancti, Deus, in saecula saeculorum. Amen.*

f. *Imparibus meritis pendent tria corpora ramis:*
*Dysmas et Gestas* ✠ *media est Divina Potestas;*
*Alta petit Dysmas, infelix infima Gestas:*
*Nos et res nostras conservet Summa Potestas;*
*Hoc versus dicas ne te furto tua perdas.*

### BLESSING OF PREGNANT WOMEN, OR ON EXPECTATION OF A DIFFICULT BIRTH

✠ Our aid is in the name of the Lord!
Who created heaven and earth.
Save, O Lord, Thy servant (give name of the woman),
Whose whole hope is in Thee alone, O my God!
O Lord, be for her like a powerful fortress,
Against all the attacks of the enemy.
Let this enemy gain no advantage over her,
And may the son of evil do her no harm at all!
From Thy heaven, O Lord, send her protection!
And may Sion defend her.
O Lord, listen to my prayer,
And let my cry ascend to Thee!

*Let us pray:*

O omnipotent and eternal God, who in order to let us confess the true faith, granted to Thy servants knowledge of the glorious and eternal Trinity, and the opportunity to admire Thy unity in the omnipotence of Thy majesty: we implore

Thee, so that Thy servant (name . . .) confirmed in the same faith, will always be guarded against every kind of maliciousness. Through our Lord Jesus Christ. Amen.

*Let us pray:*

O my Lord and creator of everything, strong and terrible, just and merciful. Thou who are always good and full of love for us: That art Thou, who made our beloved fathers Thy chosen people, guarded them against every evil and sanctified them by the hand of the Holy Spirit, prepared the soul and body of the blessed Virgin Mary to make her a worthy dwelling for Thy Son; That art Thou, who filled John the Baptist with the gifts of the Holy Ghost and made him tremble for joy while still in his mother's womb. Accept the sacrifice of the ardent and contrite heart of Thy servant (name . . .) who beseeches Thee humbly for the preservation of the child which Thou hast allowed her to conceive. Guard Thy possession (the child) and defend it against all maliciousness and subterfuge of the cruel enemy; may the hand of Thy mercy facilitate her happy delivery; may the fruit of her womb come forth happily to the light. May this holy generation not be extinguished; may it always serve Thee truly and be worthy to obtain the eternal life.

Through the name of our Lord Jesus Christ, Thy Son who lives and reigns with Thee. Amen.

Sprinkle the woman with blessed water while reading Psalm 66.

Let us hallow the Father, the Son and the Holy Ghost.
Glorify and exalt Him through all the ages.
God ordered His angels to guard you in all your ways;
O Lord, hear my prayer,
And let my voice ascend unto Thee!

*Let us pray:*

O Lord, we implore Thee to visit this dwelling and to remove from this woman (name . . .) Thy servant, present here, all snares of the enemy; and let Thy Holy angels dwell here and guard her in peace, as well as her child, and let ✠ Thy blessing always be on both of them.

O God the omnipotent, save them, and grant them Thy eternal light. Through Jesus Christ, our Lord. Amen.

May the blessings of the omnipotent God ✠ the Father ✠

the Son, and ✠ the Holy Spirit descend on you and your child and remain on you both forever. Amen.

### BLESSING OF THE WATER FOR HAPPY DELIVERY OF PREGNANT WOMEN

✠ Our aid is in the Lord's name,
Who created heaven and earth.
O Lord, listen to my prayer,
And let my voice ascend unto Thee!

*Let us pray:*

O God, who in Thy heavenly mercy, removes from human beings everything which can harm them, and who fills them with Thy good deeds, who gave back health to the sick through the water, agitated by Thy angel, in which they were merged, extend over this water the dew of Thy blessing, so that all sick persons recover their health. Let also pregnant women be delivered from all the evils which endanger them, and let them, through happy delivery, obtain for their children the grace of holy baptism.

✠ Through our Lord, Jesus Christ. Amen.

Sprinkle those present with blessed water.

## CHAPTER XXXI

# SHORT FORMULAS FOR HELP

As we already know, theurgy considers diseases to be not just an 'accidental' malfunction of certain organs or combination of harmful germs that attack a human, or animal body; but it individualizes the ailment, almost as if it were another being, coming into contact with the living tissue as a kind of unwelcome inhabitant. Actually, if we analyze the 'arrival' and 'departure' (that is, curing) of a disease from the point of view of a sufferer, this conception is fairly apt.

What do we really need when we get some kind of a disease, which was formerly absent, that is, non-existent for us? We need its *removal,* or cessation, usually termed *'cure'.*

We have little concern for the way in which a disease brings harm to our body, eventually destroying it. To be rid of it is what we really want.

Here you will find a few brief formulas, which are used in theurgy for the expulsion of the unwelcome visitors, which come to squat in our temporal quarters, that is, bodies.

In a certain kind of occult science there are well-known methods of getting rid of ailments by transplanting them into other beings, usually on a much lower scale of evolution, such as plants, trees and animals.

But the high moral standards of theurgy do not permit of such operations, where an afflicted human being tries to throw its burden on to another living entity, one which is most probably quite innocent, and defenceless against an elaborate and powerful action of occult transplantation, performed in a magic way. A condensed version of a conversation between P. Sédir and his spiritual master M. Andreas, an eminent theurgist of the not so distant past, will best illustrate this problem:

*Andréas:* 'What would you do, if you saw that a patient was not getting any help from your normal medical treatment?'

*Sédir:* Perhaps I would try to transplant the disease into a tree or an animal.'

*Andréas:* 'That is because you know that disease must find another host to live in. Well, but would you be happy if someone blessed you with the disease of a giant? For human ailments are just that in relation to trees and animals.'

*Sédir:* 'I see your point. Never again will I try such a method. But is there no other, better way of helping sufferers?'

*Andréas:* 'There is! But you should know, that even if you try to expel the spirit of disease, two possibilities exist. If you are stronger, the disease will go, but it will attack another being, and you will bear the responsibility for that, just as Mesmer has to bear the burden of all the misuses and crimes, committed by unscrupulous men because of his "discovery" of magnetism and hypnotism.

'If you are weaker, the spirit of disease will only become angry and will attack the patient with even more ferocity. In both cases you will be wrong.

'But there is a power, which is omnipotent and infallible. Ask the FATHER, who knows how to arrange things for the best because of His absolute wisdom. Is it not the shortest and most reasonable way, to turn to Him, who can solve every problem? Pray to the creator and sustainer of all life, and you will have done your best.'

And this is exactly what we do in theurgy. we omit all intermediary factors and ask directly of the Highest. Perhaps you may find some invocations and worship, as given in this work, subject to repetition, with similar formulas and method of addressing God. But our prayers and exorcisms are not literature, designed for entertainment or the delight of the reader. They are instruments designed to help, and for the proper channelling of the efforts of your good will, leading to the ONE SOURCE of all real assistance. The same elements are essential for every theurgic operation, and they vary only in the purpose of the worship, and the mentioning of the gist of our prayer.

Different tools are used in surgical work, but all of them have common properties: they can cut, drill and saw, are made of non-corrosive alloys, are highly polished and sharpened, and perfected according to the needs of contemporary surgery. No one would want to have them engraved, enamelled in bright colours and finished to please the sight of the patients.

In this Chapter I will give some short formulas, as used for emergencies, or immediate assistance, when there is no time or facilities for extended operations.

### a. PRAYER FOR ONESELF OR FOR OTHERS

✠ Blessed be Thou, O Lord, teach me Thy initiation!

✠ Bessed be Thou, O Lord, show me Thy mercy!

✠ In the name of Jesus, disease, cease to make him (her) (name . . .) suffer.

✠ In the name of Jesus, I want this, and I order thee to *go away, to return to where thou came from, and remain there forever!*

In the name ✠ of the Father, and ✠ Son, and ✠ Holy Spirit. So may it be!

(Use blessed water or oil, if available.)

### b. ANOTHER FORM OF OPERATION

✠ Disease (or other evil), no matter what thou art, from where thou comest, or what is thy nature and principle, I am ordering thee to leave (name . . .), this creature of God, in the name of Jesus, Whom everything obeys in heaven, on the earth and even in hell! I order this in the name ✠ of the Father, and ✠ of the Son, and ✠ of the Holy Ghost. Amen.

### c. A SHORT INVOCATION FOR AN EMERGENCY

O Lord, I call upon Thee,
Hear me now!
Hear me, O Lord, for great is Thy mercy,
And illimitable is Thy munificence:
Grant me Thy protection!

This is a rather personal form of addressing, to be used in the case of a sudden, unexpected and menacing trouble of any kind. It should be repeated many times, as far as circumstances permit, aloud, whispered, or said mentally, depending upon the outer conditions and the operator's own attitude.

Briefly, instead of allowing your mind to behave like a frightened bird in a cage, from which it is unable to escape, *discipline your mind* and thoughts, forbidding them to run feverishly here and there, by the *conscious* and incessant use of this invocation.

Even if it does not always effect a one hundred per cent removal of all the troubles at the time, it will nevertheless spare you a great deal of unnecessary suffering and senseless despair, transforming these things into inner peace and dignity.

If you realize that all kinds of trouble and suffering are definite lessons, then, by firmly accepting a reasonable and intelligent attitude towards them, as given in the foregoing invocation, you may learn the lesson quickly, thereby reducing the reasons for any repetition of similar troubles in the future, which then become unnecessary: a college student does not need to study the primers of his childhood again.

In spite of the evident differences between various categories of men in our present epoch, one cannot fail to recognize, that there are also problems common to all human beings, independent of their degree of evolution in intelligence and experience. We are all defenceless against physical death and suffering, and against accidents and unexpected events, which we cannot exclude or dominate. And materialistic science is helpless here.

But the knowledge that there are causes, albeit hidden for the majority of men, which produce the results, just mentioned, teaches us to turn to the *Primary Source*, which controls the events beyond our reach. Theurgy has just the purpose of influencing the all-embracing *source*. Thus it was in the ancient initiations of Egypt, Greece, and many other similar currents, which involved a deep knowledge of the human psyche and destiny. It is not otherwise in this period, in which this book has come into your hands.

Some theurgists use a mystical attitude throughout their lives. When anything favourable, pleasant, or good happens to them, they invariably say from the depths of their souls: 'It was only because of God's grace: blessed be His name forever!' When they experience the reverse, that is, bad luck, or a loss, they say: 'God gave, God took away. Blessed be the Lord's name forever.'

A strange attitude for those, who, as yet, have no spiritual spark in their consciousness. But such an attitude invariably brings peace and protection from the Highest. It can be experienced, as many of us have proved. It is difficult to speak about this mystical law. But It exists, It works! Why is this so? Nobody knows, as far as mortal men are concerned. But HE KNOWS!

# CHAPTER XXXII

# BLESSING OF A RESIDENCE OR ANY OTHER DWELLING OR PLACE

✠ Peace to this home,
—And to all its dwellers!
*Asperges me hyssopo—et mundabor.*
*Lavabis me aqua et super nivem dealbabor!*
Sprinkle me, O Lord, with hyssop—and I shall be pure.
Wash me with water and I shall be whiter than snow!

Have mercy on me, my God, according to the greatness of Thy grace; Glory to the ✠ Father, to the ✠ Son and to the ✠ Holy Spirit, as it was in the beginning, as it is now and as it will be forever!

O Lord, show us Thy mercy,
And give us Thy salutary protection.
O Lord, listen to my prayer,
And let my cry ascend unto Thee!

*Let us pray:*

O Lord, we beseech Thee, grant us, Thy servants, through the sprinkling of this blessed water, equilibrium of Spirit, health of body, assurance of salvation, firmness in faith, certainty in hope, and the ripe fruit of charity, now and unto the eternity of the ages.

Through our Lord, Jesus Christ. Amen.

Hear us, most Holy Lord, Father omnipotent, eternal God! And deign to send Thy holy angel from heaven to guard, protect, and be our friend, to visit and to defend all who dwell in this residence!

✠ Through Jesus Christ, our Lord. Amen.

Bless, O omnipotent Lord, this dwelling, and in this place may there forever be health, purity, victory, virtue, humility, goodness, sweetness, lawfulness and the grace of God the Father, ✠ the Son and ✠ the Holy Ghost. Let this blessing remain on this residence and all who are living in it, now, and through the ages of ages. Amen.

*Let us pray:*

God the omnipotent and eternal, who confers on Thy priests the grace of choice, let it be that everything which we do here in Thy name, with dignity, piety and with the greatest possible perfection, may be considered as done by Thyself.

We beg this from Thy immeasurable goodness!

Visit, O Lord, what we visit; bless what we bless; and extend ✠ Thy hand over everything we may do. No matter how humble we are, at the very moment of our entering into this house, through the virtues of Thy saints, let devils depart from here, and Thy angels come in.

Through our Lord, Jesus Christ. Amen.

*Let us pray:*

O Thou, my God, the omnipotent Father, we beseech Thee very humbly for those who live here and for everything in this dwelling, to deign ✠ to bless this house, to ✠ sanctify it, and ✠ to fill it with all kinds of goods; deign this, O Lord, because of Thy mercy, to all living here and grant an abundance of heavenly dew, the substance of life through the richness of the soil, and a fulfilment of all their legitimate desires. Just as Thou blessed the dwellings of Abraham, Isaac and Jacob, deign through our visit to this place, to ✠ bless it, and to ✠ sanctify it. Let Thy angels of light dwell in the walls of this place, to look faithfully after it and its inmates.

Through Jesus Christ, our Lord. Amen.

*Let us pray:*

Bless, O Lord, through the virtues of Thy saint (give the name of your favourite saint) this home, ✠ bless our entry, and ✠ bless every step we take here, as once Thou ✠ blessed the dwellings of the faithful Abraham, Isaac and Jacob. Did Thou not say, O Lord Jesus, to Thy disciples: 'When you come to a home, greet it with these words: "Peace be to this house",' may peace descend on this home as well as on all Thy servants present here or those who dwell here: deliver them O Lord, from every disease or infirmity, fill this house a hundredfold with fruit, wine, oil and flour, and then grant them eternal salvation. Amen.

Holy angels of God, descend through the divine mercy, into this home and all its buildings; always defend and protect them against demons and their misdeeds. Amen.

O Lord, preserve this dwelling and let it remain without any impurity; that is why here, at this moment, ✠ I do expunge from it every impure spirit, ✠ I purify it, and ✠ I sanctify it.

O Lord, may Thy mercy sprinkle it with every grace, and may Thou say to the angel, duly charged with the power to punish and to strike: 'Cease to hold thy hand over that home, let us see thy greatness and goodness, sanctifying this home.'

Let no demon hide in this home, or perform anything malicious. And you, Saint (give the name . . .) raise yourself and through the passion of our Lord Jesus Christ ✠ bless ✠ and sanctify this dwelling and all its inhabitants.

*Now read the exorcism:*

For I (name . . .), a servant of God, in the name of ✠ Jesus ✠, I destroy and I annihilate all the malicious deeds done or to be done in this house, and in every place in this house, and I ✠ bless and sanctify this dwelling in all its parts.

Demons and your deeds, you can no longer remain or rest here, since you are now destroyed and nothing remains of you. In the name ✠ of the Father, and ✠ Son, and ✠ Holy Ghost. Amen.

*The final action:*

The exorcizer takes blessed water and sprinkles it everywhere, in the house, in every one of its rooms and especially over the doors and in the corners saying:

*'Asperges me hyssopo—et mundabor.*
*Lavabis me aqua et super nivem dealbabor.'*

Then the operator take the sword (it can be in the form of a magic trident), blessed in a separate ceremony for this purpose (see former chapters), and raising it over his head, says: *'Vade retro, Satan, et da locum Spiritui Sancto!'* (Go away, Satan, and leave room for the Holy Ghost!).

After this, the concluding formulas may be used:

✠ I beg Thee, O Lord, because of Thy infinite goodness, to ✠ bless with Thy holy right hand, this house together with all its dwellers: let it be as a burning fire for all demons: let them always keep away from it, and fly from it in shame and confusion. Never let them hide in this home, neither by day, nor by night; let all its inhabitants remain in security and sleep in peace without any trouble and without fear and fright of devilish traps. But may Thy blessing always be in this house, on all who live in it and are inside it. Amen.

May the peace and blessing of the most Holy Trinity and of Saint (name . . .) descend over this home. Amen. In the name of Jesus, may all the dwellers of this house pray with faith, sleep without nightmares, eat, drink and perform all their normal activities in full freedom from every inhibition.

Through our Lord, Jesus Christ. Amen.

The person officiating may sprinkle those present with blessed water.

# CHAPTER XXXIII

# SEVEN MYSTICAL PRAYERS

The best way to practise this powerful form of worship would be to use the prescribed prayer at the beginning of each day, that is, in the morning, before meals and other daily occupations. This will bring blessing and light for the whole day, for, if the start is good, there is every chance that the ensuing hours will give of their best. We know of the wonderful results which happen to those, who made it an invariable custom to practise these prayers every morning.

### SUNDAY

✠ Deliver me (name . . .), O Lord, who am Thy creature, from all evils of the past, present and future, which touch my body and soul alike. Through Thy goodness, give me peace and health, and be propitious to me. I beseech Thee through the intercession of the blessed Virgin Mary, Thy saint apostles Peter, Paul and Andrew, and all Thy saints!

Grant me peace and health during my lifetime, so that with the assistance of Thy mercy, I never will become a slave to sin, and never will be frightened by any trouble. I conjure Thee through Jesus Christ, Thy Son, our Lord, who being God, lives and reigns in unity with the Holy Ghost through all the ages of ages. Amen.

Let the peace of the Lord always be with me! Amen.

Let this heavenly peace, O Lord, which Thou hast left to Thy disciples remain forever between me and my enemies, visible as well as invisible. Amen.

Let the Lord's peace, his soul and blood help me, console me and protect my soul and body. Amen.

✠ Lamb of God, sacrificed for the salvation of the world, have mercy on my soul and body!

✠ Lamb of God, through whom all the faithful are saved, give me Thy peace and let it be with me forever, in this life as well as in the future one. Amen.

### MONDAY

✠ O Great God, through Whom all things are saved, preserve me also from every evil. O Great God, who has granted Thy consolation to all beings, console me also in my afflictions. O Great God, who has helped and assisted all things, help me also and assist me in all my needs, my miseries, my enterprises and my dangers! Deliver me from all the opposition and snares of my enemies, visible as well as invisible, ✠ in the name of the Father, who created the world, ✠ in the name of the Son, who redeemed this world, and ✠ in the name of the Holy Spirit who fulfilled the Law in all its perfection.

I throw myself into Thy arms and surrender myself entirely to Thy protection.

✠ May the blessing of God, Father the omnipotent, whose sole word created all things, always be with me! Amen.

✠ May the blessing of our Lord Jesus Christ, Son of the great living God, always be with me! Amen.

✠ May the blessing of the Holy Ghost with His seven gifts always be with me! Amen.

May the blessing of the Virgin Mary, together with that of her divine Son, always be with me (name . . .), your servant. Amen.

### TUESDAY

✠ May the blessing of our Lord Jesus Christ, when He consecrated the bread and gave it to His disciples, saying to them: 'Take it and eat it all, for this is my flesh which will be sacrificed for the remission of all sins,' always be with me (name . . .), poor sinner! Amen.

✠ May the blessing of the saints, angels, archangels, virtues, powers, thrones, dominations, principalities, cherubim and seraphim, always be with me! Amen.

May the blessing of patriarchs, prophets, apostles, martyrs, confessors, and all God's saints always be with me! Amen.

May the blessing of all the heavens of God always be with me! Amen.

May the majesty of the omnipotent God support and protect me; may His eternal goodness lead me; may His illimitable charity inflame me!

May the power of the Father preserve me; may the wisdom

of the Son revive me; may the virtue of the Holy Spirit always be between me and my enemies, visible as well as invisible. Amen.

✠ Power of the Father—fortify me! Wisdom of the Son—enlighten me! Consolation of the Holy Ghost—console me!

The *Father* is peace, the Son is the life, the Holy Ghost is the remedy, consolation and salvation.

May the divinity of God bless me, His mercy warm me, His love embrace me with love! Amen.

### WEDNESDAY

✠ O Jesus Christ, Son of the Great Living God, have mercy on me!

O Emmanuel! Defend me against the malicious enemy and against all my enemies, visible as well as invisible! Deliver me from every evil O God, made man, who patiently suffered for us, King Jesus Christ, come in peace.

✠ Jesus Christ commands, ✠ Jesus Christ reigns, ✠ Jesus Christ triumphs!

May Jesus Christ, the good king, always be between me and my enemies to defend me! Amen.

May Jesus Christ permanently deliver me from all evil! Amen.

✠ Here is the cross of our Lord Jesus Christ! Fly! my enemies, at its sight! The lion of the tribe of Judah, race of David, is triumphant. Alleluia! Alleluia! Alleluia!

O Saviour of the world, secure me and save me, Thou who redeemed me through Thy cross and Thy precious blood: protect me, I do conjure Thee, O my God! ✠ Agios o Theos, ✠ Agios Ischyros, ✠ Agios Athanatos, Eleison imas: God the holy, God the mighty, God the immortal, have mercy on me (name . . .), Thy creature! Be my support, O Lord, do not abandon me, do not refute my prayers. God my salvation, always be my aid. Amen.

### THURSDAY

✠ O Lord, enlighten my eyes with the true light, so that they will not be closed by the eternal sleep, and my enemy cannot say that he has advantage over me.

In so far as the Lord is with me, I shall not be frightened by the maliciousness of my enemies. O sweetest Jesus, ✠ preserve me, ✠ protect me, ✠ save me! Amen.

On the sole pronouncing of the name of Jesus, may every knee bend in heaven, on the earth and in hell!

I know beyond any doubt, that immediately I invoke the Lord, no matter at what hour or on what day, I will be saved.

✠ O sweetest Lord Jesus Christ, who performed such great miracles solely by the power of Thy very precious name, and who so greatly enriched the natives (of the Holy Land), because of Thy power demons were put to flight, the blind saw, the deaf heard, the lame walked upright, the mute spoke, the lepers were cleansed, the sick were cured and the dead resurrected.

Immediately someone pronounces the sweet name of Jesus, the ear becomes charmed and delighted, and the mouth is filled with all sweet things; solely on its pronouncing demons disappear; every knee bends; temptations, even the worst, are eradicated, all sicknesses are cured; all disputes and battles which arise between the world, flesh and the devil are dissipated; and the heart is filled with all heavenly goodness; because if anyone invoked, invokes and will invoke that holy name of Jesus, he was, is and will always be saved: myself included, for I am invoking Thee and cry unto Thee: ✠ Jesus, son of David, have mercy on me (name . . .), Thy servant! Amen.

## FRIDAY

✠ O sweet name of Jesus, name to fortify the heart of a man! Name of life, of salvation and of joy; name precious, glorious and pleasant; name which saves, leads, rules and protects everything; may Thou be pleased, O very sweet Jesus, through the power of that name, to remove from me (name . . .), Thy humble servant, every evil spirit; enlighten me, who am blind; return my hearing to me, who am deaf; straighten me, who am limping; give me back speech, who am mute; give me back my health, who am ill; and resuscitate me, who am dead! Give me back my life and encircle me on all sides, inside as well as outside, purify me, who am a leper, so that I will be fortified and armed with that holy name; so that I will always live in

Thee, praising Thee, honouring Thee, because every praise is due to Thee, because Thou alone art worthy of glory.

The Lord is the eternal Son of God; through Him everything is joyful and is governed by justice.

✠ May Jesus always be in in my heart and inside me.

✠ May Jesus always be inside me, to revive me; may He be around me, in order to protect me; may He be before me, in order to lead me; may He be behind me, in order to guard me; may He be beside me, in order to govern me; may He be above me, in order to bless me; may He be below me, in order to strengthen me; may He always be with me to deliver me from all suffering and from eternal death!

✠ Praise, honour and glory are rendered to Jesus through the ages of ages. Amen.

### SATURDAY

✠ Jesus, son of Mary, salvation of the world, be favourable, sweet and propitious to me; grant me a holy and willing spirit, so that I may render homage to Thee and respect Thee duly, Thou, who art the liberator of the world, who was, is and always will be God and man, beginning and end.

Jesus of Nazareth, King of the Jews, son of the Virgin Mary, have mercy on me (name . . .), a poor sinner! Lead me because of Thy sweetness on to the road of eternal salvation. Amen.

And Jesus passed in the midst of them, and nobody could lay on Him his hands, because His hour had not yet come. . . . But Jesus, knowing the things which had to happen to Him, went forward and asked them: for Whom are you seeking? They answered Him, Jesus of Nazareth. And Judas, who had to betray Him was amongst them. And immediately as Jesus told them that it was Him, men fell flat on the earth. And Jesus again asked them: for Whom are you seeking? They again answered: Jesus of Nazareth. Jesus replied to them—I have already told you that I am he for whom you are seeking, let them (His disciples) go.

The spear, the nails, the thorns, the cross, the death I suffered prove that I eradicated and redeemed the crimes of these miserable men.

Protect me O Lord Jesus Christ from all the wounds of poverty and the snares of my enemies. May the five wounds of our Lord serve me continuously as a remedy. Jesus is the way, Jesus is the truth, Jesus is the life.

✠ Jesus Who suffered, ✠ Jesus Who was crucified, Jesus Who is resurrected from the dead, have mercy on me!

May these prayers which I have brought to Thee, O Jesus, be eternally my guarantee against my enemies, against all evil and danger! Amen.

# CHAPTER XXXIV

# OPERATIONS AGAINST OBSESSION

## EXORCISMS AGAINST SUCCUBI AND INCUBI

In ancient times, before the founding of the Christian religion, certain sexual abnormalities and extravagancies were attributed to the direct influence of evil beings from other than the physical world. This is not the place to give an extensive account of them, but, because this evil still occurs among men of the twentieth century, theurgy has had to expose it and to find the means to fight it.

Malicious beings from the astral world, who impersonate the vice of sexual perversion are of two kinds. Those that attack men and have a female appearance are called—*succubi*, while those affecting women and assuming a male form are known as *incubi*. These Latin names speak for themselves, depicting the activities of the evil creatures.

They usually attack solitary people, like monks and nuns, who are trying to subdue their physical passions. If the sexual fire in men and women is so strong that even the discipline of a monastery or convent is unable to extinguish it, the tragedy of the afflicted human being becomes similar to a boiling kettle with a tightly fitting lid: it bursts in a destructive explosion.

It would seem that the only cure for such people would be normal sexual relations, as in married life, and so on.

If this safety valve cannot be used, and the people concerned still fight a losing battle with themselves, a suitable ground is then prepared for interference from the side of the watching evil entities. Their activities take the form of sexual nightmares of extreme intensity and reality, so that the luckless people have the impression of the real physical sin of impurity, committed with irresistibly attractive beings of the opposite sex, who visit them late at night. Usually, such half-physical, half-astral relations end with the normal orgasm, and so on.

The affected persons usually speak of the extremely intense

sensuality involved in such relations, and are oppressed, being convinced that they have committed an unpardonable sin.

Actually, every form of self-abuse so often encountered in adolescents is only a mild form of actual obsession, but in these cases, the exciting sexual images do not possess such grim 'reality', and disappear after the onanist has reached his artificially induced sexual climax.

Nevertheless, this vice may sometimes cost the weak-willed person dearly. In Chapter V of *The Tarot* there is a full account of just such a case, followed by the tragic death of the self-abuser, who was even conscious of his position, and asked me for help. However, at the time, I was only starting my occult studies, so I had to consult my book and prepare myself beforehand for the action. But next day it was already too late, as the desperate man had brought a violent death to himself in an attack of fury.

I am giving below the full ritual of the operation, which is directed against the malicious influences on the *'other side'*, translated from the original Latin.

### GREAT EXORCISM OF THE RITUAL AGAINST EVIL SPIRITS, USED IN ALL CASES OF OBSESSION

✠ In the name of the Father, and Son, and Holy Spirit!
✠ Our aid is in the Lord's name,
Who created heaven and earth.
O Lord, hear my prayer,
And let my cry ascend unto Thee!

*Let us pray:*

O Omnipotent Lord, Logos of God the Father, Christ Jesus, who gave Thy apostles the power to stamp on serpents and scorpions, and to annihilate every effort of the enemy; Thou, whose power defeated Satan himself and made him fall from heaven faster than does a thunderbolt: trembling and imploringly I invoke Thy name, in order that Thou will forgive me (name . . .), Thy unworthy servant my sins, and give me the faith and force necessary to attack this powerful dragon, under the shelter of Thy all-powerful hand!

✠ Thou, who lives and reigns with the Father, in unity with the Holy Ghost. Amen.

*Let us pray:*

O God, omnipotent and eternal, before whom trembles heaven, mountains melt like wax, the earth shudders and trembles, the abysses open and hell is terrified: I make this humble prayer to Thee.

With the invocation of Thy name may the soul of Thy servant (name . . .) be freed from every vexation, returning to the sole author of its salvation, and let all stench be dissipated and replaced by the sweet aromas of the Holy Ghost, so that this soul will be able to follow its liberator, our Lord Jesus Christ, who lives and reigns forever.

(If possible, the afflicted person should here recite the apostle's creed personally, or with assistance, and all present join in in whispers.)

✠ Blessed be the Father, the Son and the Holy Ghost.

Let them be exalted and praised through all the ages of ages. The Lord is with you and with your spirit.

*Let us pray:*

O God, omnipotent and eternal, who grants to Thy servants the grace to profess the true faith, because they recognize Thy eternal and glorious trinity, adoring Thy unity in the omnipotence of Thy Majesty. We implore Thee to fortify that faith in us, and to defend us from all our enemies.

Through Jesus Christ, our Lord. Amen.

*Reading taken from the Gospel of St Matthew, 17: 14-20*

'And when he was come to the multitude, there came to him a man falling down on his knees before him, saying: Lord, have pity on my son, for he is a lunatic, and suffereth much: for he falleth often into the fire, and often into the water. And I brought him to thy disciples, and they could not cure him. Then Jesus answered and said: O unbelieving and perverse generation, how long shall I be with you? how long shall I suffer you? Bring him hither to me. And Jesus rebuked him, and the devil went out of him, and the child was cured from that hour. Then came the disciples to Jesus secretly, and said: Why could not we cast him out? Jesus said to them: Because of your unbelief. For, amen I say to you, if you have faith as a grain of mustard-seed, you shall say to this mountain: Remove from hence hither, and it shall remove: and nothing shall be impossible to you. But this kind is not cast out but by prayer and fasting.'

*Reading taken from the Gospel of St Mark, 16: 14-20*

'At length he appeared to the eleven as they were at table: and he upbraided them with their increduility and hardness of heart, because they did not believe them who had seen him after he was risen again. And he said to them: Go ye into the whole world, and preach the gospel to every creature. He that believeth and is baptized, shall be saved: but he that believeth not shall be condemned. And these signs shall follow them that believe: In my name they shall cast out devils: they shall speak with new tongues. They shall take up serpents; and if they shall drink any deadly thing it shall not hurt them: they shall lay their hands upon the sick, and they shall recover. And the Lord Jesus, after he had spoken to them, was taken up into heaven, and sitteth on the right hand of God. But they going forth preached everywhere: the Lord working withal, and confirming the word with signs that followed.'

*Reading taken from the Gospel of St Luke, 4: 31-35*

'And he went down into Capharnaum, a city of Galilee; and there he taught them on the sabbath-days. And they were astonished at his doctrine: for his speech was with power. And in the synagogue there was a man who had an unclean devil, and he cried out with a loud voice. Saying: Let us alone, what have we to do with thee, Jesus of Nazareth? Art thou come to destroy us? I know thee who thou art, the holy one of God. And Jesus rebuked him saying: Hold thy peace, and go out of him. And when the devil had thrown him into the midst, he went out of him, and hurt him not at all.'

*Reading taken from the Gospel of St John, 12: 31-36*

'Now is the judgment of the world: now shall the prince of this world be cast out. And I, if I be lifted up from the earth, will draw all things to myself. (Now this he said, signifying what death he should die.) The multitude answered him: We have heard out of the law, that CHRIST abideth for ever: and how sayest thou: The son of man must be lifted up? Who is this son of man? Jesus therefore said to them:

Yet a little while, the light is among you. Walk whilst you have the light, that the darkness overtake you not. And he that walketh in darkness, knoweth not whither he goeth. Whilst you have the light, believe in the light, that you may be the children of light. . . .'

*Place the book of the Gospels (or the present book containing the exorcisms) on the patient's head, and then impose hands on him and say:*

I exorcize thee, impure spirit ✠ through the Father, ✠ through the Son, and ✠ through the Holy Ghost, to go away and leave this servant of God (name . . .). Accursed and damned, obey Him who once walked on the waters and extended His hand to Peter, so that he would not submerge. It is He again, who opened the eyes of the blind, and resuscitated Lazarus from his tomb where he had already lain buried for four days. That is why thou, O accursed demon, know thy damnation and render homage to ✠ the living true God, render homage to ✠ Jesus Christ, His Son, ✠ and to the Holy Ghost! Immediately leave this servant of God (name . . .). This sign ✠ of the holy cross which we now make on this forehead (make the sign of the cross over the patient), thou, the accursed demon have no courage to despise. In the name of Him who will come to judge the living and the dead, and who will purify the world by fire! Amen.

Listen thou, accursed Satan, I adjure thee through the name of the Eternal God, our saviour Jesus Christ, to go away, defeated in thy hatred, go away with fear and howling: in this servant of God (name . . .) there is nothing belonging to thee. Render homage to the Holy Spirit who comes now and who deigns to descend from high heaven in order to break the snares, to complete the purification of this temple, this dwelling, to deliver completely from thy vexation this servant of God (name . . .) who will render to God eternal actions of grace and who will bless His name through all the ages of ages. Amen.

Know this well, O Satan, it is clearer than day, that a terrible punishment awaits thee, frightful torments are hanging over thy head, the day of judgment is near, the day of thy torture, the day which is coming like a fiery furnace in which thou and all the rebellious angels will perish in the eternal death.

Well! Damned and damnable one, curb thyself before the true and living God, curb thyself before Jesus Christ, His Son, before the Holy Ghost, in whose name, and through the virtue of whom, I (name . . .) am ordering thee, no matter who thou art, impure spirit, to go out of this servant (name . . .), whom our God and master Jesus Christ has deigned to redeem through His precious blood: He, who will come to judge the living and the dead and who will purify this world through fire! Amen.

Fly, impure spirit, from this creature of God (name . . .) and do not presume to return to him. This orders thee, O accursed demon, He who commands thee to return from whence thou came. So thou, spirit of the most black perversions, enemy of the human race, seller of the dead, thief of life, offender of justice, source of all evil, seducer of men, exciter of hatred, cause of discordance, father of lies, dread Him, who was sacrificed in Isaac, sold in Joseph, killed as a lamb, crucified as a man, who defeated hell and went out glorious. Retire now, in the name ✠ of the Father and ✠ Son, ✠ and Holy Ghost, from this servant of God (name . . .), and never again enter into him, by virtue of our Lord Jesus Christ who will some day come to judge the living and the dead, and who will purify this world by fire. Amen.

*The exorcizing theurgist takes the cross and says:*

Here is the wood of ✠ the most holy cross: fly enemies!

He was triumphant over you and the world, our Lord Jesus Christ, Son of God, the sovereign emperor, lion of the tribe of Judah, descendant of the race of David.

*The sufferer must now kiss the cross saying:*

We adore Thee, O Christ, we bless Thee, because it is through Thy holy cross, that Thou hast redeemed the world. O Lord, have mercy; Christ, have mercy; Lord, have mercy!

Then together with the operator, the patient says the Lord's Prayer loudly.

*The operator re-opens the service:*

Here God arises and His enemies immediately take flight!
And those who hate Him—fly from His sight!
Save Thy servant (name . . .), who has no other hope than in Thee!

May the enemy gain no power over him, and the son of iniquity not harm him!
Be for him, O Lord, like an indestructible tower,
In the face of the enemy!
O Lord, listen to my prayer,
And let my cry ascend unto Thee!

*The operator speaks to the patient:*
Lord be with you!

*The patient answers:*
And with your spirit!

*Let us pray:*

O God, whom every sin offends, whom every repentance appeases, look favourably on the humble prayers of Thy people and turn aside the punishment of Thy just anger, which we create by our errors!

God omnipotent and eternal! Eternal salvation for the faithful, hear us now as we pray for Thy servant (name . . .) who is in distress and for whom we implore Thy merciful goodness in restoring this health, expelling his enemies and allowing him to return to Thy Church with thanks for Thy blessed grace!

We implore Thee, O Lord, to crush the pride of our enemies, and may the force of Thy hand abate their stubborn opposition.

O God, who does not dislike the complaint of a repentant heart and who does not reject the love of those who are afflicted; agree with our imploring, which we renew in the midst of our suffering. May Thou listen to it in Thy goodness, so that all these evils which are directed against us, the diabolical maliciousness or human hatred become as nothing, broken by the aid of Thy mercy. May no adversity befall us, and full of joy and recognition may we render to Thee grace for Thy goodness.

Through our Lord, Jesus Christ. Amen.

O God, who has instructed the hearts of Thy faithful through the light of the Holy Ghost: grant us through the same spirit the knowledge and love of everything just, that we will be able to enjoy His consolation.

Through Jesus Christ, our Lord. Amen.

Grant to Thy servants, as we implore Thee, O our Lord and

God, the grace of perpetual health of spirit and body; and through the intercession of the blessed Virgin Mary grant us deliverance from present sadness and the possession of eternal joys.

Through Jesus Christ, our Lord. Amen.

At this point may be added a reading of the following Psalms, according to the operator's choice: 58, 65, 66, 74.

The final blessing terminates the operation:

May the blessing of God the omnipotent ✠ Father ✠ Son and ✠ Holy Spirit descend on you (name . . .), and remain with you forever. Amen.

If the devilish vexations continue, even in the smallest degree, the exorcism must be repeated, until it works completely. Other formulas, which you find in this book on related material, may also be used. Unction with blessed oil, as given in former chapters, often brings quick relief, when used in conjunction with this operation.

It has been found, that the attacks of *incubi* and *succubi* can be prevented, if the sufferer is not left alone, especially at night. Some good and courageous friend or relative should watch him, until the spell is over.

Operations against evil spirits should be performed by well-trained theurgists, who lead pure lives, so that they may be able to resist the temptations and invultuations coming from the 'other side'. Assistance must be utterly unselfish, and no payment is allowed, for in such a case the result will be nil, and, moreover, the attacks may increase in strength and frequency. An unworthy operator may easily become the target of similar attacks by the same demons, and suffer the fate of his patient. You should know, that invisible evil beings do possess intelligence and abilities, often superior to those of the average man, and they have the advantage of being indefatigable and not perceptible to the physical eye, unless they choose to be visible and materialize in some kind of body.

Our thoughts and feelings are also not a mystery to them, so they can perfectly well 'see' what kind of adversary they have against them. They will flee from a saint, a virtuous man, a great yogi or a powerful white occultist, it is true; but average people can seldom resist evil spirits, if their destiny or (karma) allows them to be targets for the dark forces from the astral world.

If the prospective operator cannot dominate fear of those whom he has to conquer and expel, or if he is only a half-hearted believer in theurgy, then the most reasonable thing would be for *no operation whatsoever to be undertaken by such a person*. This applies even more if he considers himself to be an 'agnostic' and is only curious about theurgic operations and not a sincere adept, or if he *'would like to make only an interesting experiment'*. Then in such a case he will invariably be defeated, harmed himself and the state of the sufferer made considerably worse.

The fact that one does not believe in the forces one wants to contact has no meaning as regards the consequences of an unwise action.

Ignorance of the law does not save a culprit from due punishment, and the 'non-believing' in the existence of gaols will not prevent him from being locked up, if he breaks the law.

A magic sword (see Chapter V of *The Tarot*) can be used during the operation against *succubi* and *incubi*. It should be pointed towards the patient, when the proper exorcizing words against the demon are pronounced. But many theurgists prefer to present the blessed crucifix, which is considered to be the ultimate weapon against evil forces.

# CHAPTER XXXV

# USE OF PSALMS IN THEURGIC OPERATIONS

In quite a number of theurgic operations described in Part II of this book, various psalms of King David are recommended for the strengthening of an action and thereby obtaining better results. Mystical power is hidden in this inspired stream of invocations, in spite of the fact that so many centuries have elapsed since the poet king poured the songs straight from the elation of his heart.

In our tradition, it is the accepted thing to use certain psalms as a remedy for specific conditions, which require assistance and defence. In this chapter you will find an alphabetically arranged list of troubles with the corresponding psalms, which parallel the main theurgic operations.

## PSALMS

Actions of Grace 18, 56, 95, 116
Adoration 28, 94
Adversity 33, 101
Afflictions 56
Air travel 138
Alliances 107
Ambitions 100
Anemia 21, 37, 72
Anger 4, 36, 37
Animals, protection of 35, 134

Bad dreams 90
Bad language, evil talk 5, 63, 90, 119
Bad visits (dangerous ones) 17, 27
Beasts, domestic 103, 106
Beasts, savage, 57, 90, 123
Birds, 49, 103
Bites 21, 31
Blasphemy (against) 14, 23, 113
Blessed oil 103
Blood, diseases of 6, 123
Bones, diseases of 6, 21, 33, 101
Broken limbs 37

Calumnies (against) 4, 14, 37, 39, 51, 56, 62, 71, 108, 118, 139
Cancer 37
Cattle 49, 113
Character, good 20, 21
Charity 14, 11, 132
Chastity, purity of life 11, 23
Chest, diseases of 21, 72
Child (to have one) 36, 101, 112, 126
Child, retarded 15

# PART III

# EPILOGUE

# PART III

## EPILOGUE

If human life, as well as the life of other manifestations of existence in the universe could be limited to definite, uniform and controlled patterns, there would be no religions, philosophies, occultism and, of course, theurgy. All of them are superfluous and unnecessary for the functioning of say, a machine even in its highest evolutionary form, such as advanced electronic computers, whose existence and operation are utterly dependent upon the mind which created them from different kinds of materials, which finally are nothing more than combinations of certain forms of energy, manifested in a concentrated form of physical matter.

Knowing the laws, or even, as in our own human case, only certain basic laws, which rule matter, we are able to build complicated mechanisms, which are predictable and controllable to a considerable degree, allowing us to use them for our purposes within the limits circumscribed for them by our own will and intelligence.

If an imaginary dweller of another world would arrive, intending to observe life on the surface of our earth, from his 'flying saucer' or other contraption, he would probably 'anchor' his ship at a safe distance above, beyond our immediate sight and reach. But, *what would he see* apart from immovable objects like earthly flora and our artificial constructions such as houses, cities, dams, and so on? Of course, innumerable moving objects, large and small, slow and fast; humans, animals, land and water vehicles, of every kind, flying machines, moving mechanisms in factories, and so on.

Individual or massed people on streets and roads, small or large cars, long trains, vessels, all of them would have, for a fully impartial foreign observer, a completely strange and unfamiliar appearance with one common quality: the ability to move in all directions.

Only an intensive investigation necessitating a close contact with the observed world could reveal to our interplanetary traveller, what life on earth actually is, where the intelligent beings are, which apparently rule the visible manifestations of life, and where the animals and machines are, and so on. Finally, he might be allowed to know the difference between human beings and other moving objects, just as we do.

He would then realize that all movements of machines, and to a certain degree, of animals, depended on us. And here the same problem would confront him as it does us: what makes us think, feel, act, be born, work and finally—die? If our guest will be not less intelligent than us, he would realize that, in their activities and inventions, human beings are using certain laws of Nature, which are known to them, just as he does in his own advanced world.

But, apart from the laws governing our mechanics, he would also have to try to discover those which concern our kind of life, control it and give to it, this or that form and fill it with innumerable events and accidents.

Those amongst us who are wiser might sincerely wish our visitor from far away success in this endeavour, in which, so far, we ourselves have been unsuccessful. We do not know what causes us to be born, live, think, feel, be happy or suffer, and finally—disappear in a heap of ashes or in the dust of a graveyard. We do not 'know' the Power which produces all of those conditions and events, in the sense that we may know physical laws and objects, apart from ourselves .Of course, in all religions we find efforts to present to us that great *cause* as a *Supreme Being* called God, and to instruct us how we should behave in our lifetime in order to align ourselves with the laws, which have apparently been established for the inner life of man, just as those that apply to his visible form.

Someone said that 'if a machine could think a little, it would probably imagine man as its God and creator, but it would certainly be far from any awareness of the mental processes inside its maker that led to its realization. However, all this ignorance would not impede the machine in its functions, according to the physical laws used for its creation.'

Simple as this conception is, there is one interesting idea behind it: *the possibility of using laws and facts* WITHOUT FULL KNOWLEDGE ABOUT THEIR AUTHOR.

Theurgy, as well as religions, does not attempt to give us

'knowledge' of the Supreme Power, which acts behind our life and destiny. Philosophically speaking this is understandable and logical: for knowledge necessitates two factors.

The object of knowledge (in this case it should be God Himself) and the knower, that is, man. This immediately creates an impossible consequence: that you and I can be apart from the absolute, omnipresent and omnipotent Power, that controls everything. This is a sheer absurdity, for this would deprive the Supreme Power of qualities which alone make It that power. 'Who are you apart from the Supreme Self (God)?' asked the last great Rishi of India—Sri Ramana. All religions assert that every life is possible only in God. Then every birth of life, its endurance in time, transformation and dissolution are within His law. While not knowing what it is impossible to know (God) we can be aware of His laws and then act according to them, which will produce the desired results.

Now perhaps you will be able to realize what is in the heart of theurgic methods, conjurations, exorcisms and prayers.

These are applications of the laws known to theurgic science and which face the unknowable God, who is Himself beyond all attributes, these being only limitations of the unique perfection, which is the only 'attribute' of God; but who responds if we turn to Him, even when we ascribe attributes to Him in our minds, because these minds cannot operate without the limitations of definitions and attributes.

He understands everything, for He is the only One Who really KNOWS! The creation can only guess.

So, when we worship and pray, using theurgic formulas, tuning to the illimitable goodness, mercy, wisdom, omnipresence, justice, love, power, we are NOT in the wrong at all, for, being Himself infinitely beyond any limiting attributes, He still embraces everything we can imagine or create in our hearts and minds in the matter of the highest qualities, as we conceive them. Just as a small bay, which is undoubtedly a part of the great ocean, cannot hope to enclose the wholeness of that ocean, so the ocean cannot be confined to a bay.

This is what you have to realize fully, and then your invocations and prayers will have the attribute of wisdom, which penetrates theurgic practices.

Then you will operate with faith and confidence in Him, and thereby obtain results beyond all expectation. You already know that simple repetition of even the most powerful theurgic invocations (and there are a lot of them in this book) is of little avail, if faith and confidence in the Supreme are absent in the operator. Why is there such a condition? Realize that everything in the manifested worlds is conditioned, that is, subject to certain laws. Can you tell why such powers as, say, gravitation, magnetism or vibration actually exist? WHY, (not HOW!) rays of light produce certain chemical reactions on your retina, and why they are transformed into nervous energy which affects—in quite a mysterious way—your consciousness, so that you are able to read these lines now before your eyes? This 'WHY' belongs to the CAUSE of these phenomena, not to their technicalities and effects.

The answer is one, and it alone is possible 'such is the law'. And with this our knowledge ends: we do not know 'WHY', but only 'HOW'.

And in spite of this ignorance, our actual cognition is not destroyed or rendered useless. A few, who perhaps can penetrate beyond words and mind's cognition, will object, defending the possibility of attainment of the absolute, unconditional wisdom of reality, through the transcending of the mental consciousness and the entering into the higher state, where there is no shadow, but only the light. And this light is that of God, but not—Him.

We are not ignorant of this truth, and Samadhi (see the third part of my *Trilogy*) is the answer to it.

But, in this epoch, this supreme state of consciousness can be obtained, by only a few, and it cannot be recognized as something known to everyone or attainable by all. This state is beyond the human level. On the contrary, theurgy is aimed at assisting many people, among them also being 'average' men, who can use its methods for establishing real relations with the Supreme. These methods can be applied with more or less success, and results will be obtained, according to our capabilities, which cannot be said of other paths.

The 'kingdom of heaven' means just this state full of beatitude, resulting from full attainment, and its rays are clearly perceptible in Samadhi, even when we are still in our physical bodies. This is because theurgy is for the living and not for the dead, just as God is not a God of the dead, but of the living!

In turning to God in theurgic operations, and using the most perfect attributes for Him, we are actually getting closer to the truth of Him, which is inconceivable and inexpressible in any words, and at the same time, meditation about those attributes will very positively tune the operator himself.

The conditions pertaining to theurgic operations which alone can secure success are, as I said before, *sincerity and faith* on the part of the worshipper. We know that it is different in Western Occultism, as well as in the science of Eastern Yoga. In both long preparation is essential, extending over many years of one's lifetime, and a lot of knowledge and training cannot be dispensed with. Moreover, I would like to comment that, in order to become a real occultist (see *The Tarot*), or yogi, certain innate abilities of karmic origin seem to be a definite condition. This is because a special kind of development requires special inner and outer conditions for the aspirant.

But when we turn to God, just as we are, trusting that our imperfections are known to Him in full (who else would know?), we surrender everything to Him, thus establishing a direct relation with the Source of every being.

There again lies the difference between the theurgic path and Western and Eastern aspects of occultism. But where is there any difference in relation to religions? You probably noticed, that, in theurgic prayers and invocations, the worshipper is always called a 'servant of God'. There is no mention of any intermediary between God and man. Saints and good spirits (angels), who are sometimes invoked in theurgic rituals, although superior to us, are also 'servants' of Him, but, of course, of a much more potent and higher class. They are more perfect executioners of God's will and laws than the average man. All that they do is not done in their own, but always in His name. When, many years ago, I first contacted and learned the invocations and theurgic prayers, which cater for every human need, I was a little confused by its 'business-like' attitude towards the Supreme Being. The true light came much later, when I realized that a poor man, praying for the improvement of his health, or status, or the hard conditions of his life, and a saint, who disregards all these miseries, but asks only for the highest, that is, for final union with the *Father*, are both right, and that He listens equally to their prayers. This is a powerful stimulant for action and a bright ray of light for everyone who contacts the 'Art of Effective Worship', which is what theurgy actually is.

In this book you will find little about sins, that is, transgressions of the unique Law and Will. Simply because theurgists believe that the best way to spiritual progress and attainment of the grace of the Supreme is not a constant and depressing bewailing or deliberation about one's mistakes or sins, as some erroneous religious sects seem to profess, but rather a 'raising of the head' and directing of all attention to the *perfection of Him,* as an eternal beacon on the path.

Therefore, one is encouraged to forget the sinful ways of the past, and concentrate on the righteous path for today, and for the future. You see, it is rather a process of substitution, instead of the creation of a temporary 'vacuum' through the method of 'destruction' of faults and sins, as certain religious and even some occult organizations suggest. Know, that this 'vacuum' is dangerous, even if it lasts for a short time. Support for the truthfulness of this side of theurgic science can be found in the teachings of a great spiritual Master of this epoch, in the striking advice of Ramana Maharshi (1879-1950) to the aspirants that were around him in his ashram:

*'Raise your head high, do not think about the muddy waves below. Have faith in God and in yourself. That will cure all, Hope for the best, expect the best, toil for the best—and everything will come right for you in the end.'*

Many so-called 'miraculous' cures have been noted, as being performed by eminent theurgists who practised their wisdom and faith in the field of help for human misery. But this is only a small fragment of the whole picture, as not all theurgists allow their deeds to be made public; others passed on only a part of their achievements to the knowledge of the world. Therefore I cannot speak about those who preferred to remain apart from any publicity, mentioning only a few of them, who allowed some cases to be known. The first example is that of 'Master Philippe' (Philippe Nizier of Lyons). His powers were amazing and immense. He knew the sickness of everyone of his dozens of patients, who attended the daily sessions held in his home. The procedure was simple. He stood in front of and facing each person and asked briefly what was wrong. Often, without even waiting for an answer, Philippe said: 'Well, everything will be all right, God wants it so!' Usually the results were quite dramatic and felt immediately: health returned rapidly, and cases of relapse were few. When this happened the Master Philippe explained that, despite his warning, the sick persons had returned to their former wrong ways of living, and then new suffering was the result. He did not seem to use any special ritual during the healing sessions, but those who were close to him, said that he prayed and meditated intensely before patients came. He did not remain with us for long, as his life span was limited to 55 years (1849-1905).

The second example is that of Father John of Cronstadt (a town and former czarist sea-fortress close to the Russian capital —St Petersburg, now Leningrad), a Russian Orthodox priest, who lived at the same period as Master Philippe. This saintly man apparently excelled in restoring the health of incurably sick persons, especially in bad mental cases. He used the traditional prayers and blessings of his church, but performed them with such sincerity and power of faith, that some witnesses reported that: 'It was impossible for a miraculous cure not to happen after his worship.'

A spiritual friend of Father John of Cronstadt was the famous French clergyman—Abbé Julio (Houssay), whose activities and writings make him a most prominent theurgist of the twentieth century. He recovered scores of old Christian mystical prayers and rituals from the dust of oblivion and translated them from their original Latin and Greek into the French language. Quite a few of them have been adapted by myself for Part II of this book.

There was dissension between Abbé Julio and the French governing body of clergy, because of his liberalism and uncompromising attitude towards the Roman Catholic interpretation and disapproval of numerous old inspired prayers and form of worship he used, and finally he founded his own Catholic church, at the end of the nineteenth century. In 1906 he was created a bishop of that church, and contributed a lot towards popularizing theurgic ideas and methods, based on the Western churches. He was also in contact with many of the illustrious and spiritually minded men of his epoch such as, Papus, Sédir, Maitre Philippe and Jean Sempé. Prior to World War I, his cures and other assistance to sufferers were famous.

At the present time theurgy exists in the world in the form of groups of worshippers, as well as individual theurgists, who use fragments of ideas and rituals which were used sixty or seventy years ago. There is no comprehensive book (especially in English literature) which portrays the whole of the usable theurgic science, and gives the traditional and most effective texts, arranged for collective or individual operations. This book has been written to fill the existing gap, which is practically a vacuum, in the literature of this kind.

It was most important for the writer to place an adequate, proven and spiritually correct basis for activities in the hands of those who are able and willing to serve their neighbours in a traditional and effective way, bringing them more light and happiness.

Theurgy does not ask its aspirants about their religious or philosophical background, I repeat that the only condition which must be fulfilled by the prospective theurgist or student of this ancient science is, that he must be ripe enough to realize that, in the realm of manifested life in the Universe, there cannot be any effect without a cause. No matter whether both are easy to find, or their origin hidden deeply in the mysteries of the great Source, from which emanates everything that was, is and will be throughout the eternity of time and the infinity of space.

In plain words, he must have intuitional belief in God and be on His side, which will make him a servant and friend of the Lord.

King David expressed this idea in one of his most inspired Psalms: *'And said the fool in his heart: there is no God!'*

And now, at the end of this book, the reader is entitled to ask the writer: 'Do you agree with the statement, that the existence or non-existence of God cannot be proved?' Does it not undermine the whole structure of theurgy, which is based on the axiom that God exists and rules?

I would be only too glad to answer such a question.

What is observed in the above statement regarding proof of the existence of the Supreme Power, is—at the same time—true and this is no empty paradox, because if we look deeper into the whole problem, any superficial judgment will be only void and useless.

1. *The statement is true,* since you cannot show God to any-

body saying: 'Look! Here He is!' Equally well you cannot say to me: 'Look! Can you see His absence?' This is because the infinite problem and its subject are handled in a wrong way and with inadequate tools, being only those provided by the ordinary mind-brain apparatus. Exactly the same as if someone tries to catch an atom with a blacksmith's pliers, and when he cannot, starts to deny the existence of that particle of matter. You cannot separate and eliminate for demonstration purposes, something, which by far transcends the conceptions of time and space accessible to human beings. As I have already said, the idea of the omnipresence of God can best be approached when one meditates about space without end. Actually, no one can even imagine the limits of space, for what will he find on 'the other side' of that fantastic 'frontier'? In Chapter XVI 'The Attainment of the Final Union' you heard about the usefulness of the idea of infinite space as being a prelude to the deepest possible conception of the Supreme.

The demonstration of the existence or non-existence of God is impossible, just as it is impossible to limit space, or to enclose infinity and eternity in a limited area and time.

2. *The statement is untrue,* when we direct it to the right point: being objectively unprovable, it is fully provable subjectively. If you have, say, a headache or rheumatic pains, or if you feel a sense of well-being in your body, what external proof can you present to me, apart from your statement about what you really feel?

The awareness of the Highest is supremely individual, it is a purely inner experience, which cannot be touched, seen or tasted. But it is unconditionally real for the person experiencing it. It is beyond all mortal senses, and it could not be otherwise: for it is ETERNAL, and does not perish with the mortal body and its senses. It is beyond the mind, because it cannot appear unless the mind is stilled and silenced, for that purpose. There is no need to mention here about experiences of God, which have happened to innumerable human beings such as saints, true philosophers, yogis and rishis of the East.

All of these people are firm in their descriptions of these experiences as surpassing mental and sensual ways of cognition. This means that the existence of God can be proved beyond any doubt, but only individually, that is, through personal experience. So the initial statements as analyzed in

1 and 2 now becomes *untrue,* for man can be convinced of and experience the existence of God, *to live Him and in Him.*

This is my own statement and it can be confirmed only by those who have had a similar experience of truth, which is only another term for the Lord. It is hard to express such experiences in words or thoughts and perhaps it would be best to remain silent about them, as have done and still do so many great souls on this earth.

But in the course of the last few years I have had the proof, that if one does speak (even in the inadequate and clumsy language of the mind) about higher experiences accessible to human consciousness, numerous individuals are often inspired and supported in their own, still perhaps timid attempts to approach the super-sensual experiences, for which they are ripe enough and are but seeking only a trigger to be pulled, a confirmation of their own inner reality. That is why I am writing chiefly for them.

The use of the pronoun 'Him' is utterly wrong in relation to the all-embracing, omnipresent Supreme Being, because we are all in that Being and not apart from IT, which cannot be limited to comparatively infinitesimal awareness of man. But how otherwise can one speak? So, listen if you can, and open your own door to accept Him, who does not comes uninvited or unwanted!

He comes when man leaves his everyday anxieties. It is impossible to know (or rather to guess) whether this state of inner tranquillity is His act of grace, permitting further, deeper experiences, or, that man, enforcing this state in himself, by stilling his lower nature, invites the high Visitor into his innermost sanctuary of awareness. Then comes peace, bringing with it the realization of the futility of every kind of life, except that of merging in Him. On this degree man usually perceives the direct influence of the Highest. And it becomes so natural: He is the perfect Peace, therefore our first contact with Him must be peaceful. But this reasoning does not exist in the real experience: one only *knows,* without any thinking.

After the elimination of anxiety and the obtaining of the *peace,* there comes the *joy.* It is indescribable bliss, purposeless unconditioned, full of certainty of life—of *joy.* And then we *know,* that He is joy itself, and we know that His presence has been called—paradise.

This *joy* of Him is full of *love*. But, as then, there is no difference between the human 'I' and the 'I' of the Whole-Him. We are unable to define the cause of this merging in love, whether He floods us with It, or we ourselves dive into the ocean of Him. But it does not matter any more, for then nothing counts except the discovered PRESENCE.

This experience is on the deepest level of one's consciousness, beyond all other levels. And this may explain the strange fact, that such a spiritual ecstasy does not dim our awareness of the outer world. It is not lost or sunk in oblivion, simply it is put on the last plane of consciousness, deprived of any interest for us: neither hated nor loved, and hence it is hard to find anything more to describe this state. The difference as regard the state of Samadhi, seems to be twofold:

*Firstly* there is no trance for the body, only final and absolute lucidity of consciouness.

*Secondly* there is the all powerful awareness of the great, impossible to describe PRESENCE. We may call It—God. So did the saints. But it is *neither outside* us, *nor inside*: It only—IS.

The we know that He IS, and that He can be with us. Then we realize who helped us in apparently hopeless situations, when we had even no thought about Him in our anxiety and despair. Then we know who answered our prayers, who arranged and is arranging our circumstances in the best possible way, about which we were not even hoping or dreaming. And we know, who will do the same, beyond time and space—forever.

From all this dawns the realization of what is *faith*—that power which may move mountains: and its mystery seems to be in our reach, but never described.

Such an experience cannot be forgotten, and the only reality remains in Him, although from the outside of *mortal man* it seems as if nothing has been changed. But he also knows the mystery of resurrection.

This all brings the presence of the Lord. There is nothing beyond entering into His joy.

The outer shape of the world may have changed since the first records about the relationship between man and the Supreme were made. And those who experienced the PRESENCE thousands of years ago could perhaps hardly recognize the altered face of the planet, on which they spent their lives which they successfully dedicated to the search for Him.

But the inner core of man remains unchanged, and the same problems of search for the imperishable faces the man living in the atomic age as they did for his predecessors, the humble shepherds and primitive agriculturists. Their mortal dust has returned back into the same soil from which it arose, and from which were and are built the bodies of the later generations, our own included.

'And restless remains the heart of man, until it finds its final repose in Thee, O Lord!' said St Augustine, thus concluding his life that was so fruitful and rich in spiritual experience.

I feel that the earnest reader would like to put a question to me. What is your own experience in theurgy, and does it corroborate all you have said about it? I think he is entitled to a sincere answer, for in spiritual matters, especially for beginners, the ascertaining that it is possible to follow the path and to obtain real results is of too great a value to be lightly dismissed.

The operations, when performed exactly according to tradition (as given in this work) seem to produce deep changes in our nature. One comes closer and closer to the solution of the tremendous problem, which is put to every human being in the form of an ageless binary: *Man and his creator*. When you proceed with all the sincerity and *faith*, which you are able to find in your innermost recesses, your prayers and invocations simply cannot remain without response from HIS side. No matter how developed you are intellectually, your creeds, your personal philosophy, belief or disbelief in religious dogmas, when one turns to HIM, HE invariably enters into one's everyday life. And more and more of HIS virtues are then revealed to the genuine devotee. I do not pretend to have exhausted all of them, for I am firm in the belief, that in such earnest matters man dares to speak only of what he knows from his own experience: everything else would be only guesswork, utterly incompatible with one's true achievement.

He comes in manifold forms and ways. Then He is the most tender Father, showing the path to Himself in an incredibly subtle way. The heart melts in Him. The glorious dawn of the union of our limited consciousness with the eternal joy of

Him produces a silent and indescribable ecstasy of limitless love and surrender. Just as a small child snuggles up to its parent, so the happy soul enters into His unimaginable spiritual 'hug' (words lack the ability to express what lies beyond them). The most wonderful thing in this experience is the absolute lack of selfishness in man in the moments of spiritual ecstasy of His Presence: one does not seek any advantage from It. It matters little, whether It will bring worldly luck or suffering, everything will be accepted with an equal and immense thankfulness and love, if only the Presence will continue.

The world becomes *His world*, no matter how ugly it might have appeared *before*: in the face of the Presence there cannot be any more ugliness. His wisdom penetrates man, who then seems to participate in It. Nothing unknown, but nothing attracts man anymore, except the awareness that in Him is the wholeness of all possible wisdom. All this is realized in the comparable way of *direct perception*, without any trace of thinking or desire.

The great mystery of love is then revealed and stands in the full beauty of its nakedness, without any veils or conditioning. All becomes understandable and crystal-clear: the love between the Lord and His creation, between creatures and men, planets and their suns, galaxies and comets.

Do any 'miracles' happen when I am facing the Presence? They do, but at the time I do not care about them. When friendliness looks at me from every face, when the sun shines in a glimpse of unusual beauty, when good news comes unexpectedly, and the most beloved melodies start to flow from my radio, if it happens to be switched on in these moments of happiness: all of these become personal miracles. But I feel that it could not be otherwise. The inner certainty embraces everything. Unending garlands or words could then be plaited, but they will be unable to reflect the truth lived through. Perhaps deep silence would best reflect It, so let us cover the most guarded secrets of the living soul with the silence, until you will come, in due course, to the Diamond Gate, behind which He has been waiting for you since the beginning of time.

That is the only real thing which we have to know. It is as real as these lines before you now.

# BIBLIOGRAPHY


AMBELAIN, Robert. *Le Dragon d'Or,* Paris, 1956.

ANGELUS SILESIUS. *Saemtliche Werke,* Muenchen, 1922.

BARBARIN, Georges. *L'Ami des Heures Difficiles,* Paris, 1955.

HASTINGS, James (Ed.). *Encyclopaedia of Religion and Ethics,* Edinburgh, 1921.

INGE, William Ralph. *Christian Mysticism,* London, 1933.

JULIO, Abbé (M. Houssay). *Grands Secrets Merveilleux,* Paris 1906.

—— *Le Livre Secret des Grands Exorcisms et Benedictions,* Paris, 1902.

—— *Petits Secrets Merveilleux,* Paris, 1906.

—— *Prières Liturgiques,* Paris, 1900.

LÉVI, Eliphas. *Le Grand Secret,* Paris, 1878.

MEISTER ECKHART. *Die Deutschen Werke,* Stuttgart, 1936.

PARACELSUS. *Saemtliche Werke,* 1904.

PREL, Charles du. *Raetsel des Menschen,* Saulgau, 1951.

REUCHLIN, J. *De Verbo Mirifico,* Basel, 1494.

ROESEMUELLER, Wilhelm Otto. *Gebetskraefte, Hilfe aus dem Jenseits,* R. Ebertin, 1936.

RUYSBROECK, J. *Mystic und Pietismus,* Muenchen, 1925.

SADHU, Mouni. *Concentration,* London, 1959.

—— *The Tarot,* a Contemporary Course of the Quintessence of Hermetic Occultism, London, 1962.

—— *Ways to Self-Realization:* A Modern Evaluation of Occultism and Spiritual Paths, New York, 1962.

SÉDIR, Paul. *Les Forces Mystiques et la Conduite de la vie,* Rouen, 1948.

—— *Le Sermon sur la Montagne,* Rouen, 1948.

—— *Les Guerisons de Christ,* Rouen, 1948.

—— *Le Royaume de Dieu,* Rouen, 1948.

—— *L'Energie Ascétique,* Rouen, 1948.

—— *Le Sacrifice,* Rouen, 1948.

—— *Initiations,* Rouen, 1948.

SCHWENKER, Pastor Friedrich. *Das Gebet,* Erlautert durch mehr als Tausend Beispiele, Leipzig, 1934.

SIMON, Jules. *L'Histoire de L'Ecole D'Alexandrie,* 3 Vol., Paris, 1844.

STEINER, Rudolph Dr. *Das Christentum als Mistische Tatsache,* Wien, 1920.

STRAUSS, Alfred Dr. *Theurgische Heilmethoden,* Lorch, 1936.
SURYA, G. W. *Theurgische Heilmethoden,* Lorch, 1936.
—— *Vereinfachtes Heilsystem,* Lorch, 1934.
—— *Macrocosmos und Microcosmos,* Lorch, 1936.
—— *Hermetische Medizin,* Lorch, 1936.
VACHEROT, E. *L'Histoire Critique de l'Ecole d'Alexandrie,* 2 Vols., Paris, 1846-1851.
VAUGHAN, Robert Alfred. *Hours with the Mystics,* London, 1860.
VINDEVOGEL, J. *La Gnose,* Bruxelles, 1906.
WHITTAKER, Thomas. *The Neoplatonists,* Hildesheim, 1961.
WILDER, Alexander (Translator). *Theurgia,* or: The Egyptian Mysteries by Iamblicos, London, 1912.

# INDEX

Printed in the United Kingdom
by Lightning Source UK Ltd.
116466UKS00001B/301-321